W9-BKO-200

Twayne's
Filmmakers Series

Warren French, Editor

Woody Allen

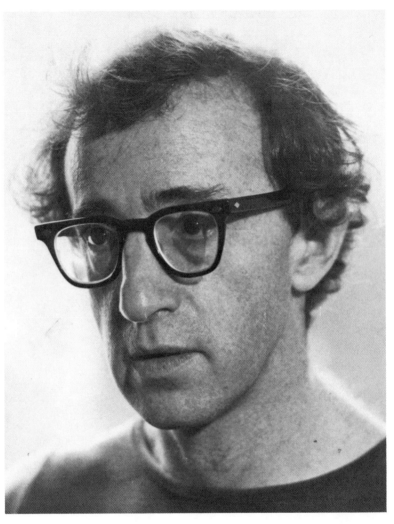

Woody Allen as Isaac Davis in *Manhattan* (1979). *Courtesy of Woody Allen and United Artists.*

WOODY ALLEN

Nancy Pogel

TWAYNE PUBLISHERS • BOSTON
A Division of G. K. Hall & Co.

Woody Allen

Nancy Pogel

Copyright © 1987 by G. K. Hall & Co.
All rights reserved
Published by Twayne Publishers
A Division of G. K. Hall & Co.
70 Lincoln Street, Boston, Massachusetts   02111

Copyediting supervised by Lewis DeSimone
Book design and production by Janet Zietowski
Typeset in 10 pt. Aster with Rockwell display type
by Compset, Inc., of Beverly, Massachusetts

Printed on permanent/durable acid-free paper
and bound in the United States of America

First Printing

Library of Congress Cataloging-in-Publication Data

Pogel, Nancy.
  Woody Allen.

  (Twayne's filmmakers series)
  Filmography: p. 231
  Bibliography: p. 224
  Includes index.
  1. Allen, Woody—Criticism and interpretation.
I. Title. II. Series.
PN1998.A3A5676   1987   791.43'028'0924   86-29521
ISBN 0-8057-9297-X (alk. paper)

CONTENTS

About the Author   vi
Preface   vii
Acknowledgments   xi
Chronology   xiii

1. Little Men and Dialogues: An Introduction   1

2. Will the Real Little Man Please Stand Up?   17

3. Humble Beginnings:
    The First "Woody Allen" Films   33

4. Sex, Sci-Fi, and Sophisticated Philosophy   57

5. The Little Man's Screwball Comedy   81

6. Beyond Allegory   99

7. Between Bridges   117

8. 8½ or 9½   133

9. Recapturing Lost Moments   153

10. The Little Man Becomes a Legend   171

11. Allen's Rose Period   189

Notes and References   215
Selected Bibliography   224
Filmography   231
Index   241

ABOUT THE AUTHOR

Nancy Pogel is a professor of American Thought and Language and teaches in the Film Thematic Program at Michigan State University. She received her A.B. in English and journalism from Grinnell College, her M.A. in American studies from the University of Wyoming, and her Ph.D. in English from the University of Wisconsin–Madison. She has delivered papers on film comedy, women in film, and American literary humor at PCA, MLA, MMLA, and CEA meetings. Her articles and reviews appear in *Literature/Film Quarterly, MidAmerica, American Literature, American Humor,* vol. 2 of the *Dictionary of Literary Biography, American Women by Women, Midwest Miscellany, Dictionary of American Biography, Twentieth-Century Romance and Gothic Writers,* and *Heritage of the Midwest.* With Paul Somers, Jr., she is coauthor of a chapter on "Literary Humor" in *Genres of American Humor* and a chapter on "Editorial Cartooning" in vol. 2 of *The Handbook of American Popular Culture.*

PREFACE

This book began in 1977 as a series of papers for a Woody Allen film festival shortly after Allen completed *Annie Hall*. Since that time Allen has grown considerably as a filmmaker, and he has become more prolific. Allen's increased productivity as well as the complexity of his recent films makes it difficult for interpreters to keep pace with him. This explains why his most current films are not included here; it also bears on my decision to concentrate on the films following *Annie Hall* and to limit my study to films over which Allen exercised most control—those for which he wrote the original screenplay or which he both wrote and directed.

Like so many of our greatest humorists, Woody Allen appears to see the world in terms of contrarieties and oppositions. My readings of the major films from *Take the Money and Run* to *The Purple Rose of Cairo* are primarily concerned with Allen's dialogues and debates, his reflexivity, and the role of his "little men" characters within his dialogic structure and style. Although Allen's films fit no critical categorizations securely, Mikhail Bakhtin's discussion of intertextuality and the dialogical imagination provide a spacious framework for interpreting Allen's densely allusive, inconclusive films. Prominent intertextual references to film genres, to individual films, to literature, and to popular culture are means of entrance into most of the films considered here. I regard these references as more than casual in-jokes; they are integral to understanding Allen's contemporary critical sensibility, his techniques and effects.

My first chapter recalls Allen's links with twentieth-century literary humor and with a genre of comic films; however, the focus is on how Allen's work is also distinguished from those backgrounds and represents a conversation, as well as a quarrel, with these and a great many other influences. A portion of that chapter first appeared in an essay I wrote for Stanley Trachtenberg's *American Humorists* (Detroit: Gale Research, 1982). The biographical section that follows is a helpful compilation from secondary materials—interviews and the like—but Allen aficionados, who are familiar with Allen's public attitudes and what little we know about his private life, may wish to skim those discussions.

Because of my special interest in the later films, analyses of the early comedies in chapters 3 and 4 should serve as an introduction and background to the films following *Annie Hall*. While examining Allen's more recent efforts, I have tried to respond to several negative critical estimations of *Interiors, Stardust Memories*, and *A Midsummer Night's Sex Comedy*. Although the issue could have been raised earlier in the book, the final chapter offers a convenient opportunity to deal with Bakhtin's views of the carnivalesque in relation to Allen's work, but especially with regard to *Broadway Danny Rose* and *The Purple Rose of Cairo*.

In order to retain more of the flavor of the films as we experience them in the theater, I look at the details of Allen's productions within their narrative context as much as possible. I have generally left consideration of the specific contributions by Allen's fine ensemble of cinematographers, editors, and production designers to someone else. Although the films represent a group effort, the unusual amount of authority that Allen retains over his films justifies such an attitude.

No consideration of Allen's cinema can avoid dealing with his little-man protagonists. Now that Allen has completed his fifteenth film and is probably working on his sixteenth and seventeenth, it is appropriate to ask again what has become of the humble victim of *Take the Money and Run*. Poised at the intersection of competing options, he has been a surrogate for both spectator and filmmaker. He has been both self-conscious and unaware; a character to take seriously and a mockery of himself. Recently, Woody Allen's little man has been jostled about by more intense currents in his film environment than were evident in the early films. While he remains, even today, a remarkable antihero, he has become an insider as well as an outsider. His image has become, in one sense, less distinct; he has compromised and been compromised by those closest to him and by time and history. Even as Allen's heroes and heroines remain representatives of his (and our) "fighting for a faith," when we encounter Allen's central characters in some recent films, they may evoke a sense of loss.

In dealing with little-man main characters and their place amid a great many choices and alternatives, Woody Allen's reflexive cinema also deals with the role of the spectator and the artist in relation to film itself. His films explore critical questions that tie culture and ideology to the nature of the mass media as well as to psychological and metaphysical concerns. They carry on debates between fabulation and realism, between illusionism and anti-illusionism. While Allen's dialogic films, especially following the early comedies, never leave us with clear solutions to aesthetic, psychological, or political problems, Allen's active experimentation with style and idea heightens our ability to feel and to observe, to know ourselves and our world. Allen's sad and funny films make us look anew at the fundamental questions of our existence; they express our utopian hopes and they deconstruct them and their expression. They explore the advantages and limitations that come with time, sophistication, and self-awareness; and they consider our absurd but powerful dreams of an authentic innocence—our longing for satisfaction beyond frustrated desire.

Nancy Pogel

ACKNOWLEDGMENTS

Were this book to have a dedication, it would go to my family, my teachers, and my friends who have actively supported my work. I am particularly grateful to David D. Anderson for years of professional encouragement and for introducing me to Twayne. And I am indebted to Charles Cleaver, Hamlin Hill, and John S. Tuckey for introducing me to Mark Twain—whose dialogic novels prepared me to take on Woody Allen's films. I am also thankful to colleagues in the MSU Department of American Thought and Language film program: Herbert Bergman, Edward Recchia, Douglas Noverr, William Chamberlain, and Erik Lunde read parts of the manuscript, opened their libraries to me, and offered good advice. Harold Currie, Henry Silverman, and Jennifer Banks juggled schedules so I would have time to write. Portions of this manuscript were completed with the aid of Michigan State University research grants.

My work would have proceeded even more slowly were it not for the assistance of Charles Silver and the Film Study Center of the Museum of Modern Art, Sue Wilt of the MSU Instructional Media Center, and Anita Evans of MSU Libraries. Pauline Adams, Pat Anderson, Robert Eberwein, Barry Gross, Perry Gianakos, Jim Limbacher, Marilyn and John Nathan, and Dr. Michael Salesin responded to inquiries and/or helped me to obtain documents. Betty Uphaus typed early drafts of the manuscript.

Warren French has been a most patient and perceptive field editor; over eight years ago he was farsighted enough to recognize Woody Allen's significance for this series. Borgna Brunner was the in-house editor, Lewis DeSimone supervised the copyediting, and Janet Zietowski guided the book through production. Woody Allen kindly checked the chronology for errors.

Finally, my husband, Larry Landrum deserves special thanks for reading the manuscript and for repeatedly reminding me that my enterprise was worthwhile.

CHRONOLOGY

1935	Born on 1 December in Brooklyn, New York, Allan Stewart Konigsberg is the first of two children, of Martin and Nettie Konigsberg.
1948–1952	Attends Midwood High School in Brooklyn. While still in high school attracts the attention of David O. Alber, who engages the seventeen-year-old to ghostwrite jokes for Guy Lombardo, Sammy Kaye, and Arthur Murray.
1952	Signs with William Morris Agency. Writes TV comedy skits for Pat Boone, Herb Shriner, Peter Lind Hayes, and Buddy Hackett. After high school briefly attends New York University and City College of New York. Fails course in movie production at NYU and drops out of CCNY.
1953	Writes for Sid Caesar's specials. Works with Larry Gelbart, Mel Brooks, and others.
1953–1954	Goes to Hollywood at eighteen as part of NBC Writer's Development Program. Works on "Colgate Comedy Hour." Collaborates with Danny Simon. Marries Harlene Rosen. Moves back to New York and writes nightclub material for Kay Ballard, Carol Channing, and Stubby Kaye.
1958	Leaves William Morris Agency and manager Harvey Meltzer. Begins long-term association with managers Jack Rollins and Charles Joffe.
1960	Divorced from Harlene Rosen. Special nightclub audition at the Blue Angel.
1961	First major nightclub engagement at the Duplex in Greenwich Village.
1962	Tours college campuses. Meets Louise Lasser and Dick Cavett.

1964   Charles Feldman sees Allen's act at the Blue Angel and asks him to write and appear in *What's New, Pussycat?*.

1965   Marries Louise Lasser. *What's New, Pussycat?* opens in New York to mixed reviews but is a box-office success.

1966   Dubs *What's Up, Tiger Lily?* First play, *Don't Drink the Water,* opens on Broadway. Begins contributing pieces to the *New Yorker.* Frequent appearances on television.

1967   Appears in *Casino Royale.*

1968   *Play It Again, Sam,* second play, opens on Broadway.

1969   *Take the Money and Run,* first film that Allen writes, directs and stars in. Film version of *Don't Drink the Water,* starring Jackie Gleason. Divorced from Louise Lasser.

1971   *Bananas,* second major film. Publishes *Getting Even,* first collection of essays and stories. Writes "The Woody Allen Comedy Special," for PBS, which is never aired because it contains "controversial material." Lives with Diane Keaton for about a year.

1972   Film version of *Play It Again, Sam,* starring Allen but directed by Herbert Ross. *Everything You Always Wanted to Know about Sex* (*but were afraid to ask).*

1973   *Sleeper.*

1975   *Love and Death.* Publishes *Without Feathers,* second collection of writings.

1976   Appears in *The Front,* directed by Martin Ritt.

1977   *Annie Hall.*

1978   *Interiors.* Allen directs and writes but does not appear in his first noncomic film. Appointed to directorate of the Vivian Beaumont Theater at

Lincoln Center in New York. *Annie Hall* wins four Academy Awards.

1979   *Manhattan.* Academy Award nomination as Best Director for *Interiors.*

1980   *Stardust Memories.* Publishes third collection of writings, *Side Effects.* Begins long-term personal relationship with Mia Farrow. Ends ten-year business relationship with United Artists to join a former UA team at Orion Pictures.

1981   *The Floating Lightbulb,* a play, opens at Lincoln Center in New York, 27 April.

1982   *A Midsummer Night's Sex Comedy.*

1983   *Zelig.*

1984   *Broadway Danny Rose.*

1985   *The Purple Rose of Cairo.* Academy Award nomination as Best Director for *Broadway Danny Rose.*

1986   *Hannah and Her Sisters.*

Woody Allen and his "comedian comedy" ancestors (clockwise from top left): Charlie Chaplin, Harold Lloyd, Buster Keaton, and Bob Hope. *Courtesy of Woody Allen and United Artists.*

1

Little Men and Dialogues: An Introduction

"How wrong Emily Dickinson was!" writes Woody Allen. "Hope is not 'the thing with feathers.' The thing with feathers has turned out to be my nephew. I must take him to a specialist in Zurich."[1] Like his films, Woody Allen's joke involves both a distrust of optimism and a funny "little man's" perspective that innocently and matter-of-factly mocks its own seriousness. In this "Selection from the Allen Notebooks," as in all of his films, Allen carries on dialogues with others' worldviews as well as with his own, and he recalls an earlier, more innocent vision of life that contrasts with sophisticated contemporary experience. From his first comedies to his later more earnest experiments, Allen's paradoxical films confront the ambiguities of our times. His finest work exposes a culture that simultaneously promises and frustrates the fulfillment of our desires, while his comic spirit reminds us of our humanity and of our stubborn resistance to all life-denying, closed systems.

Allen is regarded today as one of America's most important humorists and filmakers. Although his films ultimately achieve their impact because of his ability to reach audiences with his particular style and concerns, his work also participates in a definable tradition of American literary and film comedy. The most consistent qualities of his inconsistent films, his little-man main characters and his reflexive,[2] dialogic style[3] have arche-

typal roots,[4] but their immediate ancestry is traceable to patterns in twentieth-century American humor that first appear as
a trend with the rise of modernism following World War I.

Walter Blair describes the history of American humor as occurring in two consecutive but overlapping movements. From
its beginnings through the nineteenth century, native American
humor, also called "horse sense" or "common sense" humor,
predominates, while twentieth-century humor is a "dementia-
praecox" variety, or humor of "the little soul."[5] Blair sees the
older native American sort as a humor of "gumption" and
"mother wit."[6] Born out of the frontier experience and national
self-confidence, its tall-tale or down-home regional heroes know
who they are, usually exhibit control over their environment,
and see their world as relatively predictable and stable. Their
values are firmly grounded in common-sense experience. Often
racy and vigorous, nineteenth-century humor regards sex as
good, natural fun.

Dementia-praecox or little-man humor, on the other hand, has
been associated with the decay of a unitary national mythology,
the loss of national self-confidence, and the diminished lot of the
ordinary individual in modern times. Modern humorists find
their world bewildering and unreliable rather than stable; rapid
changes constantly threaten their values, the environment often
seems overwhelming. As a result, their tone is often anxious,
neurotic—even hysterical; they sometimes retreat into "inner
space," into fantasy worlds of impossible dreams and self-deni-
grating nightmares. Hamlin Hill once suggested that this more
"urbane humor . . . reflects the tinge of insanity and despair of
contemporary society."[7] The American little-man character, who
came into his own with the rise of modernism in the 1920s, is
beleaguered by big business; by even the simplest machines; by
Darwinian biology and survival-of-the-fittest morality; by the
rise of social science, progressive education, Freudian psychology, and the mass media. He is also bedeviled by women.[8] In
dementia-praecox humor, sex is "a source of anxiety and frustration";[9] although the little man longs for intimacy, he usually
has trouble finding it.

If the exuberant backwoods adventures of Davy Crockett and Mike Fink are examples of the native American tradition, essays and stories by James Thurber, Robert Benchley, and S. J. Perelman, the *New Yorker* humorists of the 1920s and 1930s, as well as many of the silent-film clown comedians, provide early examples of twentieth-century little-man humor in America. Amid Perelman's patchwork of hysterical rhythms, his imitations and parodies of literary styles, his distrust of nature, and his longing for an easier life (where there are also delicatessens); amid Benchley's gentler attacks on scientific and political solutions to human dilemmas; or amid Thurber's satire of books that "explain" sex, and his little man's triumph over arrogant empiricism in "The Unicorn in the Garden," lies the understanding that the languages through which their forebears made their worlds comprehensible have become problematic.

If the sound of native American humor is the "barbaric yawp" of a "ring-tailed roarer," the sound of little-man humor is a deep sigh and a whine. Beneath the little man's lamentations about his difficulties with modern life, lies an outrage with indeterminacy and instability. The early little-man humorist stands at the intersection of contradictory options; he feels himself to be a stranger in his own culture; familiar settings come to seem dreamlike, artificial, and unreal. Behind the little-man humorist's jokes lies a sense of innocence lost to time and the complexities of a fast-paced modern life; these humorists, however, are not merely negative or nostalgic; they hasten to cover their vulnerability before they become sentimental. They both criticize their society and make fun of themselves.

Despite the fact that conventional meaning and value systems no longer offer solace, the little man tries to remain a basically ethical character, one whose attempts to be honest set him apart from the modern mob and serve as a positive contrast to the modern environment in which he tries to maintain his sanity. Norris Yates observes that despite all the opposition he faces, the twentieth-century humorous type embodies certain desirable values: "a sense of the golden mean, everyday common sense, personal integrity, a belief in monogamy and stability

. . . , a measure of personal and political freedom." According to Yates, the little-man humorist is "the conscience of the twentieth century," and little-man characters are one version of the "wise fool": "either as the *naif* or simple fellow with direct, clear insight like the child who saw the emperor had nothing on at all, or as the 'eccentric' jester who slashes his alleged betters with satire that would sting if it didn't come from an apparently stupid or disreputable character."[10] Sanford Pinsker found that "the typical Perelman creation is an irritated innocent . . . who sets his particular 'No!' in thunder against our culture's expectations and its junk."[11]

While some degree of self-consciousness and self-parody was present in native American humor as in all humor, it appears more pointedly in the twentieth-century literary tradition. Using highly artificial prose, asides, authorial interruptions, fantasies within their fantasies, and other reflexive, anti-illusionistic narrative devices, Perelman and the little-man literary humorists often made fun of their scapegoat characters and their medium, even as they wrote in it, and of their own modicum of romanticism, even as they fought to retain it. They are both outside or above the worlds they satirize and in them, debating with themselves and with others about the possibilities for survival. Like Woody Allen's response several decades later to issues even more difficult, their humor is both a cry of rebellion and a self-protective reaction to future shock.

The little man became a major figure in comic films during the same period in which the literary humorists created their little-man characters. The little-man "outlaw/fugitive" or "loner/reject" is the central figure in "comedian comedy," a genre which Steve Seidman traces back to our earliest comic films.[12] The little man or woman who appears to be eccentric, childlike, mad, and/or creative and fantasizing in film comedy evolves from the entertainer's role as a figure historically regarded as being outside of the dominant culture. Comedian comedy's typical use of reflexive techniques is closely related to performers' prefilmic backgrounds in vaudeville, music hall, or stand-up

comedy, and to their special awareness of the spectator or audience whom they entertain.[13]

Comedian comedy shares with other film genres a double appeal to audiences' repressed anticultural desires and to their
need for censorship of such desires and the validation of cultural
values. In little-man or comedian comedy, as in its literary humor analogue, the opposition involves an apparently confused
or eccentric individual identity in conflict with an identity that
the dominant culture can accept. Unlike many of the literary
little-man essays and tales, however, most film treatments
transform the little man in order to resolve this conflict and to
reaffirm culture's faith in social conformity.[14]

Some of the same cultural climate that produced the literary
little-man humorists influenced the first little-man-and-woman
comedian comics, silent-screen clowns such as Buster Keaton,
Harold Lloyd, Marie Dressler, Mabel Normand, Harry Langdon,
Charlie Chaplin, and the transitional Laurel and Hardy. Of
these, Woody Allen speaks most frequently about Keaton and
Chaplin, in whose work one finds some of the best early visual
examples of little-man style. Although Allen's films must number such reflexive classics as Keaton's *Sherlock Jr.* among their
ancestors, Allen is fonder of Chaplin than he is of Keaton, whose
comedy he feels is "colder."[15]

It is Chaplin who consolidated the little-man tradition in film.
In Chaplin's best-remembered films, the little tramp (whose costume informed us of his marginal social status), was distinguished both by his fallibility and by his ability to survive in the
face of intimidating enemies and an overbearing environment.
Caught in the oversized cogs of a huge machine or bewildered
by the speed of the assembly line, Chaplin's innocent little man
became a commentator on his times, a human alternative in a
dehumanizing world. Most fascinating, perhaps, were his attempts to alter an unpleasant situation by means of fantasy or
the imagination. Behind Chaplin's need to maintain tenuous illusions for the sake of survival, as he winds his shoe's laces
around his fork for spaghetti or dreams of performing the

oceana roll for dance hall women in *The Gold Rush,* is a brave triumph over a precarious reality. But these dreams of desire also offer flimsy solutions. Like Allen's films, Chaplin's often reflexive art is ambivalent about the powers of the imagination, holding faith and skepticism in delicate balance.

Like several of Allen's main characters, Chaplin's tramp is remembered as being childlike—sometimes playfully creative, sometimes the aggressive smart aleck, but always a countercultural figure, and a survivor. Indeed, Chaplin's films, such as *Modern Times,* eschew the conventional resolution that favors cultural, as opposed to countercultural, values. Like Allen's persona, the little tramp speaks to us about loneliness, the fragility of innocence, the survival of human spirit and the need for human connection in an increasingly more unpredictable world. Under such conditions, the only consistency exists in the main character himself; in Chaplin's last films, even that consistent clown character may become only a memory. Chaplin's most enduring images of the little tramp waddling down an open road are inconclusive—they involve a blend of pathos and comedy that just escapes affectation. Chaplin's ability to pull his images up just short of sentimentality is a characteristic Allen admired. According to Allen, "It says a lot about love."[16]

In addition to learning his craft by reading the work of writers like Perelman and Benchley and by seeing the films of the silent clowns, Allen saw a great many comic and noncomic movies of the 1940s and 1950s. Some were clearly illusionistic films that created the sorts of perfect heroes the little man wanted to become but could never be. Predominantly, such classical Hollywood films fostered a seamless, empathic, and passive relationship between audience and film world, so that the audience felt it was participating in the "reality" on the screen. The most illusionistic of such films were closed worlds that tended to resolve contradictions and to reinforce traditional social mores rather than to question them in any significant manner.

Some comedian comedies in the 1930s, following the more aggressive middle and later Chaplin films, were made by such iconoclastic little men and women comics as Mae West or the Marx Brothers, but during the 1940s and 1950s, American comedian comedy, shaped in great part by economic pressures—by television and a changing marketplace[17]—became less aggressive, both philosophically and stylistically. While comedian comedy in the 1940s and 1950s contained reflexive elements, these were seldom used as creatively or as provocatively as in some early film comedy, where filmmakers were closer to the apparatus and where audiences and comedians were still delighted and puzzled by the illusions that the new medium produced.

Reflexive devices continued to play a minor role in films of the forties and fifties; however, they were usually not essential to the films' structures or primary motifs and did little to seriously interrupt or question the audiences' empathic participation in "transparent" films—to make audiences aware of the film as a constructed series of illusions and of their roles as spectators, or to encourage active rather than passive viewing. Rather, what reflexivity did appear usually took the form of superficial puns or light jokes that operated on the surface of what was predominantly a realistic narrative, complete with a comfortable resolution and a restoration of status quo values. Similarly, although the little man was an outsider who temporarily evoked anticultural alternatives, such "otherness" in the work of Jerry Lewis, Jack Benny, or even the early Bob Hope, whose timing and smart-alecky routines Allen especially admired,[18] did not often explore any truly unsettling alternatives to classical cinema. Such films probably did not attempt to raise, nor succeed in raising political, metaphysical, or psychological issues in spectators' minds; rather the films' comedy served to reaffirm conventional wisdom.

While Allen's work is clearly indebted to a long tradition, especially to immediate antecedents in twentieth-century American literature and comedian comedy, his little-man humor is also distinctive. Beginning as a comic writer who recalls Ben-

chley and Perelman as special inspirations,[19] Allen eventually
elaborates on his little-man character and on the comedian
comedy genre—extends the tradition into stand-up comedy and
then into a more intense and unsettling contemporary filmic
experience.

In Allen's postmodern films, the little man appears in a more
perplexing set of contexts. Indeed, Allen's work is densely "intertextual" or dialogic—made up of intersecting texts that provide commentary on one another or that "mutually and
ideologically interanimate" or "illuminate" each other.[20] In Allen's films, as in Mikhail Bakhtin's view of the dialogic novel,
one text or style "argues with [another], agrees with it (although
with conditions), interrogates it, eavesdrops on it, but also rid-
icules it, parodically exaggerates it."[21] Bakhtin contrasts dialogic texts (or texts that carry on dialogues with other texts, but do
not resolve them in favor of a unitary or unproblematic meaning) with "monoglottic" or "monologic" texts, which tend to as-
sert an unproblematic single truth. Ultimately, dialogic texts
are reflexive: they have as their concern the very language or
medium of representation itself. However, although dialogic
texts are antiunitary, "at the same time there does exist a center
of language. . . . The author cannot be found at any one of the
[work's] language levels: he is to be found at the center of or-
ganization where all levels intersect."[22] As the little-man humorists are both inside and outside their comic situations, so
the dialogic author and his text. He is inside the text and part
of it, but he also looks at language, "from the outside, with another's eye, from the point of view of a potentially different language and style."[23]

Allen films carry on a great many dialogues over ideas, style,
and form. The little man becomes the focus of Allen's existential
predilection for dismantling monologic belief systems and social conventions with a greater tenacity then most early little-
man humorists or filmmakers were willing to pursue. Allen has
no sure solutions, but he effectively questions our most comforting cultural norms or fundamental beliefs and lays doubt on
the claims of those concepts that pretend to offer meaning, and

prevent people from facing the crucial problems of existence. Resisting the closed perspectives of conventional comedian comedy, Allen appears to be opposed to all that is "ready-made and completed, to all pretense at immutability."[24] But, like Bakhtin, he also questions the dangers of unconditional pluralism and radical anti-dogmatism. His perspective allows for no assurances, not even finally a confidence in the mind "as itself the basis of an aesthetic ordered at a profound level and revealed to consciousness at isolated 'epiphanic' moments,"[25] as in the ending to Federico Fellini's *8½*. For all his existential affinity, Allen also appears to recognize the weaknesses in existential arguments on behalf of both art and self-consciousness as the highest forms of authenticity, and even as he takes such oases seriously, he also questions them as yet other means of rationalizing contradictions.

While Allen provides no answers to explain away the apparent meaninglessness of life, and while he appears to question in one film what were his own favorite refuges in another, his films are not mere formalistic exercises that evoke quietism, nor are they merely examples of radical-subjectivism or narcissism, any more than they are wholly negative satires, on the one hand, or optimistic polemics for moral reform, on the other. They portray a weave of interrelationships between the individual and the social contexts and history within which he or she struggles for definition and transformation. His films are always *of* this world, and they deal with the everyday concerns that make up the hope and hopelessness of the human condition. They criticize dehumanization; they evoke a longing for renewal, for authenticity, for human connection—but they convey doubt about such utopian possibilities at the same time. Allen recognizes the restrictions inherent in contemporary life, but his films carry sympathy for the human predicament and encourage people to continue to struggle honestly and to remember their humanity amid life's confusion and difficulty.

Allen's work depends for its effects upon a complex set of relationships among spectator, artist, and little-man character. In his initial films, the little-man figure, usually played by Allen,

is the viewer's surrogate. The little-man character is a particularly apt mediator between the world of the film and the spectator sitting in the theater. He is a conduit for what some film
theorists describe as the cinema's greatest power over the spectator: our desire to return to a primal dream state, that lost authentic experience of childhood fulfillment and unity, in which
subject and object, mother and offspring satisfied each other's
desires.[26] The little man permits us to identify with the source
of our own desire for fulfillment, precisely because he is so bereft
of satisfaction for his own desire, because he appears to be so
physically and linguistically inexperienced and inept, so small
of stature, so needy.[27] His emptiness and alienation remind us of
our own, while his helplessness mediates between our needs and
the promise inherent in his being on the screen—our longing for
childhood unity lost to adulthood and sophistication, our trust
in the satisfaction of desire that wish-fulfilling patterns of transparent cinema have told us can be attained.

Yet at the same time that he invites empathy, the little man
does not make the audience so vulnerable as to make the identification dangerous; initially, he also evokes from the spectator
a comforting adult superiority, for even in our alienated lives,
we arrogantly think ourselves far more at one with our worlds
than he. Given our experience with recurrent patterns of comedian comedy, we anticipate that our sense of security will be
validated and that Allen's little man will join us in the adult
community before his adventures are over.

Like earlier little-men characters, Allen's figures also appeal
to our countercultural needs; they are childlike, fantasizing, destructive, eccentric, neurotic—filled with updated versions of
the modern anxieties that plagued the little-men characters of
the 1920s. Sometimes Allen's little man is the spectator; sometimes he is the artist seeking authenticity. In either case, he is
balanced at an intersection of competing possibilities. Although
the little man as artist is somewhat more self-aware, both he
and the little man as spectator are associated with a tentative,
innocent notion of language; they do not belong to established
language patterns. They search among languages; they question, experience, seek satisfaction among contradictory world-

views. They are never clearly identified with a single philosophy, but like their most provocative literary and filmic ancestors, they innocently arouse conscience in the twentieth century. Their childlike demeanor, fallibility, and humanity serve as contrasts to the dehumanizing pressures they inevitably encounter. As Allen's little men's desires are constantly frustrated, so one can hope, we recognize the frustrations in our own existence and identify and reject those dogmatic and dehumanizing forces within our culture that thwart our needs.

For all his importance as a searcher, however, the little man of Allen's films is also at times a ludicrous anachronism, a foolish character—even a corrupted one. While he invokes our sympathy and our conscience, while he represents our hopes for renewal, he is also part of a larger joke that mocks his (and our) innocence, his (and our) search for integrity, his (and our) longing for authenticity. The little-man's never-ending struggles between inner and outer worlds leave Allen's characters both caught within a gap amid dialogues, and always open to possibilities. Allen's attitude toward his little man is ambivalent: the laughter he creates is "gay, triumphant and at the same time mocking, deriding."[28]

It is true that some of Allen's little men eventually appear to succeed in terms resembling the resolutions of traditional classical films. They may therefore seem to fulfill, as little men in comedian comedy usually do, not only our countercultural needs, but our cultural needs—our desire for stability and reaffirmation of the status quo (success for the Allen little man usually involves some degree of fulfillment in the form of love, defined as an authentic human connection and sexual communication with a woman, which alleviates the little man's loneliness and alienation without invalidating his "otherness"). But even these successes or resolutions are conditional. There is, in fact, some evidence that even from the earliest films, Allen intended to deny his little men (and his spectators) satisfaction, that he wanted to leave his films' endings and the fate of his little men even less conclusive than they came to be.[29] Even those conclusions in which the "loser" appears to "take all"[30] are to varying degrees subverted by the reflexive references that qualify the reliability of the narrative in which the little man's successes take place. Allen does not deny the potency of human connection and love, but he demonstrates how difficult it is for genuine communication to break through the encrustation of doctrinaire ideology and dehumanizing social conventions. Allen does not devalue genuine feeling; he even emphasizes its importance precisely in terms of the oppressive conditions that circumscribe it. But that does not mean that he ever settles into a belief that such recoveries provide salvations any more enduring than the fleeting moments in which they occur.

As much as reflexivity and self-consciousness have been part of American film comedy from the days of the silent clowns, today, the modern filmmaker assumes that spectators have more experience with film than they did earlier in the century. The opportunities for intertextual filmic references are therefore greater now, since film has a well-established history and an audience that has been raised on movies and socialized on visual imagery. Thus, Allen is able to impersonate a larger number of film styles and conventions than the creators of earlier comedian comedies, and he can provide more resonant dialogic relationships between the little man's search for fulfillment and a postmodern world that is "singularly uncertain, insecure, self-questioning and culturally pluralistic."[31]

The dialogues Allen creates utilize a sense of play with verbal and visual language that is typical of densely intertextual postmodern films: self-reflexive imagery (cameras, mirrors, etc.); retrospective structures; autobiographical allusions; appearances by the filmmaker in his own films; casting based on an actor's or actress's earlier films or personal life; use of real-life, theatrical, and nontheatrical figures in the midst of fictional film; narrative frames; discussions of art and filmmaking; and allusions to plays, novels, cartoons, short stories, television, and especially to other films. Such techniques "defamiliarize" the audience from Allen's films and achieve a variety of consequences.

Even Allen's earliest movies, which tend to use reflexivity in a conventional fashion and for purposes of light comedy, carry

hints of the larger questions that will dominate Allen's later seriocomedies. They may emphasize the problem we have sepa-
rating the fictional quality of reality from the reality of the
fictional world; they present our world as one where visual imagery indoctrinates, and roles are difficult to distinguish from
authentic experience. In doing so, they undermine the last remaining belief system, the very art we are seeing; they draw
attention to the role film plays as part of the very problem it is
exploring. They also represent a defensive tactic, used to create
distance, not only between the audience and the medium, but
between the filmmaker and his own fears of sentimentality.
They may even be interpreted as a dramatization of an Oedipal
struggle between identity and influence. Yet, while such techniques can emphasize the domination of the spectator by the
medium and the dominant culture the medium reflects, conversely (and simultaneously) such techniques may also be
freeing, for they disorient us and shock us into a reexamination
of conventional perceptions and mythologies, preparing the way
for new understanding and change. In this sense Allen's reflexive
cinema both "asserts and denies, it buries and revives."[32]

Paradoxically, then, just as Allen comes to mix comedy and
tragedy in his films, so he also mixes realism with anti-illusionistic, reflexive, or surrealistic techniques. Realistic conventions
help to make Allen's films accessible; they help to retain a film's
contact with the social world; sometimes they function within
a comedic context to enable the spectator to perceive the contrast between an inflexible norm, or valued convention within
an apparently orderly or consistent world, and the less conventional, often outrageous or subversive alternative to that regularity. Thus, traditional realistic-illusionistic surfaces serve as
referents with which the questioning or deconstructive reflexivity can carry on its dialogue. Because Allen combines these
realistic-illusionistic conventions with anti-illusionistic conventions in a variety of ways, his work is characterized by its ex-
perimental quality and by a tendency to remain in-process with
regard to both content and form.

The effects of the continuing dialogue between illusionistic and anti-illusionistic perspectives create some puzzling recurrent motifs in Allen's films. Although, overall, Allen's work is inconsistent and recursive rather than strictly progressive, several of his films, both individually and in groups, depict patterns of awakening or developing awareness in the films' littlemen characters and their surrogates. Such growing awareness is achieved only in the face of obstacles that multiply even as the awareness grows. The developing self-consciousness in the little-man character, because it is attached to his identification not only as spectator but also as film critic, writer, artist, or filmmaker, heightens the reflexivity and defamiliarization of the film to the point where the spectator is also forced into additional levels of self-awareness. While self-awareness helps the little man (and the spectator) to see what is wrong with the world he finds himself in, it also becomes part of the problem. The growing awareness evokes additional frustrations as it interferes with the search for innocence, naturalness, and authenticity that are the utopian hope and alternative to the dehumanizing contexts that plague the little man. Among their many paradoxes, then, Allen's films deal with a basic paradox of time and human existence. Adulthood and civilization may be incompatible with the innocent satisfaction of desire. The search for authenticity (or genuine innocence) is paradoxical because its objectives may not be able to coexist with the very selfawareness and urge for demystification that comes with experience.

At the same time, however, the pattern of increased self-consciousness in Allen's little-man heroes and the accompanying multiplication of reflexive techniques in his films help to create for the spectator (by contrast) an awareness of memorable brief occasions in the films—captured moments of innocence, of genuine sentiment, of human connection. These "loopholes" are saved from the depredations of self-consciousness and time, and at the same time they are circumscribed by them. Ultimately, such contradictions are not resolved within the films; they are left to the interaction between the spectator and the film. Allen's films come to seem like Escher drawings; what they say depends upon the active participation of those who read them.

To varying degrees, then, Allen's films are both open and closed worlds—dialogic, reflexive films that challenge confining ideologies with the very process of continuing inquiry, but films that do not remain at rest long enough to adopt a unitary stance. In their refusal to accept a comforting stasis in the face of uncertainty, Allen's films explore our longing for innocence, all the while making us aware of the burden that time, history, memory, and self-consciousness give us to bear in our attempt to achieve both individual authenticity and a more meaningful society. By creating a tension between our desires and our self-awareness, Allen produces films at once personal and social, funny and unsettling.

Lately, the little-man character has become less reliable, and his image has been threatened by increasingly more ominous conditions. However, even in some of Allen's recent films, where innocence may be only the memory of an image and where the little man and his integrity may be only a fading dream, Allen's main characters remain indications that, however absurdly, the filmmaker still clings—sometimes grimly—to a comic perspective. Even the films that convey most emphatically the emptiness and the frustrating ambiguities of our age, contain delicious, rebellious moments of affirmation that remind us how, remarkably, we manage to hope and to survive in an unstable world we are always helping to create.

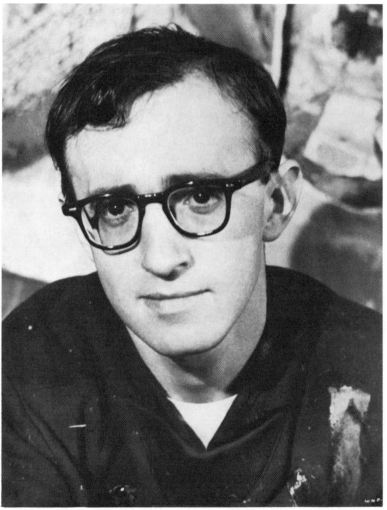

Woody Allen in the 1960s. *Courtesy of Woody Allen and Movie Star News.*

2

Will the Real Little Man
Please Stand Up?

Fans have always had difficulty distinguishing between Woody Allen's little-man character and his creator, but Allen takes pains to emphasize that he is a far cry from his persona; and recent writers tend to see the successful director, actor, and writer Allen as distinct from his creation. In fact, interviews with Allen reveal that he is unlike his little-man characters in a number of ways, but very much like them in others. Any picture of Woody Allen we attempt to construct will be as inconclusive as his dialogic films.

Critics of Allen as moralist and philosopher like to remind us that Woody Allen complains about the world's misery but lives in a Park Avenue duplex apartment designed by an interior decorator and filled with oriental rugs, Kokoschka watercolors, and expensive antiques.[1] He moves about town in a Rolls Royce, and he is making so much money today that nobody will discuss how much he is worth. He is a pretty good tennis player, a conscientious musician, and he is seldom without female companionship. For several years Mia Farrow has been a steady friend. He is acknowledged to be a financial, as well as an artistic, success.

Unlike his several disorganized little-man characters, Allen leads a disciplined life and tries to control his environment in order to save energy for his work. He is an early riser who regularly spends his mornings writing when he is not making a film. He never misses two hours of clarinet practice, and he often uses his exercise bike and takes walks. He may continue writing into the night or go out for dinner with one or more of his close friends; he employs a cook to make meals he eats at home. He frequently goes to the movies or to the theater. He seldom takes vacations.[2] He neither smokes nor drinks anything beyond an occasional glass of wine, and he does not like drugs.

Unlike his little-man character on the job, Allen has confidence in his writing talents and his comic gifts, which have seldom failed him. He doesn't worry so much that his sources of inspiration will dry up, but that he will not be able to develop all the ideas he has; what he does worry about is which idea to pursue next.[3] Although he has a workroom with a typewriter, he likes to write in longhand sitting on his bed. Of the three major stages in filmmaking, he enjoys writing and editing more than filming. Like many screenplay writers, rather than producing a finished script, Allen writes his films in note form, and his movies are not improvised so much as actually written on location once he can see the set and the actors; he preserves a sense of freshness in his films because he usually doesn't rehearse them. Allen's jokes come either during the writing or filming stages. "Sometimes," he told Robert F. Moss, "I'll just think up one joke and I'll try to set it up in the film. For example, I did a scene in *Annie Hall* with Paul Simon. We improvised and I just said to Paul: 'Try to get to the word "mellow" eventually because I have a joke I want to tell.' "[4] Allen writes about three to five hours a day, steadily, rather than in single bursts of inspiration, and he can't stand noise as he produces the half-dozen drafts he usually goes through. Because he discovers themes while he is filming and editing, Allen does not pick his film's titles until the movies are completed.[5]

On the set, Penelope Gilliatt has observed, Allen is "like a conductor":[6] clearly in control. Gordon Willis, frequently Allen's cinematographer since *Annie Hall*, says Allen "is one of the most meticulous men I have ever dealt with. He doesn't let anything slide. He's quiet but determined."[7] Allen is also precise in the editing room. When he worked with Ralph Rosenblum up through *Interiors*, Rosenblum preferred to make a rough cut of the film and then "fine tune" it, but Allen likes to make a careful first cut so that it more closely resembles the final film. In 1980 Allen said: "To this day, I can't thread a movieola or splice two pieces of film together. I have no interest in movies from that point of view. But regardless of the limited technical background you start with, you quickly begin to make distinctions between good and bad lighting, good photography and bad, sophisticated and unsophisticated editing."[8]

Allen does not overpower the ensemble of the people who help him make his films, but he is even more involved today than he was when he made his first movie. Because he knows more, he considers himself more "obsessive," and he says: "I work much, much harder at filmmaking today. I'm much more involved with sets, costumes, photography, all aspects of the picture." After showing his film to a small group, Allen tests it on a larger one of perhaps a hundred people, to learn what has to be changed. Allen is exacting about continuity in lighting and composition. In the old days, he would have cared more about the laugh than the visual image, but today Allen budgets three or four weeks reshooting time to correct imperfections in his work.[9]

Over the years, Allen has also gained a reputation as a competent businessman. He controls not only the script, the casting, the shooting, the editing, and the final cut of his film, but the film's marketing. According to a former executive for United Artists, which marketed *Bananas* through *Manhattan*, Allen budgets films so they'll turn a small profit or create only a small loss. "His business sense is extraordinary. He knows that his fiscal conservatism and preplanning are what allow him to make other movies. If he had spent $20 million on *A Midsummer Night's Sex Comedy* instead of 5½ million, he would have had trouble getting the financing for *Zelig*."[10] *Annie Hall*, which initially grossed only $20 million but has now grossed between $80 million and $100 million, cost only $4 million to make. *Everything You Always Wanted to Know about Sex,* which by 1985 had grossed $16 million in studio rentals, cost just $2 million to produce.[11] Even Allen's films that do not do well in the United States recoup losses in Europe. Initially, *Annie Hall, Interiors,* and *Manhattan* all made more money abroad than at home.[12] Allen refuses to permit misleading promotion and advertising. Not only does he authorize the marketing, publicity, and advertising for his pictures, but he is also involved in the details of choosing good quotes from reviews, and the design of coming-attraction trailers, publicity posters, and advertising formats; he even suggests to distributors what sorts of theaters his films should appear in.[13]

In a highly competitive medium Allen manages not only to be a good businessman, but to retain his integrity, to take risks, and to grow artistically. Allen told Richard J. H. Johnston as early as 1969 that he feared becoming a "specialist" who would not develop and use all his talents.[14] Allen admires filmmakers like Chaplin who took chances and failed, but did not rest in one place throughout their careers.[15] In 1976, before *Annie Hall* was released, Allen described his long-term goals: "I'd like to keep growing in my work, I'd like to do more serious comical films and do different types of films. . . . And take chances—I would like to fail a little for the public. . . . What I want to do is go on to areas that I'm insecure about and not so good at."[16] Allen believes failure is a good indication that you're not just playing it safe. When you only try to make films that are hits, he believes that "compromises and concessions" begin to show up in the work.[17]

Allen is aware of his audience, of his critics, and of the fact that his films have to make profits if he is going to survive as a filmmaker, but although he believes that the primary object of the artist is to entertain,[18] he also believes that audience reactions to films are almost "totally subjective," that you can't please everybody, and that the filmmaker has to make the film he wants. Thus, although he listens to audiences and critics, and is willing to take material out of a film when it is not effective, he never violates his own intentions in order to put something in a film that audiences like but he doesn't.[19]

The first real evidence of growth in Allen's major films since 1969 occurs with *Sleeper*, where he begins to become more interested in the visual qualities of his films. "Since then," says Allen, "I've gotten deeper and deeper into visually arresting films. It's not just decorative, of course, but hopefully part of the storytelling. . . . With each film, one struggles to utilize photography, light, colors, sound track, performances more effectively and integrate them better into the character of the film."[20] Mel Bourne, Allen's most frequent production designer since *Annie Hall*, says that "working with Woody Allen is a lot like going back to school. He has ideas that really push techniques."[21]

The greatest risk Allen has taken in the course of his career, however, has been his movement from comedy to more solemn films and seriocomedies. Although Allen insisted early in his career that he didn't "differentiate between 'comedy' and 'serious' work" and that he resented the word 'serious' used in contrast with humorous,[22] he also told Frank Rich that even as a child he was attracted to tragedy. "There was something about the moodiness, the austerity, the apparent profundity of Elia Kazan's films then that sucked me in. With comedy you can buy yourself out of the problems of life and diffuse them. In tragedy you must confront them and it is painful, but I'm a real sucker."[23]

As Allen was finishing *Annie Hall*, Jack Kroll observed that "inside this clown there's a tragedian who's not only struggling to get out, but who's just about made it."[24] By the time he made *Manhattan*, Allen's little man had matured and Allen's film style had grown considerably. Allen took his greatest risks with *Interiors*, his first entirely noncomic film, and it received mixed reviews in the United States. Although he was not satisfied with the results, he did not regret taking chances making it. "If you try for something and it fails honorably, it's better failing that way than to succeed with something exploitative," he said.[25] Today, Allen tries to reach a balance of comedy and drama that he did not feel he achieved with much success in *Annie Hall* and *Manhattan*. "The pitfall," he says, "is the temptation to do comedy, then stop and do something serious, then back to the humor, then some more drama. The trick is to truly integrate the comedy and the drama, to intertwine them. I've decided that the only really effective way to mix the two modes is to do drama and interpolate comedy into it."[26]

Although Allen has seen phenomenal success, there are still significant relationships between the man and his anxious little-soul persona. Allen actually does not like machines and has trouble with cars; he also dislikes "bugs, country life, and sex manuals."[27] He prefers gloomy to sunny days, and like Alvy Singer in *Annie Hall*, he sounds like he suffers from anhedonia, the inability to enjoy life. In 1970 Allen said, "One thing I know is that there is no real correlation between economic success and freedom from your fears. The hang-ups remain hang-ups, however much money you make."[28] There are no indications that this view has changed in recent years.

Allen has been in psychotherapy for twenty-nine years, and he says that therapy has helped him with his shyness and his relating to people. While he does not think that it has helped him dramatically with his work, he believes that there have been small effects, and he holds out hope for long-term influences. "I feel that if I lost some of these anxieties," he has said, "I'd be able to reach more of humanity with my work. A comedian like W. C. Fields who was an enormous comic talent, spoke to a smaller audience because there was a certain lack of personal integration, a certain neurotic quality, whereas Chaplin had a greater feeling for the human condition."[29]

Allen acknowledges that on the surface of things he has no reason to be dissatisfied, but he admits to a "genetic dissatisfaction" with everything.[30] "Early in life," Allen says, "I was visited by the bluebird of anxiety."[31] From childhood he recalls being "terrified of death, of being kidnapped, of being on boats, and especially of the dark." He concedes that he's "still not thrilled with the dark."[32] Allen believes that S. J. Perelman summed up the character of great comics in one phrase, "Baby, it's cold inside."[33] Like many comedians and comic writers, Allen is seldom "on" in private and seldom cracks jokes on the set. "We're like people in a concentration camp," he said in 1974.[34]

Allen is also disheartened at least as much as the early little-man humorists were by civilization's "junk," by depersonalization and inauthenticity in modern life. "There's such a widespread religious disappointment," he has said, "a general realization about the emptiness of everything that's very hard for the society to bear. . . . It's a society with so many shortcomings—desensitized by television, drugs, fast-food chains, loud music and feelingless mechanical sex. Until we find a resolution for our terrors, we're going to have an expedient culture, that's all—directing all its energies toward coping with the nightmares and fears of existence, seeking nothing but peace, respite, and surcease from anxiety."[35] Allen says that the only meaning of life is that "nobody knows the meaning of life."[36] "Until we reach some understanding of who we are, what the purpose of creation was, what happens after death," Allen said, "we're caught in a maze of certain hysterical desperation. . . . Even sex won't improve until we've deciphered these ultimate meanings." Although he doesn't think much of modern life, Allen thinks about love and death a great deal. He sees "the whole thrust of human existence as one enormous escape from the fear of dying."[37]

Despite his many artistic successes, Allen, like his little-men characters, is often dissatisfied with his work. While making films brings Allen a certain amount of self-fulfillment, he does not speak of their giving him any real pleasure. "I always think the next thing I do will be fun. Then when I do it I don't like it at all."[38] Although Allen believes that his work is an authentic attempt, he longs for a day when he will make a film that he's totally satisfied with himself.[39]

Although Allen's anxieties about life's absurdity and about the spiritual aridity of contemporary culture make him a close relative of his later little-man characters, Allen is as complex and contradictory as most little-man humorists and their best little-man figures. For although he frequently describes the world as a grim place, he apparently still hopes for a recovery of human-itarian feeling and an improvement in the human condition. Allen worked for George McGovern's 1972 campaign although he preferred the more radical platform of Benjamin Spock.[40] He also supported Eugene McCarthy and John Lindsay—all liberal, progressive candidates for public office. He was disappointed with Ronald Reagan's election in 1980 because he felt that Reagan's domestic programs denied the poor and because he disliked Reagan's stance on nuclear weapons and the environment.[41]

Allen does not think of himself as a political person, however. "I'm not that political," he said in 1974. "I believe . . . change has to be voluntary, that you've got to get to a situation where people will act not because there are laws making them act that way but because they see the benefit, the enjoyment, of the hu-manitarian ideal. . . . Until they see it, it can't be foisted on them, it has to be achieved through a change of consciousness. It can't come about by violent revolution because as Hannah Arendt says in her book *On Revolution*, any violence only breeds more violence. . . . I guess you could call me a *probable* nonvi-olent revolutionary."[42] Allen reduces some political controver-sies to what he considers the essential opposition between "fascism" and "a basically humanitarian type of approach." He believes the only hope is that people will "realize the obvious worth of honesty and integrity."[43] "Either we've got to accept that life is *not* meaningless, for reasons as yet unknown, or we've got to create some sort of social structure that offers us the op-portunity for real fulfillment. . . . We've got to give up the im-mediate self-gratifying view," he said. "We've got to find the transition to a life style and a culture in which we make tough, honest, moral and ethical choices simply because on the most basic, pragmatic grounds—they are seen to be the highest good."[44]

Similarly, although Allen is suspicious of organized religion, he appreciates genuine religious feeling. Raised in a Jewish home, Allen went to Hebrew school for eight years and was bar mitzvahed, but while he writes about Jewish characters and plays them, and his films are often haunted by a post-Holocaust sensibility, he does not attend synagogue today, and he told Natalie Gittelson that being Jewish never consciously enters his work. "It's not on my mind; it's no part of my artistic consciousness. There are certain cultural differences between Jews and non-Jews, I guess, but I think they're largely superficial. Of course, any character I play would be Jewish, just because I'm Jewish."[45]

He says that he doesn't approve of organized religions because they are really "social, political and economic organizations."[46] He is also frightened by "religiosity" in this country. After debating religion on TV with Billy Graham, Allen complained about the many hate letters he received which called him (among other things) "a nigger loving atheistic Jew."[47] While he finds organized religions "silly,"[48] he is interested in a religious sensibility such as that which he finds in existentialists like Sartre, although Sartre was an atheist.

Allen is skeptical of social and economic organizations, but he speaks more positively about loyalty among friends, and about intimacy between two people. Although Allen has gone through two divorces, he has not given up on long-term monogamous relationships. Jack Kroll has reported, in fact, that "Woody agrees with Camus that women are all we know of paradise on earth."[49] Allen sees women much as Ingmar Bergman portrays them in his films, as more natural and more honest about their feelings than men. As he told Roger Ebert: "I've always felt more sanguine about women than about men. . . . They're more mature, less bellicose, more gentle. They're closer to what life's supposed to be about. They bring up kids. Men are stiffer, don't cry, die of heart attacks. Women are just more into nature. They know what sex *should be*. They never disassociate sex and love."[50]

Although Allen, like Bergman, has tended to reinforce stereotypes, because he has portrayed sympathetic women primarily as intuitive creatures, his little-man alternative to macho movie heroes suggests his awareness that traditional sex-role models have prevented men as well as women from achieving self-fulfillment. In feminist terms, Allen has been a slow learner, but over the course of his career he has grown from a comedian who used women as straight people for sexist jokes to a filmmaker who now shares billing with more complex female characters and represents female perspectives with greater insight and sensitivity than in his earlier films.

ALLEN STEWART KONIGSBERG BECOMES WOODY ALLEN

Even though Woody Allen has occasionally been open with interviewers, the problem of identifying the real Woody Allen in relation to his work is still difficult because of Allen's understandable reluctance to make his personal life public record. We know little about Woody Allen's formative years because Allen's private life, and especially its implications for his work, remains a well-guarded secret. Perhaps because he dislikes the publicizers who grow rich from celebrities' revelations, perhaps because he wants people to concentrate on experiencing his films' broader implications rather than seeing them only as narrow reflections of the personal experiences that motivate his work, only a few details relevant to his early years are available.

Allen Stewart Konigsberg grew up in the heart of urban America. No child of the quiet village, he lived a part of his life in what he describes as "an old world" setting at Avenue K and 15th Street in Brooklyn. Born in December 1935 to Martin and Nettie Konigsberg, residents of Flatbush, he was destined to become as street smart and as cleverly defensive as any local Jewish boy. He would also learn to feel uncomfortable outside of New York, and to regard that city, rather than Hollywood, as the place to make authentic films.

Although Allen rarely speaks directly about his family, and it is difficult to know his attitudes with any certainty, a number of his one-liners and stories are suggestive of his early relationship with them. When Allen says his parents were most interested in

"God and carpeting," it is typical Allen humorous juxtaposition—perhaps containing some truth as well. His parents appear in Allen's jokes to be puzzled by his views and by his humor. Allen is very fond of his parents, now retired, but according to him, they always enjoyed "a broader kind of comedy," like the work of Georgie Jessel. "My kind of comedy is whimsical . . . often slightly surrealistic," he said in 1974. "It seems to float right over my parents' heads."[51]

Allen and his only sibling, sister Letty, eight years his junior, lived at home together until he left when she was ten. Trained as a schoolteacher and married to a psychologist, Letty has always been Woody's fan and friend. Although personal relationships may sometimes have been strained—his parents wanted him to be a pharmacist—his comedy probably gained from his family experience. According to Allen, "Relatives were always running in and out of rooms. It was like living in the middle of a Marx Brothers movie."[52]

Moreover, Allen's parents probably provided some indirect encouragement for his interest in film. His father liked westerns and his mother liked romances, so Allen saw a great many of both. His parents took him to movies, and he escaped from them and from school into movies. According to Eric Lax, Allen saw every film that came along and listened to every comedy radio show from "Duffy's Tavern" to "Fibber McGee and Molly."[53] When he was only seven, Allen's mother took him to Loew's theater near his home to see Bing Crosby and his later hero, Bob Hope, in *The Road to Morocco*. It may have been then, suggests Foster Hirsch, that Allen realized he wanted to be a comedian.[54] In any case, by the time he was ready to enter high school, Allen knew from their films and radio performances how Bob Hope and other well-known comedians worked. He also watched lesser-known comics at the Flatbush Theatre, an old vaudeville house. Jack Kroll reports that Allen watched five acts at a sitting on Saturdays and sometimes sat through a show twice, taking notes about comedy routines on boxes of Raisinets.[55]

Allen's school record is mediocre, as he preferred the New York Giants, movies, radio, comic books, magic tricks, and boxing to classrooms and lessons. "Magic," he remembers, "fit into everything I needed at the time. . . . It was so much better than school, which was boring, frightening. The whole thing was ugly. I never had the answers. I never did the homework."[56] The only assignments he describes more positively were compositions. He remembers that "by the fifth grade I had some innate knowledge of how to write funny, so much so, that I would be doing references to Freud and sex, too, without knowing who he and what it really was but sensing how to use them correctly. Teachers would read my compositions and bring other teachers into the room and they'd read them together and point at me."[57]

At sixteen, while attending Midwood High School in Brooklyn, Allen learned to play the clarinet, and when he has time, he now plays Dixieland Jazz on Monday nights at Michael's Pub in Manhattan. His continuing interest in music can be seen in the careful attention he pays to musical backgrounds in his films. Although some versions of his life portray Allen as so shy that he dropped pencils on the floor so he wouldn't be called on by teachers in high school, others suggest that he developed into a comedian by being the class clown. His success in amusing his classmates probably encouraged Allen at age sixteen to send his jokes to columnists like Walter Winchell, Ed Sullivan, and Earl Wilson. This was his entrance into the professional world of comedy. At the same time he also took the name Woody Allen because unlike Allen Stewart Konigsberg "it had all the glamorous appeal of show business one imagines in Flatbush."[58]

Those frequent one-liners sent to columnists eventually caught the attention of press agent David O. Alber, who engaged the seventeen-year-old comic on a regular basis to ghost jokes for stars like Guy Lombardo, Sammy Kaye, and Arthur Murray. Allen produced thirty to forty jokes a day after school for twenty-five dollars a week.[59] While he was still in high school Allen was signed by the William Morris Agency.

After high school, Allen attended college, but with little interest. He failed a course in movie production at New York University and dropped out of film courses at City College of New York after a week. At eighteen, he went back to being a full-time comic writer, producing jokes and sketches at first for Herb Shriner, then for Pat Boone and Art Carney, for seventy-five dollars a week. In 1954, at nineteen, he went to Hollywood as part of the NBC Writer's Development Program and worked on the "Colgate Comedy Hour." During this time he teamed with Neil Simon's brother Danny Simon, a collaboration that taught Allen plot construction and, in his own estimation, "took me out of fantasy and into [the] reality" of comic writing as a business.[60]

At nineteen, Allen wed his first wife, sixteen-year-old Harlene Rosen; the marriage that lasted only five years. Allen's explanation for the breakup was that the two were simply too young, but Rosen later sued him for telling jokes about her that defamed her character.[61] Although Allen had little faith in learning within institutional settings, with his marriage to Harlene, he began to follow in earnest a schedule of reading for self-education that has made him very well-read today. Harlene was a philosophy student at Hunter College, so Allen learned philosophy with her, and together they hired a tutor from Columbia to teach them a Great Books course. Allen, now a voracious reader, reads for "survival." "People who read for pleasure are wasting their time," he has said. "Reading isn't fun, it's indispensable."[62] Allen likes philosophy best of all, especially the existentialists. Among the many authors whose works Allen has referred to in interviews since 1969 are Arendt, Flaubert, Kafka, Chekhov, Dostoevsky, Ionesco, Genet, Joyce, Borges, Beckett, Jung, Freud, Woolf, Benchley, Perelman, Shulman, Plath, Mishima, Sartre, Kierkegaard, Heidegger, Camus, Russell, Dewey, Hegel, Berdyayev, and Wittgenstein. When Jack Kroll talked to Allen in 1978, he observed "an image of an American mind creating itself, with passion and irony."[63]

After the "Colgate Comedy Hour," Allen wrote for Sid Caesar. By this time he was making $1,500 a week. Working for Caesar, he associated with experienced comedy writers like Simon, Larry Gelbart, and Mel Brooks. Allen left the William Morris Agency and his manager, Harvey Meltzer, in 1958, and Jack Rollins and Charles Joffe became his managers; they continue to manage Allen's professional affairs today. In *Broadway Danny Rose*,

Allen pays tribute to Joffe and Rollins's "personal management"; and until recently (when Allen moved from United Artists film company to Orion Pictures and a more lucrative
contract, in which Allen began earning a percentage of the gross
"from dollar one" in studio rentals), he and his "partner" managers, at Allen's insistence, split 50 percent of the net profits after the film company took 30 percent off the top for distribution
and kept another 50 percent.[64]

Joffe and Rollins convinced Allen that he could provide a
more successful delivery for the jokes he was writing and ad-
vance his career if he told those jokes himself, so Allen gave up
his higher-paying job as a comedy writer for other people and
became a performer. He debuted at the Duplex in Greenwich
Village, where, Charles Joffe recalls, "Woody was just awful. Of
course, he had good lines. But he was so scared and embarrassed
and—rabbity." Allen tried to quit the Duplex five or six times,
but his managers sat up nights talking him out of it.[65] After the
Duplex, he appeared at the Blue Angel in New York, Mister Kelly's in Chicago, and the Hungry I in San Francisco, becoming
more experienced as a stand-up little man with each move. His
material, as it is today, was true, but exaggerated. Allen told
jokes about his former wife, his old neighborhood, and his parents. He also began appearing frequently on talk shows, using
some of the material he had developed in his nightclub act. At
twenty-six he was a recognizable public figure, and his persona
grew more definite with each successful appearance. His record
album of those performances, "Woody Allen: The Nightclub
Years," has become a classic today.

The years between his first nightclub appearance in 1961 and
his first major film in 1969 were busy ones. He met actress-co-
medienne Louise Lasser in 1962 and married her in 1965. They
were divorced in 1968, but remain friends today, and Lasser has
appeared in several Allen films. In 1966 Allen's first play, *Don't
Drink the Water*, opened on Broadway, and in 1969 it was made
into a film starring Jackie Gleason; however, Allen had little
connection with it beyond writing the stage play.

During the same period, Allen contributed his first essays and stories to the *New Yorker;* he has since published three collections of writings, *Getting Even* (1971), *Without Feathers* (1975), and *Side Effects* (1980). A number of his comic ideas that appeared originally in the *New Yorker* and elsewhere surface again in his films. Allen was also invited to work on *What's Up, Tiger Lily?* (1966), a Japanese production originally entitled *Kagi No Kagi* (Key of keys), a hard-boiled detective film, which Allen dubbed with comical lines so that it became a wearisome parody about a search for an egg salad recipe. Allen also appeared briefly in *Casino Royale* (1967), an attempt to parody the top-grossing James Bond films, which Allen has never seen and prefers to forget. A far less embarrassing early enterprise was his second play, *Play It Again, Sam,* which opened on Broadway the next year to good reviews, and began the long-term friendship between Allen and his costars, Diane Keaton and Tony Roberts.

The most important moment for Allen's film career, however, occurred earlier during this period, while he was still appearing at the Blue Angel. One night Charles Feldman caught Allen's act and was impressed enough to ask him to rewrite the script of *What's New, Pussycat?* for sixty thousand dollars. It was *What's New, Pussycat?* that really opened the way for Allen to become the relatively independent filmmaker he is today. By this time, too, the little-man persona was a developed character, and he was ready to make his first major appearance in a Woody Allen film—*Take the Money and Run.*

Allan Felix (Woody Allen) and his former wife, Nancy (Susan Anspach), climb San Francisco hills in *Play It Again, Sam*. The struggles and dialogues of Felix's life are underlined in the mise-en-scène. *Courtesy of Woody Allen and Paramount Studios.*

3

Humble Beginnings:
The First "Woody Allen" Films

The first three films that helped establish Woody Allen's reputation as a comic filmmaker, *Take the Money and Run* (1969),
Bananas (1971), and *Play It Again, Sam* (1972), share several parallel patterns despite variations in narrative situation and setting. These films involve a meek central character, a reflexive
context, and a dialogic, jokelike structure. The little man is
tossed between two conflicting circumstances, the second of
which often promises to be more rewarding than the first. Ultimately, however, neither situation proves satisfying; inevitably,
the little man's encounter with a promising alternative only
highlights its meaninglessness and the main character's foolish-
ness and alienation—yet also, a third and more human possibility that he himself represents.[1]

Unlike the more complicated and self-conscious little men in
several of Allen's later films, the figure in these early movies is
an innocent and humble victim. He serves to expose the anxieties and absurdities of contemporary life, to examine the threat
such a life poses to coherent identity, and to reveal the problems
in attempting to live up to heroic images born out of Hollywood
fantasy. While filmic allusions suggest how significant visual
impressions have been in creating unreliable contemporary values and behavior patterns, those same images also contribute to
the little man's survival. Like many modern examples of Amer-

ican humor and comic film, Allen's early work evokes skepticism, but it is not without hope; Allen explores a double-edged view of American dreams and false illusions in terms of his own language and medium. Even in his earliest films, he recognizes that film is part of the problem it describes, and even his earliest films are more inconclusive than they may first appear to be.

Although *Play It Again, Sam* has a tighter, more conventional narrative line than the other two early comedies, all three films are episodic and filled with slapstick, one-liners, and comic shtick transposed from nightclub performance and literary production to film. Always a remarkable mimic of visual as well as verbal styles, Allen used visual puns and relied heavily on reflexive allusions and references in his earliest films, but unlike the later films, his early efforts are not the work of a sophisticated visual artist. The jokes take precedence over composition, lighting, color, and carefully controlled mise-en-scène; and the films' overall coherence and depth appear to be secondary to entertaining dialogue and relatively simple comic effects.

"THE JUNGLE IS NO PLACE FOR A CELLIST":
Take the Money and Run.

Neither the critics nor Woody Allen considered *What's New, Pussycat?* an artistically important movie, but it was such a commercial success that Allen's managers, Joffe and Rollins, were able to launch Allen as a director, actor, and writer of his own films. After a year and a half of looking for the right situation, Charles Joffe finally sold the script for *Take the Money and Run* to Palomar Pictures, who put up $1.6 million for its production and gave Allen the right to direct and star.[2] For his first film, Allen told Eric Lax, "I stayed with my safest stuff, which is the stuff I know: abject humility. I was very timid in that picture. But there was no way I could have been anything else. I had never made a film, I was never the star of a picture before."[3]

Allen, however, sought assistance. In addition to Joffe, who would produce, and Mickey Rose, who coauthored the script, Allen drew on the expertise of veteran cinematographer Lester Schorr, production manager Jack Grossberg, and Fred Gallo, who served as unit manager and right-hand man on this film. Allen also called upon editor Ralph Rosenblum, whose credits include *The Pawnbroker* (1965) and *Long Day's Journey into Night* (1962). Rosenblum, who would go on to edit *Bananas, Sleeper, Annie Hall,* and *Interiors,* was called in to save the film after screenings of a rough cut failed with trial audiences. Allen lacked confidence. As he put it later: "I had been too harsh on myself and lopped out gobs and gobs of material. His [Rosenblum's] big thing was to say, 'Put it back' "[4] Rosenblum believed the film's greatest problem was its uneven tone. He objected to the very combination of qualities that would characterize Allen's best films of the late seventies and eighties,—the pathos and seriousness that ran through what was supposed to be a comedy. Rosenblum especially disliked the ending, a bloody *Bonnie and Clyde* parody in which the little man was gunned down following a bank robbery. Rosenblum suggested a more upbeat conclusion.[5]

Allen claims to have thought seriously once about becoming a gangster. He said, "I never would have stopped trying to beat the law in the face of persistent defeat."[6] Before he began making *Take the Money and Run,* Allen had done a spoof of *Bonnie and Clyde* (1967) with Liza Minnelli on the "Kraft Music Hall Comedy Hour." Later he would write a piece on organized crime for *Getting Even,* his first collection of humorous essays.[7] Allen notes that he was thinking about Dillinger when he made the film, but Allen's little man, with the meek first name Virgil, takes his last name, Starkwell, from Charles Starkweather, a notorious 1950s killer. Virgil takes his story not only from the lives of real gangsters, but from countless moving pictures—from *Little Caesar* (1930) to *Bonnie and Clyde*—that created the gangster-hero myths so endemic to the American imagination.

Take the Money and Run is a genre fantasy involving all of the American gangster film conventions. Within a pseudodocumentary frame, Jackson Beck, the film's narrator, provides a Movietone-newsreel grittiness with his staccato voice-over that imitates the style of fifties films like *Walk East on Beacon* (1952). The narration, the newsreel-like footage, and the burlesque Pathe-style vignettes of Virgil's parents, his teacher, his cello instructor, his probation officer, and a fellow convict all spoof crime films' cinema verité techniques. Other moments in the film parody a variety of gangster genre paradigms. Represented are biographies of single criminals, the bad-kid-grows-up-to-be-a-gangster stories, the prison pictures, the organized crime movies, and the chain gang, big escape, and hostage films. In addition, *Take the Money* alludes to other films, such as *The Hustler* (1961) and *West Side Story* (1961), which lie on the outskirts of the genre.

But on each of the typical occasions drawn from gangster films, Virgil is far less than the macho masters of circumstances who have swaggered across American movie screens since James Cagney chucked his mother on the shoulder in *Public Enemy* (1931). Virgil Starkwell bungles one opportunity for stylish behavior after another. Virgil is no dapper young tough, who eludes the police and grows up to be a fearless criminal; he is a slight child with tousled red hair and freckles whose hands get stuck in the gumball machines he tries to rob. He violates all the old patterns: instead of being a Horatio Alger success, he fails as a young entrepreneur because he can't give a spit shoeshine without hitting his customer's trousers. He is not a frustrated artist led to crime, but a failure at mastering the cello—he blows into it. And he creates a classic moment of comic disorder when he attempts to perform sitting down in a marching band.

Unlike Paul Newman's Fast Eddy, Virgil plays an embarrassing game of pool. In a *West Side Story*–style street fight, Virgil's is the only switchblade that won't work. He is not the dapper, debonair hoodlum with a platinum blonde on his arm—he falls in love and marries a laundress, and on the day when he is preparing to rob a bank, squabbles with her over who has first rights to the bathroom. Even his bank robberies lack the élan of the classic robber: during his first attempt, the bank officials cannot read his holdup note. Appearing to say, "Apt natural I have a gub," the note highlights the little man's innocent use of language in contrast to sophisticated social protocol, and it leads to his imprisonment.

Neither of Virgil's options permits success or satisfies his desires. Attempting to be a criminal or attempting to go straight, Virgil's schlemiel persona is Allen's response to the romantic conventions of the classic American crime film. Virgil is victimized in prison by a treacherous shirt-folding machine in the laundry, by officials whose medical experiments turn him into a Hassidic rabbi, and by his fellow inmates, who don't bother to inform him that a planned escape is off and leave him outside the cell-block doors, banging to get back in. When he tries to be Cool Hand Luke and escapes from a work gang, he must do so in lockstep with five other prisoners to whom he is chained. Allen is also playing off such films as *20,000 Years in Sing-Sing* (1933), *The Big House* (1930), *I Was a Fugitive from a Chain Gang* (1932), *Dillinger* (1945), *The Asphalt Jungle* (1950), and *The Defiant Ones* (1958) in his depiction of Virgil's failures to live up to the heroic images of dashing gangster types.

Take the Money and Run, like other early Allen films, finds a humble little-man main character caught between two unsavory possibilities. He is no freer outside than inside prison, and his confinement becomes a representative contemporary predicament, and in comic form refers to greater modern paradoxes than innocent Virgil ever consciously considers. Virgil's confinement also involves a reflexive burlesque context, a comment on films and filmmaking.

Virgil is confined not merely by worlds inside and outside prison, but by the rigid demands of the genre he finds himself in; however, while he epitomizes our propensity to glorify false illusions, he also re-creates our impotence in a comic fashion and represents our hopes. His frustration in the face of everything from stubborn shirt machines to conscientious cops lies well within the conventions of twentieth-century literary and filmic humor, wherein mechanical contrivances of the smallest sort and authority of any sort are the stuff that nightmares are made of. But against the rigidities of bands marching in orderly formation, depressing domestic problems, the deadly routine of prison life, or the requirements of formulaic genres and their desensitizing macho codes, Virgil Starkwell's disorderly ineptitude signifies antistructure and makes us laugh at our reluctance to acknowledge our own very human flaws.

A more significant affirmation lies in Virgil's persistence, derived from his innocence and his unknowing attempts to imitate Hollywood images. The same illusions that entrap him encourage him to believe in love, freedom, and survival. Although later little men will be far more self-conscious about time and aging, Virgil has as little sense of time's tyranny as he has of the limits suggested by Allen's metaphors of place. Even though he has been sentenced to eight hundred years in jail, and even though life outside jail provides no haven from adversity, Virgil refuses to give up. Despite several earlier unsuccessful attempts, at the end of *Take the Money and Run*, he is planning to escape from prison again. Although he failed before when a gun carved out of soap and painted with shoe polish (à la Dillinger) turned to suds in a rainstorm, we see Virgil whittling away at yet another bar of soap. Just as in the movies, he has no doubt that his next attempt will succeed. Virgil's naïveté makes him a victim, but it also presumes a creator behind the character who still toys with the idea of renewal. Although Virgil's persistence clearly has its pathetic side, we see him endure because, like Don Quixote, he believes and acts upon his faith. The film is inconclusive about whether we should value Virgil's innocence or reject his illusions.

In carrying on dialogues with the social codes that have become literary, political, or filmic conventions, Woody Allen reflects on the sophistication of his day—textbook history, the social fantasies that underlie the genre, his audience, and the customs of his medium. The parody and the self-reflexive comedy in this early Allen film are handled so gently and with such a sense of familiarity with filmic conventions, however, that Allen doesn't just expose our failures to ridicule and unsympathetic laughter. *Take the Money and Run*, like later films from *Play It Again, Sam* to *The Purple Rose of Cairo* (1985), implies that unrealistic figures created by the American film industry in complicity with an undiscerning audience may be damaging, but they are also woven into the American mythos as the fabric of hope. Paradoxically, they are related at once to our worst self-deceptions and to a modicum of genuine romantic faith that, like Jay Gatsby's dream, is difficult to abandon.

MORE JUNGLES IN *BANANAS*

The 1960s were the politically intense years of Castro, revolts in South America, civil conflicts in the Dominican Republic, assassinations in the United States, and student unrest over civil rights and Vietnam. Woody Allen's second major film, *Bananas*, explores the issues of its times—politics, revolution, and violence—with surprising aggressiveness. In *Bananas*, the critical themes that are to interest Allen throughout his filmmaking career take on sharper definition. One of Woody Allen's major concerns is the individual's search for authenticity in the face of dehumanizing modern manners, ideologies, and technologies. Allen's film deals with contemporary living that fosters depersonalization, uniformity, alienation, and loneliness.

Bananas's Fielding Mellish (Woody Allen), like Virgil Starkwell, is a humble little man. Like Virgil, he is interested in love, sex, and survival; however, the little soul's instinctive longing for an innocence that requires trust is in constant conflict with the painful realities of modern experience. Allen demands an open-eyed look at the world, a look that leads to doubt and militates against the modicum of faith that his main character unconsciously seeks to retain; but despite the odds against individual fulfillment, Fielding Mellish, like Allen's other little-man characters, is a reflection of his creator's best wishes. In *Bananas*, the media can desensitize and act as an analogue to both depersonalizing corporations that define the quality of work experience, and to power-hungry politicians who devalue life; yet Fielding's comic struggle to win his girl stresses the quest for intimacy and the importance of personal relationships—the longing for a world where love may still triumph over death.

Although it contains a number of minor movements, *Bananas* is basically orchestrated into two major parts—the spatial pattern of the film sends Fielding Mellish away from a sophisticated American civilization and into a more primal setting where he tries to find greater satisfaction, but like the parallel worlds inside and outside prison in *Take the Money and Run*, the jungle in the banana republic is not unlike the urban jungle. The rebels are as egomaniacal and fascistic as the dictators they oppose; justice is expedient in both places; and for the little man, problems with machines, food, and women are common to both locations. As a result of his confrontation with two equally unsatisfying possibilities, the little man in *Bananas* becomes somewhat more self-aware and discerning. *Bananas* suggests that if meaning is to be found, it lies in a recovery of humane instincts and in close personal relationships rather than in political abstractions. But while Allen's film apparently denounces political approaches, it cannot escape some of its own political implications, and while the little man appears to achieve some success at the end of the film, like all Allen's endings, this one is not without its important qualifications.

The opening sequence explores the roles of television and Hollywood in desensitizing viewers to violence, and sets the tone for the remainder of the film. Wearing Sunday afternoon sports announcers' uniforms, complete with decals on their blazers, Howard Cosell and Don Dunphy provide a play-by-play description of political assassination in San Marcos, a banana republic. Without inflection, Dunphy reports that he has witnessed "many colorful riots . . . the traditional bombing of the U.S. Embassy," and the beating of a labor leader—one of "the most exciting spectacles [he] . . . has ever seen."

Visual allusions to violent moments from *Bonnie and Clyde* and *Potemkin* (1925) make the brutal assassination that follows a witty filmic ritual. While creating comic irony, the references suggest how quickly older films and the meaningful responses they originally evoked can become conventionalized. On the one hand, Allen's reflexive film appeals to a nostalgia for great film moments, and on the other, it demonstrates how even this film participates to some extent in the distancing and desensitization of an audience.

Following this prologue and the credits, set off by an appropriately ironic sound track—a happy Spanish love song and a barrage of machine-gun fire—the action moves to the Execuciser Corporation offices in New York, where Fielding Mellish is a products tester. The sequences's opening shot includes two profiles, one of the salesman and the other of the buyer, one on the far left and the other on the far right of the screen. The composition suggests that the seller and buyer are two parts of the same face and also emphasizes how corporate protocol encourages social distance. The stale discourse of this sequence is the sales pitch, but the nasal voice and rhythms resemble Cosell's.

The sales representative tries to sell a device that permits busy executives to exercise at their desks. One of the potential buyers, who looks remarkably like former vice president Spiro Agnew, supplies a connection between business and American politics. The irony is not only in the interchange that follows, but in the disparity between the businessmen's uninterested reactions and Mellish's predicament. The camera also emphasizes corporate power and expansionism by contrasting a tiny paperweight globe of the world with the huge execuciser desk on which it sits. A more important contrast finds small Fielding Mellish sprawled awkwardly on his hands and knees beside the orderly massive desk, as he tinkers with the execuciser apparatus. In addition, Mellish's costume emphasizes the lip service paid to individuality in the corporate setting; he wears a typical gray work uniform with a personalized touch: his given name, Fielding, embroidered over the pocket.

Initially, keeping time with the salesman's descriptions, Mellish confidently demonstrates the execuciser's bicycle and weight-lifting equipment. When Mellish's speed falls behind the pitch, however, the salesman fills in with gibberish until Mellish can catch up. The emptiness of the salesman's spiel is obvious from his syntax, as he announces that "basketballs as handled by Mr. Mellish develop reflexes." Indeed, as Fielding continues, the machinery, like Chaplin's assembly line or the eating machine in *Modern Times*, seems to come alive and outdistance him. The salesman and his customers are oblivious to Mellish as he is hit on the head with basketballs and pummeled by gadgets until he lies struggling on the floor. The proxemic contrast between Fielding alone at the big desk and the executives standing far across the room underlines the businessmen's ability to divorce themselves from the little man's misfortunes.

If Mellish is made to feel like a marshmallow at work, his personal life is no more satisfying. His fellow workers will not fix him up with a date, and the "easiest" woman in the office rejects him; so Fielding, like so many film spectators, is driven to voyeurism—in this case, to adult bookstores where he tries to hide a copy of *Orgasm* among *Time* and the *Saturday Review*, only to have the cashier broadcast his purchases. Mellish is reduced to mumbling transparent excuses for his natural desires: he says he is engaged in "a sociological study of aberrant sexuality."

Boarding a subway where commuters keep unneighborly distances from each other, Mellish soon runs into violence New York–style: two hoods taunt the passengers and attack a crippled old woman sitting next to him. Although Fielding tries to camouflage himself behind a copy of *Commentary*—and transcend the greasy punks—he cannot maintain intellectual distance. His better instincts lead him to attack the hoods—unsuccessfully, of course. A final irony occurs in the sequence's last shots; as Fielding runs away from his pursuers, the hoods' female victim enjoys his sexy magazine. Not only is Mellish a thwarted hero, but circumstances prevent him from having his orgasm, even as vicarious experience.

Fielding's home life is no more gratifying. Mellish battles not only with bullies, but with food. The choreography is related to the later lobster scene in *Annie Hall*, but instead of live lobsters, Mellish fights a slippery package of frozen spinach, which like twice-removed sexual experience or execucisers, further verifies the distance between life in a sophisticated society and people's basic needs.

Like little-men characters throughout Allen's collection, Fielding also has problems with romantic relationships. His love interest, Nancy (Louise Lasser), is a political activist who urges Fielding to sign a petition against General Vargas's dictatorship in San Marcos, but Fielding sees her as an answer to his loneliness. Despite the disparity between her activism and his lack of commitment, both Nancy and Fielding are more human than the sportscasters or executives in preceding scenes. Their fumbling attempts at communication stand in sharp contrast to the lack of communication in the porn shop and subway, and to glib sportscasting or sales jargon.

The little man is not experienced in political courtships, however. When he tries to join picket lines to please Nancy, Fielding only gets caught in the crossfire between police and demonstrators. Even ordinary romantic occasions are fraught with problems. So inept is Mellish as a romantic and political figure that Nancy eventually tells him that he is not enough of a "leader," and that "something is missing." This rejection scene, played in a pastoral setting with soft focus and sweeping camera movements, burlesques itself and frothy film love stores.

Cast off by Nancy and dissatisfied with his job, Mellish leaves the United States for San Marcos to see the revolution. He evades General Vargas's army and seeks asylum with the revolutionary opposition; however, Fielding finds no more satisfaction among the rebels than he found in New York.

The jokes about rebels in San Marcos grew out of a parody of popular revolutionary diaries as well as solemn films like *Viva Zapata!* (1952). Allen first wrote "Viva Vargas" for the *Evergreen Review,* and it appeared later in *Getting Even.* Like the filmic allusions in *Take the Money and Run,* the references in *Bananas* involve a paradox. Allen's film parodies the false sentimentality film helps inspire for political solutions, while at the same time, heroic images bred by films such as *Viva Zapata!* inspire the innocent little man to achieve stature despite himself.

Fielding's first reaction to the rebels, conveyed in a wide-angle subjective shot that draws attention to the medium, makes them appear as disreputable as the New York subway hoods. Their leader, Esposito, speaks in high tones, telling Mellish, who has just escaped death at Vargas's hands, "You have a chance to die for freedom." But Esposito's attempts to evoke spirit with an unpoetic "Song of the Rebels" produce no reaction at all from his dirty, lethargic men.

Whatever romantic illusions Mellish retains about rebellion after this introduction are shattered further in a series of vignettes structurally paralleling an earlier montage in the "civilized" section of the film. Fielding naively orders a conventional breakfast, but receives a glutinous mash that turns out to be lizard. If New York is the home of overprocessed frozen spinach, then the San Marcos jungle is the home of food that is too primitive. Neither extreme is easy for Fielding to digest.

Mellish exchanges his gray work outfit for equally homogenizing rebel fatigues, but his failures at military maneuvers resemble his problems with the dehumanizing execuciser. Fielding can manage neither machetes nor more sophisticated technological weapons, and in an old Marx Brothers–type joke, Allen demonstrates Fielding's bad luck not only with military technology, but with politics—both right and left. When Fielding throws the pin and holds a grenade, the grenade detonates in his hand. His wound bandaged, he makes a second try; he pitches the grenade properly, but now the pin explodes in his other hand. The comic structure of the grenade episode replicates the form of Allen's early films and reminds us of a more profound joke about the absurdity of life in general.

Similarly, Fielding's attempt to avoid notice by camouflaging himself behind a copy of *Commentary* in the subway has its counterpart in Mellish's attempts to disguise himself as a tree in the jungle, only to have a rebel soldier urinate on him. When the rebels' trainer teaches new recruits to "suck out the poison" from snake bites, Fielding, using the kind of intellectual dodges he employed earlier in the adult bookstore, assumes an air of indignant propriety, insisting that "I cannot suck anybody's leg

I am not engaged to." Yet when a female rebel runs through the camp with a snakebite on her breast, Mellish races to offer first aid.

Fielding's attempts to win women in San Marcos are also no more successful than they were in New York. Imitating the flirtatious dinner sequence in *Tom Jones* (1963), Mellish only manages to drool water down his chin and get hit with a faceful of food. When he finally lures a reluctant woman to his cot, Allen burlesques love scenes just as he did in the first part of the film. The camera that so frequently leaves through a window or door to avoid showing love consummated in traditional Hollywood romances, searches hopelessly for an opening in the tent. After lovemaking, Fielding's romantic aspirations are depreciated further with a close shot of his lover's bored face; then, the camera pulls back to reveal that she is smoking and has worn her boots to bed. Here, even more than in Mellish's romance with Nancy, "something is missing."

After the rebels overthrow the government, the little man finds himself uncomfortably compromised by his political commitments, as he is forced to prepare the enemy for annihilation. When Esposito says that his own people are "too ignorant to vote," Fielding observes that the rebel leader, now as much a dictator as Vargas, looks "glassy eyed" with power. Esposito ignores Mellish's rejoinder, "But they [the people] have common sense," yet it marks an insight that separates Fielding Mellish from Virgil Starkwell, and it anticipates a developing self-awareness and concern for personal integrity in Allen's little-man characters.

Esposito's followers eventually depose him and select a reluctant Fielding to lead them, but Mellish's return to the United States to seek aid for San Marcos and his subsequent arrest and trial only further emphasize the universality of injustice. Where Esposito regularly eliminated the opposition by firing squad, in the United States, Fielding is hounded by the CIA and brought to trial for "subversive acts." The trial, made ludicrous by references to courtroom scenes in *Inherit the Wind* (1960), *Witness for the Prosecution* (1957), and *Duck Soup* (1933), also recalls the unreality of political trials of the 1960s. Fielding is decried as "a New York Jewish intellectual Communist crackpot" and condemned by a banal Miss America as "a traitor to this country because his views are different from the president and others of his kind." After such telling evidence, Fielding is, of course, convicted—but his sentence is suspended when he promises not to move into the judge's neighborhood. When the outcome of the trial is announced on a newscast sponsored by New Testament cigarettes, the film's suggestion that "The Word" is brought to us compliments of Wall Street, Washington, and the networks is hard to ignore.

Where, then, is Fielding Mellish to turn, and how is the film to end? Once more Ralph Rosenblum suggested a happy conclusion despite the odds stacked against the little-man antihero.[8] The finale offers a note of positive human communication even in the face of uninterested media hype, dehumanizing technology, and depersonalizing politics. However, the moment is a qualified one that does not violate the film's larger dialogic design, because the ending returns to a sequence reminiscent of the prologue. Surrounded by an audience, Howard Cosell calls the action during Fielding and Nancy Mellish's honeymoon night in bed. Lovemaking becomes a public sporting event, a TV spectacle, and Nancy is less than enthusiastic about Fielding's performance. Nevertheless, as Fielding tenderly kisses Nancy on the nose, he affirms à dimension of personal coming together that neither politics, big business, nor the media can thoroughly destroy. Allen's film depicts its main character as an innocent fool, but a fool whose priorities are humane, and whose sense of love is both affirmed and qualified by the constraints of the film's rules and the corresponding unreality of a world where images of experience and experience itself are too confused for comfort.

Neither the sophisticated United States nor the more primitive jungle, neither politics on the right nor politics on the left provide refuge from dehumanization, and the media finds its way even into the bedroom. The little man, in all his human clumsiness and his simple attempts to win his girl and do the right thing according to his best instincts, is still both a victim and the representative of an alternative sensibility in a comically senseless world. Fielding Mellish, however, is somewhat more aware and articulate than his counterpart in *Take the Money and Run*, and in this second major film Allen begins to stretch the significance of the oppositions that, like an ironic contemporary Colossus, the little man must straddle. Eventually, apparently conflicting values will become more difficult to distinguish and to assess. Allen uses the little-man protagonist as a focus through whom increasingly more complex and ambiguous social, moral, and philosophical issues can be explored.

PLAY IT AGAIN, SAM

It is difficult to decide where to place *Play It Again, Sam* in any discussion of Allen's development, because the Broadway version was written before any of Allen's major films were produced. It is also the only major film that Allen wrote and in which he played the lead, but that someone else directed. In *Play It Again, Sam*, as in *Take the Money and Run* and *Bananas*, the little man is humble and less aggressive than in later films, torn between two conflicting points of view, and the ending of the film may appear to resolve itself more easily than is typical of Allen's later, most problematic comedies. In *Play It Again, Sam*, however, the little man's persona is complicated because of his developing self-awareness; as a film critic, he also alerts spectators to the film's reflexivity. Moreover, the little man's ability to betray a friend on one hand and fight for integrity on the other, and the stronger story line with more integrally related allusions are characteristics that anticipate later films.

Although time and memory are not such central issues as in the films beginning with *Annie Hall*, this is also the first film in which Allen's little-man hero tries consciously to come to terms with an event in his past. And, while Allen does not explore a concern with change and instability as fully in *Play It Again, Sam* as he will in later films, this film looks forward to such concerns, for it alludes to *Casablanca*, a movie that deals not only with heroic personal sacrifices and with romantic interludes, but with an attempt to understand and relive lost opportunities.

The joke about the confusion of artifice and life, so crucial to most of Allen's films, is also explored more frankly here than in *Take the Money and Run* and *Bananas*, and the little man deals with it more self-consciously. Like so many of Allen's little men (and women), the main character in *Play It Again, Sam* is a familiar figure in American humor, the greenhorn who has difficulty distinguishing between tall-tale lies and reality, between artifice and life. The little man's confusion is exacerbated because neither the tale-teller nor the audience can consistently determine where fiction ends and reality begins. Thus, even in this early Allen film, there are foreshadowings of the later films where filmmaker, audience, and characters will all be implicated more seriously in a modern viewpoint that permits no comforting certainties about what constitutes fiction.

Just as most of Allen's films are dialogic and open-ended, Allen seems to prefer that portions of his films remain open to shape themselves during production. According to director Herbert Ross, Allen did not want to direct *Sam* either as play or as film because he had structured it so carefully when he wrote it.[9] Ross helped to transform the play for the screen; he suggested using clips from *Casablanca* in the film's first sequence, modeling the final scene on *Casablanca*'s ending, setting the narrative in hilly San Francisco, and shooting characters as they moved from one place to another to accompany the dialogue.[10]

The film deals with little man Allan Felix's attempts to rebuild his shattered life after his divorce—to reintegrate his fragmented personality and to attain self-esteem in light of confusing options and models. Like the other early films, *Sam* portrays a main character caught between two unsatisfying extremes. Allan Felix is buffeted between a self-defeating underestimation of his potential, prompted by his ex-wife, Nancy, whom he cannot forget, and a romanticized self-image proposed by macho film hero Humphrey Bogart.

In this film, unlike the other early movies, one of the two pos-sibilities is bifurcated even further to accentuate a familiar problem in Allen's films. Both Allan Felix's most positive aspi-rations and his most self-deceiving illusions are embodied in his relationship to Bogart; as Maurice Yacowar puts it, Allen ex-plores "the ambivalent effects of film upon our self-concep-tion."[11] For a lonely Allan Felix, who longs for a woman to replace Nancy and to bolster his self-image, Bogart is the epit-ome of what a lover should be. He is a Hollywood ideal of tough-guy style who prevents Felix from accepting his own more nat-ural, fumbling self as worthwhile. At the same time, Bogey is a sympathetic mentor who gives Allan fortitude and hope.

From the film's outset, Bogart's self-possession contrasts with Allan's self-doubt. A film critic, Felix is an observer, not a doer like Bogey. As *Play It Again, Sam* begins, wide-eyed Felix watch-es the conclusion of *Casablanca*, where Bogart graciously re-nounces the woman he has loved for many years in the name of a greater political and social good. So engrossed is Allan Felix that for a moment before *Casablanca* ends, he affects Bogart's mannerisms. The little man's connection to the spectator is also accentuated, as *Casablanca* fills the frame we watch, and as we participate intimately in Allan's responses by means of close shots and reaction shots. When the lights go on in the theater, however, Allan looks to the vacant seats on either side of him. In these empty seats and in the emptying theater, an emblem of hard reality is set against the softer glow of the film's illusions; the distance between Allan's identification with heroic models and the limitations of his real world becomes an important part of *Play It Again, Sam*'s comic design. As Felix puts it while he is leaving the theater: "Who'm I kidding? I'm not like that. I never was. I never will be—strictly the movies."

Despite Allan's (and our) apparent understanding of the dis-tinction between film and life as *Casablanca* ends, however, film has become a major part of his reality, and Ross does not permit us to forget that it is also a major part of ours. Allan's apartment is dominated by Bogart memorabilia; lying on his bed, Allan is dwarfed by a large Bogart poster above him, and instead of his own image, Bogart's photograph faces Allan in a dresser mirror. Allan's reliance on filmic models becomes still more obvious when Bogart appears to him periodically throughout the narrative. While Allan is having trouble getting over the loss of Nancy, he is reminded of *Casablanca* and Rick's tough-minded attitude toward the love he left in Berlin. On Bogart's first visit, Allan says: "I'm not like you. At the end of *Casablanca* when you lost Ingrid Bergman, weren't you crushed?" Bogey replies, "Nothin' a little bourbon and soda wouldn't fix." But Felix's "body will not tolerate alcohol," and when he tries Bogey's remedy, he gags and passes out.

As Felix contemplates his romantic hopes and his sexual frustrations, the film continues to exploit the comical disparity between the Bogart ideal he aspires to and the postdivorce self-conception that leaves him incompetent. He has difficulties with food (he eats TV dinners, but doesn't cook them—he sucks on them frozen). He talks about the risky swinging life he plans to lead, but wears a bathing cap in the shower. Ross captures the diminutive figure with a hat pulled down over his ears as he climbs a steep San Francisco hill to do his laundry; for Allan Felix, unlike Bogart, even the smallest domestic tasks resemble Sisyphus's trials. Ross uses those hills on several other occasions to suggest the ups and downs in Allan's moods, his fluctuating fortunes, and the antithetical patterns of both film and life.

While Allan welcomes Bogart because Bogey encourages him, he also has flashbacks of Nancy that shake his confidence. She tells him that she couldn't stand their marriage because he wasn't any fun, because he suffocated her, and because she didn't "dig" him physically. Then she admonishes him, "Oh, for God's sake, Allan, don't take it personal." Allan's view of himself is built on his past experience with what he regards as reality; it explains his need for Bogart. On one hand, the reality and the negative self-image are too depressing to bear, while on the other, Bogart as a representative film hero offers an aspiration impossible to obtain. Neither Allen's retreat into the past nor his attempts to become his romantic movie hero in the future promises to satisfy his needs.

Felix's best friends, Dick and Linda Christie, fix him up with women, but despite lessons Bogart gives him, he is no more adept at dating than other little men in Allen's early films. Preparing to go out, he is nearly propelled from the room by his own hairdryer; he overuses aftershave; and he frantically scatters evidence of his accomplishments about his apartment to make an impression. He is so nervous and inept, however, that one date thinks he "is on something," fakes a headache, and leaves him still poised for action as she slams her door in his face. Other attempts to win women are no more successful. Like Virgil Starkwell and Fielding Mellish, Allan is victimized by hoodlums and comes home battered, having given up his girl to a bunch of bullies at a bar. With deep focus, the camera highlights his loneliness as he enters an empty apartment, an echo of the emptying theater in the film's first sequence.

However, Allan and Linda Christie (Diane Keaton in her first film with Allen) are drawn together because their very human irregularities contrast with the dehumanizing and orderly rituals of the less-sensitive world around them. Linda shares insecurities with Allan. She is a model, surrounded like Allan by tantalizing images that promise intimacy in a society where such intimacy remains elusive. They both have analysts and get migraine headaches and cold sores; they both like to throw up at the Cleveland airport. As Dick says, "The two of you should get married and move into a hospital."

Dick is of the business world. He tells Allan that he won Linda because even though he loved her, he pretended to coolness. Like the execuciser people in *Bananas*, he is a creature of the corporate age—more involved in commercial dealings than in personal relationships. Dick continually interrupts social occasions as well as intimate moments to report his whereabouts to his answering service, and he talks about romance in business terms. When Allan says that he loved his former wife, Linda cries, but Dick says: "Why do you feel like crying? A man makes an investment, it doesn't pay off." It is the businessman's version of the protective distance Bogart-like heroes display in films. Neither Dick nor Bogey (as portrayed in this film) is able to expose his vulnerability, as Allan and Linda do.

Linda, on the other hand, comes to be another mentor for Al-

lan, a friend who offers an alternative to the extremes represented by Bogart and Nancy. Linda tells Allan he doesn't need
"an image." "You're bright—and you're funny and I think you're
even romantic. . . . Why not just be yourself; the girl will fall in
love with you." Later Allan meets Linda in a park, where they
sit together amid long rows of empty park benches that recall
again the empty theater seats in the film's first scene, but now
Allan is with someone despite the emptiness around him. Once
they plan to have dinner together, however, Allan fluctuates between anticipating the romance with Linda and feeling guilty
because of his friendship with Dick. As he walks home, a row of
parking meters dominates the lower-right-hand portion of the
frame to suggest the regulations and social taboos he believes
he is violating as he plans the rendezvous.

Bogey and Nancy appear to Allan together at a supermarket,
where Bogey encourages Allan to court Linda, while Nancy
plays on his guilt and tells him that Dick will beat him to a pulp.
The two polarities do battle as his own growing self-esteem battles with his remaining false fears on the one hand and his inflated romantic ideals on the other. Allan calls on Bogey for help
as he tries to make advances with Linda that night; but Nancy
again confronts Bogart, and this time she shoots him, leaving
Allan to seduce Linda all by himself.

He does it, but their successful romance causes Allan even
greater guilt, and in a pair of additional filmic allusions, Allan
experiences the various kinds of confrontations he might have if
Dick discovered his deception. One scene, recalling *Separate Tables* (1958), presents a formal British dinner in which all conflict
is translated into polite conversation, and the other imitates a
much more passionate Vittorio De Sica neorealist drama. Like
his experiences with Bogey and Nancy, the confrontation scenes
suggest the extremes toward which Allan's mind moves in his
anxiety. The contemporary little man stands caught within
debates—between passion and indifference, between inflated
dreams of perfection and nightmares of inadequacy, between
civilization and natural instinct.

Bogart appears for the last time in the film's final airport sequence, where Allan sees off Dick and Linda, who have reunited. Although Linda has already made a choice to go with Dick, Allan's concluding gestures are significant. Echoing Bogey's last speech to Paul Henreid in *Casablanca*, Felix convinces Dick that his wife is guiltless and sends his friends on their way with grace and style. In doing so, Allan replays with dignity the renunciation he could not face in his divorce. At the end of *Play It Again, Sam*, Allan Felix is left with a self-conception that is on the mend, a more confident figure than he was when the film began. Although Allan has not become a macho hero, he has begun to deal both with fears of inadequacy on the one hand and with unattainable aspirations on the other. Despite dilemmas that cause anxiety, images that discourage naturalness, and countless other obstacles, the little man has acted, he has achieved a memorable moment of intimacy, and he has shown personal integrity.

But the film's ending also leaves unresolved problems. The confusion of art and life, already aggravated throughout the narrative by Ross's refusal to consistently mark Nancy's and Bogey's appearances with transitions that usually signal fantasy, is complicated further by the replication of *Casablanca*'s finale in the conclusion, now with Allan, Dick, and Linda as key players. At the very moment that Allan seems to choose reality over fiction, and the spectator decides that *Play It Again, Sam* demonstrates that film images can and should be distinguished from reality, the ending reemphasizes that real life remains more difficult to separate from fiction than we thought.

Bogey affirms Allan's growth when he wishes him goodbye, noting that Allan doesn't need the movie star anymore since he has developed his own style, and Allan acknowledges that "the secret's not being you; it's being me." But Ross saw some of the more problematic implications of Allen's play and accentuated them. The little man's growing autonomy in *Play It Again, Sam* is not merely lip service paid to the easy " '60's bromide" "just be yourself and the world will love you," nor is the film's denouement "unqualifiedly sanguine."[12] Even this early movie hints that Allen's is a more complicated vision, which insists on taking uncertainties into account and which acknowledges that all resolutions are conditional in a world where fiction and reality have begun to merge. Moreover, pain cannot be overlooked from the film's perspective. Allan is able to act more courageously, but unlike the little man in Allen's play, who was immediately provided with a new love interest, in Ross's film, Allan is left as lonely as Rick in *Casablanca*, and he acknowledges his sense of loss. In such a vein, Allan Felix admits that his is no easy world; he tells us that he is heartbroken even as he tells Bogart that he—Allan—is "short and ugly enough" to succeed on his own.

The Fool (Woody Allen) faces a "beheading" in a medieval costume episode from *Everything You Always Wanted to Know about Sex* (*but were afraid to ask)*. *Courtesy of Woody Allen and United Artists.*

4

Sex, Sci-Fi, and
Sophisticated Philosophy

Woody Allen advances technically over the course of his next three films—*Everything You Always Wanted to Know about Sex** *(*but were afraid to ask)* (1972), *Sleeper* (1973), and *Love and Death* (1975); and his self-assurance as a director makes his parodies of both society and visual conventions more incisive, while asserting the little man's tentativeness, naturalness, humanity, and fumbling quest for meaning as an alternative to social affectations, monologic art, and unitary worldviews. In these films Allen mimics a greater variety of texts, both American and European—but his reasons for doing so go beyond the novice's glib references that seem to mark his earliest films. His parodies and burlesques continue to reflect both his affection for older films and his sense of the falseness of the sophisticated social forms that film, television, and the print media present to us as desirable. His is not a love-hate relationship, however, but a love-distrust one—an exploration of, rather than a polemic against, the alienating quality of his world and the role played in it by his medium.

His little man remains a victim of false models, but as he participates in films, he is also a preserver of them. In these next films, however, he becomes increasingly less humble, less passive, more self-conscious, and more smart alecky; his growing self-awareness anticipates the little man's more conscious search for authenticity in Allen's later films, where self-consciousness also becomes a more prominent part of the problem and figures in Allen's more varied use of metafilmic strategies to develop his themes.

At the same time that Allen emphasizes the universality of human frustration and human needs through his little-man persona, he anticipates his later more conscious concern with time, instability, and the unreliability of individual subjective perception, by placing these next films in settings that explore more variegated spatial and temporal perspectives than did the earlier films. The variety of texts and perspectives also permits him to practice his craft. For example, in the seven short episodes that comprise *Everything You Always Wanted to Know about Sex*, he moves comfortably among realistic and imaginary landscapes, between present and past time, from familiar American scenes to foreign—and from the world as our eyes see it to the world as the movie camera presents it to us. In *Sleeper* he utilizes much the same type of thematic opposition that he did in the earlier *Bananas*, but his imitation of Stanley Kubrick's consciously artificial comic-book style in *A Clockwork Orange* (1971) also marks a major step forward in Allen's handling of color and production design. And *Love and Death*, set in nineteenth-century Russia, not only alludes backward to classic Russian novels and films, but also to philosophical issues that bedeviled the intellectual of the sixties and early seventies—and that continue to bedevil the little man even today. Allen, however, makes fun of spectacular epic adaptations and treats Tolstoy and Dostoevsky, as well as lofty philosophical abstractions, on a less grandiose, more human scale than we have come to expect in dominant cinema.

SEX AND THE LITTLE MAN

Following Hiroshima, Americans of the late forties and fifties longed for normalcy, even if this meant refusing to acknowledge discomfiting anxieties that lay just beneath placid surfaces. Dr.

Kinsey's surprising reports on America's sexual habits were only one indication that the country was keeping the lid on disturbing issues. By the 1960s, however, a reaction had set in; a new sexual frankness bred glossy magazines with centerfolds and a series of how-to books. The extremes of 1950s repression, as well as such popular 1960s sex manuals as Dr. David Reuben's *Everything You Always Wanted to Know about Sex* (*but were afraid to ask)* (1969), provided the catalyst as well as the title for Woody Allen's 1972 film.

David Reuben's "utterly candid guide to the facts of life" had a self-consciously chatty tone ("In the Western world the hymen is a big deal") and used a question-and-answer format to make inquiries like "Why do women have only two breasts?" or "What about down below?" seem like snippets of coffee klatch. In the language of its time, the book dealt with everything from impotence to a long list of sexual "perversions." As Penelope Gilliatt observed, the manual was littered with technological and space-age metaphors[1] ("The labia minor is a crankshaft"; "Ejaculation can be compared to firing a missile").[2]

In Reuben's book, sex acts were also great performances on stage and screen. Impotence was "the show that is over before it starts. . . . No normal woman is going to wait for an encore."[3] Although the manual was intended to reduce sexual anxiety, sensitive readers must have been unnerved to find full-scale space programs operating in their erogenous zones or to learn that satisfying sex requires an Academy Award–winning performance.

Woody Allen's emphasis on naturalness, his search for an authenticity beyond programmed responses, and his interest in dialogic comedy involving the confusion of artifice and life made both the media's evasion of sexuality and Dr. Reuben's frank emphasis on technique at the expense of feeling appropriate comic targets. Reuben's performance metaphors especially may have prompted Allen to explore a series of different visual styles drawn from his experience in television and films, and to burlesque the performance metaphor in terms related to media.

As in his other early comedies, Allen makes fun of two extremes—in this case, sexual repression and inhibition on the one hand, and sexual license on the other. The film also provides a reflexive and deconstructive commentary on the extremes of pornography and prudery, which conventional cinema juggles in order to control audiences and to provide an authorized outlet for rebellious excesses. At the same time, the film also urges tolerance for a broad variety of human experience. In each episode the joke involves a little man working out his sexual problems within circumstances that are either too restrictive or not restrictive enough. In each case, little-person characters experience an unconventional or playful moment of freedom in which they drop their masks and reveal their natural impulses. In that process, the little-man characters also deconstruct the inauthenticities in the visual styles and forms in which they are captured. While in some episodes the sexual schlemiel wins a round—even if he does not give the year's top performance in his four-poster—he never wins the whole fight. Together, the episodes create a funny, inconclusive picture regarding the possibilities for human freedom and self-realization.

Everything You Always Wanted to Know about Sex is divided into seven sections, each with a question or title that borrows directly from Reuben or plays on Reuben's chapter headings. In all seven of the episodes that make up the film, Allen parodies popular film styles and the social conventions that gave rise to them. For example, in "What Is Sodomy?" he parodies the dark naturalism of 1950s film adaptations like *Carrie* (1952) and *A Place in the Sun* (1951) by having a respectable psychiatrist (Gene Wilder) fall in love, not with a beautiful woman of a different social class, like Jennifer Jones or Elizabeth Taylor, but with an uninterested sheep (Daisy), whose torso is treated in a burlesque of the slow revelation (ankles on up) that characterizes titillating presentations of movie love-goddesses as seen by the male gaze. The psychiatrist's obsessive love drives him to drink (Woolite) and ultimately to his destruction.

Likewise, one of the other episodes, "What Are Sex Perverts?", parodies the prim and popular early TV quiz show "What's My

Line?" with a real-life panel of experts (Pamela Mason, Regis Philbin, Robert Q. Lewis, and Toni Holt) trying to determine guest contestants' perversions within the required time and question limits. In addition to spoofing prime-time programming's false propriety, Allen exposes the hypocrisy in commercials. Despite Allen's careful mimicry of weak television signals and fuzzy early kinescope images, we are still able to make out the two he-men embracing in the background of a hair tonic advertisement.

And an earlier episode, "Are Transvestites Homosexual?", parodies popular domestic situation comedies. The style is the flat two-dimensional look of TV and film melodrama, involving little camera movement, traditional medium and medium-long perspectives, and conventional familial settings and compositions. Rather than portraying the all-too-familiar problems that beset the typical early sit-com family on "Leave It to Beaver" or "Father Knows Best," Allen presents Lou Jacobi, a middle-aged husband, father, and transvestite on a visit to his daughter's future in-laws. Bored by his better-heeled suburban hosts' self-satisfied small talk, Jacobi sneaks away and tries on his hostess's "sweet dresses." After a series of misadventures, he is , of course, discovered.

Yet for a moment, he—like Wilder's psychiatrist, like Rabbi Chaim Baumel (who on the quiz show admits to enjoying being tied up with silk stockings and spanked by a leather-clad model while his wife eats pork at his feet)—achieves a moment of playful freedom. The dreams may be false; they may only be desperate fabrications in response to social values that have nothing to do with the human animal. But the little man, even in moments of embarrassment, of humiliation, affirms our sense that moments of even apparent freedom, amid the false conventions with which we have to live, are worth having.

This feeling is probably strongest in the episodes in which Allen appears. In fact, the first of the seven episodes, "Do Aphrodisiacs Work?", plays off most of the film conventions that depict a fantasy world of the past as a magical, heroic era where all is possible, and it contrasts the harsh reality the little man faces in his everyday life with these fantasies. Allen plays an unsuccessful medieval court comedian, reminiscent of Danny Kaye's little-man role in *A Court Jester* (1956), in scenes and settings that recall the lighting for *A Man for All Seasons* on one hand, and the dark tones of film and stage versions of Shakespeare's *Hamlet* and *Macbeth* on the other. The difference is that, unlike Kaye's heroic fool, who wins the maid at the end of his 1950s film-version success story of the rise of the little man, Allen's jester, who had hoped to restore his comic gifts by sleeping with the queen, only gets his head chopped off after being discovered with his hand caught in her chastity belt.

There is little affirmation in decapitation. But there is in having taken a risk and won the queen, even temporarily, from a king who can "swim the moat lengthwise." And defeat is defused because we do not see the jester's head rolling off the block at the end of the episode; we see only the jester's bauble (a replica of Allen's face) tumbling across the screen. If the little man has not quite reached his goal by successfully making love to the queen, neither is he quite punished for his attempt to live up to his medieval sex fantasy. Unlike Kaye's jester, whose story ends in a clear triumph and resolution, Allen's does not quite succeed and he does not quite fail, but filmic slight-of-hand allows the comic spirit a chance for survival.

The little man does succeed in a later episode, "Why Do Some Women Have Trouble Reaching Orgasm?" This segment alludes to the ultramodern settings and existential concerns of contemporary Italian cinema. In this episode, Allen plays a frustrated Italian husband, Fabrizio, whose wife, Gina (Louise Lasser) is frigid. Eventually he discovers that she can only be aroused in public places where passion would be impolite; therefore, Fabrizio and Gina make love in such fashionable settings as expensive restaurants and trendy furniture stores. The couple's sexual activities, played against such a respectable social backdrop, constitute a rebellion against the stuffiness and conventionality of social norms.

The settings and the shots of the action that takes place in those settings—even the characters themselves—are reminiscent of the scenes in which romantic heroes created by directors like Bertolucci and Antonioni suffer their Italian version of metaphysical angst. Like Marcello Mastroianni, Allen's Fabrizio wanders within a mise-en-scène of large, empty rooms, brightly lit and sparsely furnished. He takes long, thoughtful walks. He searches for answers from priests and photographers. But his philosophical musings revolve around how to make his wife respond in the bedroom so that "she won't lie there like a lox."

Against arid interiors and alienated characters, Allen deals with mundane, rather than grand metaphysical, issues; Fabrizio's is not a spiritual journey as in *La notte*, but a down-to-earth physical one, and Gina's discovery of a solution is an affirmation of spontaneity in the face of contemporary disillusionment. Like the jester who clumsily courts the queen in her geometric Versailles-like gardens and proclaims his humanness by trying to "cop a feel," like the transvestite whose behavior does not look right on well-manicured suburban lawns, like the doctor who makes love to sheep in the clean white offices his mother bought for him, Gina and Fabrizio's "irregularities" make us recall an innocence and naturalness beyond the Italians' sophisticated sets and intellectual pretensions. Rascally children in a compulsively well kept house, Fabrizio and his Monica Vitti–like wife present a disheveled contrast to the carefully composed cold, white walls and chrome fixtures as they emerge, still buttoning and zipping from each forbidden sexual rendezvous. Allen's couple implies that love, sex, and life may still have their disorderly way, upsetting fixed systems and leaving established filmic conventions in disarray.

At least Fabrizio succeeds—if only on the floor of a famous restaurant. So, to a lesser extent, does Allen as Victor Shakopolis in the episode "Are the Findings of Doctors and Clinics Who Do Sexual Research Accurate?"—or perhaps he succeeds to a greater extent, since his grand achievement is trapping a gigantic female breast that has been terrorizing the countryside and drowning people in half-and-half, by confining the breast in a huge bra. In an imitation of gothic and 1950s sci-fi film codes, a sexologist, Dr. Bernardo, played by gothic veteran John Carradine, represents scientific overkill. Aside from creating the breast, Bernardo attempts to produce orgasms of incredible duration and to create a 400-foot diaphragm. Reluctant hero Victor's ingenuity and courage in counteracting this kind of speculative meddling in human activity is one of Allen's strongest affirmations of the little man's rebellion in this film.

But Allen's funniest moments come in the final episode of the film. Dressed in a white parachutist's outfit and a pilot's cap, and recalling countless heroic war films, Allen is one coward in a line of sperm, waiting to see if their man, Sidney, will finally get a chance to send them into battle. Reminiscent of science-fiction films like *Fantastic Voyage* (1966) that reduce, rather than expand, the sphere of action, the entire episode is depicted internally: within Sidney's head and body.

Tony Randall, in charge of operations control in an all-white war room, gives directions to the fumbling Sidney, who is trying to make love to a "college graduate" in a car. There is foreplay to think about, and Sidney has not read Dr. Reuben's book very well: he blows into his date's nose instead of her ear. In addition, he is feeling guilty, because there's a priest, signifying superego, in his brain, sabotaging his seduction attempts, and he forgets the proper technique, prompting Randall to yell orders to sex technician Burt Reynolds (playing a spoof of himself as macho star) to "maintain hands on breasts!" In the meantime, Sidney's sperm counterpart, Allen, is worried about the battle he will have to fight if Sidney *does* succeed: Will he be hurt going in? What about birth control pills? No matter: the time comes; Sidney succeeds. Allen prepares to disembark. While Sidney wins his war and achieves fulfillment, however, the sperm's future remains inconclusive; all the other sperm shout their versions of "Geronimo" as they leave the "plane." With less enthusiasm and expressing a more qualified sense of victory, Allen's little-man sperm sighs, "At least he's Jewish."

THE LITTLE MAN FACES THE FUTURE: *SLEEPER*

With *Sleeper,* critics believe Allen began to awaken to his finest comic and cinematic gifts: his little man is more self-confident and aggressive, his allusions continue to become more integral and complex, and his compositions and sets are more visually attractive than in earlier films. The title is a well-chosen introduction to the film's plot, themes, and style. While the little man appears to be a literal sleeper, it is actually the world around him that is desensitized and sleeping, and like the offensive player in football who is stationed in an obscure field position with the hope that he will not be noticed by the other team until after he has performed his function in a play, the little-man's role in the plot is to achieve a goal for the rebel underground before anyone realizes what he is doing. The title may also be a reflexive comment on the film—Allen's hope that it will be a sleeper, or surprising success, awakening passive spectators to the quality of modern life even as they experience an entertaining comedy.

Sleeper is a science-fiction spoof about little man Miles Monroe (Allen), who, like leftover food, is bundled in Reynolds wrap and frozen cryogenically in 1973, then defrosted two hundred years later by some rebel scientists who want him to help depose "The Leader." The situation is amenable both to the kind of social theme Allen wants to develop through his comedy—and specifically through his parody of various science-fiction film traditions—and to Allen's growing concern with the visual qualities of his films.

Of the latter concern, both cinematographer David Walsh and production designer Dale Hennessey noted Allen's developing visual skill. Walsh told Eric Lax that "Woody will find a frame . . . that some cameramen and artists couldn't find in a lifetime."[4] And Hennessey observed that "Woody has a marvelous visual eye. Maybe it's from watching all those films. He wants everything real but slightly funny. . . . Sketches don't mean anything to Woody. He has to see it with his eyes."[5] As for Allen, he complained to Lax that "the trouble is I want to make it funny *and* pretty, and the two are opposite."[6]

Appropriately to *Sleeper*, Allen makes the machines look nearly organic while the people, in contrast, are too mechanical. To accent the merging of artifice and life in an unreal futureworld that is an extrapolation of our own times, Allen also imitates Stanley Kubrick's primary color scheme in *A Clockwork Orange* to achieve a surrealistic comic-book look. So convincing are Allen's effects that above the explosions of a futuristic police wagon, we almost expect to see a bubble that reads "Boom!" Some futureworld apartments also contain bizarre "antiques" collected from the 1970s.

Allen's knowledge of older comic films, together with his familiarity with science-fiction films of the past, helps create the dialogues in this film. He uses images borrowed from Chaplin, Harold Lloyd, and Buster Keaton, combining them with plot complications and thematic motifs typical of most science-fiction genre films. Allen alludes directly or indirectly, for example, to the active physical comedies of the twenties and thirties in the film's opening wheelchair sequence; in Miles's acrobatic flight from the laboratory using a ladder; in his escape from a robot-repair center; in his escape from pursuers, where he deflates his hydro-vac suit and scoots across a lake like a giant balloon; in a vegetable scene where Miles pratfalls on an oversized banana peel; and in various other man-versus-machine sequences. Such activity forms a metaphoric contrast with the Leader in a wheelchair, and with the sleeping, unaware world that he regulates.

When viewing such scenes, it is difficult not to think of Chaplin battling the assembly line in *Modern Times* or Harold Lloyd defying gravity by hanging from a gigantic clock; but the empty futuresque settings within which these comedic sequences occur recall other, more solemn films as well—science-fiction films as far removed in time as *Things To Come* (1936), and as recent as *2001* (1968). The comic defrosting parodies such grade-B disasters as *The Frozen Dead* (1967); a fight with a giant pudding recalls *The Blob* (1958); and at the film's end Allen spoofs several cloning movies when Luna and Miles pretend to re-create the tyrannical leader from his nose. Combined with a plot that echoes the same fears of "Big Brother" articulated in Michael Anderson's adaptation of Orwell's *1984* (1956) and François Truffaut's *Fahrenheit 451* (1966), the playfulness of classic comedy contrasts with the themes of restriction, as well as with restrictive conventions of classic science fiction, to express Allen's fear of a mechanized, programmed society, an unreal pop art world that ignores the human element—a society where the little man must fight for his identity, his freedom, and his life.

Perhaps the strongest thematic and pictorial inspiration, though, is Stanley Kubrick's *A Clockwork Orange*, which was current as Allen conceived the idea for *Sleeper* with Marshall Brickman. Like Kubrick's film, Allen's lighter version deals with the same issues: a society programmed to be happy and placid at the cost of its humanity; and the individual's battle to retain his authentic identity as a complex, often confused, sometimes unhappy human being, in the face of society's attempt to turn him into a well-regulated robot. Like Kubrick's film, Allen's self-consciously considers its own role in drugging audiences into passive viewing. In Allen's film, Miles wakes up in 2173 to discover that he has been defrosted only because the rebels against the Leader can use him for their ends, since he has no record to be identified by in this highly regulated, regimented, computerized society. The allusion to *A Clockwork Orange* is directly suggested when our introduction to the film is Miles's doctor, sporting a derby like the ones Alex's "droogs" wore in the first half of Kubrick's film. Even though he purports to be against the Leader's dehumanizing policies, that same doctor is willing to "eliminate" Miles "in the usual way" if anything goes wrong during the defrosting.

Miles later discovers that much of the regulation in the future-world involves not force but a mindless pleasure principle that keeps people at the level of docile pets. Miles meets Luna (Diane Keaton), who enjoys a world (similar to the kitschy world that

Kubrick presents in *A Clockwork Orange*) where sexual satisfaction is mechanically induced by an "orgasmatron," where group sex is in vogue, where people get high by simply fondling "the orb," where Rod McKuen is considered a poet of great profundity, and where paintings of large-eyed children, reminiscent of Walter Kean's painting of the 1960s, are considered great art. ("It's more than Kean," Luna gushes over one painting. "It's Cugat.")

But the parallel to Kubrick's world is even stronger. Like the violent Alex, who disrupts the serene mindlessness of England's futureworld, Miles is a disruptive element in this new world—not because of viciousness, but because of his disorderly little-man inadequacies. He spreads his food on the doctor's clean smocks soon after he has been brought back to life; he walks backward instead of forward; he rolls his wheelchair dizzily over the feet of intimidating security policemen; his bubblecar, flying suit, and laser gun won't work for him. He does not even feel comfortable with the satisfaction supposedly to be offered by the orgasmatron ("I'm a hand man," he protests. "I don't like moving parts not my own"). He does not fit into this world—not because he is an inadequate human, but because he is too human. The little man's inadequacies become virtues in the face of the dehumanized values Allen indicates we may be developing as we move into an increasingly more mechanized, more orderly high-tech society.

Even *Sleeper*'s plot reflects this concern as it imitates the two-part structures of both *A Clockwork Orange* and *Bananas*. In the first part of the film, Miles is the social outcast, whose twentieth-century humanity clashes with the "auto-psyche" of the twenty-second century. Alex and his droogs inflicted destruction willfully on their contemporaries; Miles does so unwillingly and innocently, but just as tellingly—when, for example, he disguises himself as a robot and is sent to a robot-repair shop. He has to fight his way out, littering the shop with robot arms, heads, and legs; but his comic determination to survive says a great deal about the threat of automation to our humanity. Later,

Miles is captured, given an electronic cap like Alex's, and brain-washed (the ultimate test of the process is to see if he can answer questions as vacuously as a Miss America contestant).

Ironically, Miles is rescued from his state of mental limbo by Luna, who has since joined the rebels with a vengeance. (As in *Bananas*, Allen suggests that a lack of personal integrity and clear identity makes one susceptible to political enthusiasms of all sorts, and he underlines the concern by having Luna sing Esposito's awful rebel song yet another time.) She spirits him away from the authorities, and in an echo of Alex's second re-programming in *A Clockwork Orange*, Miles is reprogrammed back to his original bumbling self. While the first brainwashing involved teaching the patient's mind that pleasure is its only principle, the second brainwashing is designed to make Miles remember guilt and human misery; thus, he is made to attend an imaginary Passover seder at his parents' house and tell them of his impending divorce. Even more excruciatingly, he is con-fused by Luna and Erno's bad Jewish role-playing and ends up adopting a role as inappropriate for a Jewish boy as their Jewish parent roles are for two Wasps. Painfully (for Miles and for the audience), he plays Blanche Dubois in Tennessee Williams's *A Streetcar Named Desire* opposite Keaton's unbelievable Stanley. Then, as in *Bananas*, Miles and Luna work to foil an attempt to clone a new Leader from his nose (all that is left of him after an accident). In a final reference to playful silent comedy, Miles throws the nose beneath a steamroller, wins Luna, and the film implies that he and Luna may manage to restore a much less perfect, but far more human, social environment.

Although Allen's *Sleeper* spoofs Kubrick's *A Clockwork Orange*, taking the serious comedy into the realm of zany absurdity, Miles warns Luna against believing in ideological panaceas, whether they be political, religious, or scientific (he only be-lieves in sex and death); and Allen's film also carries disquieting echoes of Kubrick's warning regarding the loss of free choice and the triumph of a dehumanized fascistic state. In its obvious filmic allusions and artificial style, *Sleeper* also qualifies its own hopeful ending by acknowledging, as *A Clockwork Orange* does, the dangers of its own complicity as a film in this process. These undertones anticipate the mood and the meaning of Allen's more solemn later comedies.

LOVE AND DEATH

The burlesque setting in Allen's next film is not Dillinger's Chicago, Castro's Cuba, or Kubrick's futureworld; it is nine-teenth-century Russia, where Allen exercises his imperfect hero to the music of Prokofiev and to the moral and ethical lessons of the great Russian novelists and filmmakers. It is a film that confronts death to ask whether life has meaning. "Is there a hell? Is there a God? All right, Just one key question, are there girls?"

The film's burlesque patterns resemble those in earlier Allen movies, but now there are resonances that make this film, like *Sleeper,* a bridge to his later work. *Love and Death* is still for laughs; the film spoofs the pretensions of intellectual pomp and circumstance; yet Allen's jokes, based on the incongruity between the weighty concerns and abstract rhetoric of philosophy and literature, and ordinary peoples' down-to-earth needs, help emphasize the little man's search for authenticity and his desire to preserve his humanity. The film also draws attention to languages both verbal and visual. Reflexively, this film also helps us to understand why Allen makes human and "small" films, as opposed to popular cinematic spectacles.

In *Love and Death* Woody Allen tells us not so much what he believes, but how his mind, and the contemporary mind, conditioned by existential thought, deals with the possibility of belief—at once sifting through the past and present for meaning, yet constantly finding inadequacies in all carefully wrought systems, including even its own favorite philosophies and its own skepticism. While Allen goes beyond modernism in his desire to recover a trust in feeling and genuine empathy, he also fears shallow sentimentality.

Allen told Eric Lax: "I think I am sentimental. I think I'm a sucker for cheap sentimentality—as long as it's my own. I always hate the other guy's self-indulgence. As far as romantic, if you think being against the universe is a romantic position, then I agree. Take *Love and Death*, I guess you could say it's vaguely romantic in concept. But any existential obsession, even as frivolous as my film, carries with it romantic overtones automatically. Philosophical thought of men like say, Russell and Dewey or even Hegel may be dazzling but it's sober and uncharismatic. Dostoevsky, Camus, Kierkegaard, Berdyayev—the minds I like—I consider romantic. I guess I equate 'dread' with romance. . . . The trick, as I see it, is to be Byronic without appearing Moronic."[7]

The film is about an undersized Russian with an oversized name, Boris Petrovich Dmitrivich Greshenko, a handle that links him to both Tolstoy and Dostoevsky. Boris (Woody Allen) loves Sonia (Diane Keaton), whose character is drawn from Natasha of *War and Peace*, Grushenka of *The Brothers Karamazov*, and Anna Karenina for good measure. Sonia loves Boris's brother, but spurned by him, she accepts the hand of a herring merchant, Voskovec, who almost immediately drops dead.

Meanwhile, a reluctant Boris has been sent to war, where he experiences a usual series of little-man misadventures before accidentally becoming a hero. His medals lead him to a countess's bedroom and quickly from there to a duel with her cuckolded lover. Boris survives the duel to marry the widowed Sonia, and their love prospers for a short time before Napoleon invades Russia. Then, instead of fleeing, as Boris would prefer, Sonia insists that they assassinate the general. Boris fails in his attempt and is captured; although the moral little man is unable to kill another person, he is executed by a firing squad and led away in a dance of death.

The central thrust of the film is suggested as early as the joke imbedded in the title. Made in the manner of *War and Peace* or *Crime and Punishment*, Allen's title moves beyond evasive philosophical and social issues to the most basic, down-to-earth human questions as Woody Allen understands them. The remainder of the film follows a similar pattern of puncturing not only large philosophical debates with everyday considerations, but reducing the conventions associated with lengthy films of cinemascopic proportions to more manageable, human dimensions.

The film opens with portentous clouds floating across the frame in the manner of Bergman's opening for *The Seventh Seal*. Despite the score from *Alexander Nevsky* that haunts the background, however, we recognize that the voice-over belongs to a little man in large glasses who likes to whine about his problems. Boris's familiar monologue sets up the film's irony: "Absolutely incredible, how I got into this predicament—to be executed for a crime I never committed." And he adds the greater existential irony that also justifies his direct address to the audience: "Of course, isn't all mankind in the same boat? Isn't all mankind ultimately executed for a crime it never committed?" Then, however, Boris deflates his own seriousness with a joke: "The difference is that all men go eventually, but I go at six o'clock tomorrow morning. I was supposed to go at five o'clock, but I had a smart lawyer. Got leniency."

Although there were brief asides to the audience in earlier films, *Love and Death* includes the first instances in a major Allen film where the little man self-consciously addresses the audience directly to comment on his story. This technique, which helps to establish an intimate connection between the little man and the viewer, looks back to Allen's confessional persona in his nightclub years and forward to *Annie Hall*. Its immediate inspiration, however, for purposes of comedic contrast, may have been Tolstoy's first-person narrations and Dostoevsky's intimate authorial voice.

Anticipating *Annie Hall*, the film is a retrospective in which Boris tries to understand and to explain how he arrived at Death's doorstep. Thus, in the manner of Tolstoy's *Childhood, Boyhood, Youth*, Boris introduces those people who were important as he grew up. Allen's growing interest in the visual quality of his films is reflected in the arresting compositions, more careful use of lighting, and close shots that create a gallery of family faces and childhood recollections. Unlike Tolstoy, however, Allen develops a series of unsentimental comic portraits. Grandma and Grandpa still hate each other after fifty years of marriage; his father is a "landowner" more in the sunbelt than the Russian sense (the land is so small it fits into his coat); and in a departure from *The Brothers Karamazov*, Boris's brother is a Neanderthal who can barely spell his name in the dirt with a stick. Like the family memories that Allen will develop more completely in *Annie Hall, Stardust Memories*, and *Zelig*, Boris's remembrances are no monument to the glories of family life. Boris's mother, an enthusiastic Russian nationalist, wants nothing more than to send her son off to war to be killed.

Boris also recalls his cousin Sonia, whom he loved in part because of their "deep" discussions. Philosophical and idealistic, Sonia tries to interest him in "essences," "first causes," and "immanence"; she finds nature wondrous—a sure sign that God exists. More skeptical, Boris sees nature as "a giant restaurant" and asks for a single miracle as proof of God: just once, he'd like to see his Uncle Sasha pick up a check. Later, when Boris tries to commit suicide in Dostoevskyan fashion because he feels "an empty void at the center of [his] being," Sonia seeks advice about "what is best," what is truth, what is meaningful from a wise mentor modeled on Father Zossima in *The Brothers Karamazov*, but Allen's man of wisdom is a senile fellow billed as "the most wrinkled man in the world." "His grubbiness" teaches Sonia no great lessons about life, only that "the best thing is blond twelve-year-old girls, preferably two of them."

Similarly, with Boris, Allen also declares open season on false patriotism and the celebration of war. Boris, a "militant coward," prefers chasing butterflies to killing people. "What good is war?" he asks. "We kill a few Frenchmen; they kill a few Russians. Next thing you know, it's Easter." Against Ghislain Cloquet's beautiful camera work that imitates both King Vidor and Sergei Bondarchuk's majestic battle sequences in film versions of *War and Peace*, Allen reduces epic warfare on film with a silly World War II skit that warns soldiers of VD, with Frank Adu's bellowing drill sergeant who barks like Lee Marvin in *The Dirty*

Dozen, and with a battlefield hawker who sells blini like Harpo Marx sold the navy in *Duck Soup.* As Boris imitates Prince Andrey ruminating on how different war looks to generals and footsoldiers, Allen intercuts a herd of sheep to mix Eisenstein with Chaplin and the Marx Brothers. Unable to handle a rifle or keep step, Boris brings disarray to the battle formations typical of three-hour epic films. While Napoleon is slaughtering the Russians, a soldier tells Boris that "God is testing us." "If he's going to test us," says smart-alecky Boris, "why doesn't he give us a written?"

The serious business of dueling in *War and Peace* and countless other costume films is similarly fractured with classic comic dialogue. "My seconds will call on your seconds." "My seconds may be out. Call on my thirds. If my thirds are out, call on my fourths." Boris tries to choose both pistols when weapons are presented, and like Bob Hope in *Never Say Die* (1939), although he has made witty remarks about his opponent, he also hides behind his enemy instead of facing off as the ritual requires.

Allen also deconstructs conventional love and conventional death scenes. While Boris goes to war, Sonia, who has spoken of a perfect love with a man whose mind she respects, whose spirituality equals hers, and who has the lustful appetites she has, lives a life of quiet desperation with a smelly fish merchant whose dinner conversation runs the gamut from herring to herring. And while the herring salesman has important business to attend to with a large fish in his bedroom, Sonia carries on downstairs with a grotesque violinist in a spoof of intense love scenes from films such as *Dr. Zhivago* and commercials for Arpege perfume. When Boris finally takes Sonia to bed, Allen makes fun of the little man's sexual prowess with intertextual references to the sleeping stone lions who rise to herald the people's revolt in *Potemkin;* Allen's lions rise only briefly, then quickly fall down again, exhausted.

When Sonia's herring man dies, Sonia does not linger in a lengthy mourning as do Prince Andrey's loved ones or Petya Rostov's family in *War and Peace,* nor does the occasion provide an opportunity for one of Tolstoy's long analyses of the meaning of death, suffering, and loss. Sonia is quick to suggest that those attending the body go to a tavern on the edge of town where they make a great sausage. When Boris dies, Sonia makes one of the film's several long speeches about "wheat," in parody of *Anna Karenina*. In a similar spoof of long intense bereavements in Tolstoy, Ivan's wife, Anna, and Sonia console one another as Natasha and Marya consoled each other in *War and Peace*. In *Love and Death*, however, the mourning women divide Ivan's belongings, Sonia receives his mustache, half of his letters (the vowels), and pieces of his string collection.

The film also parodies classical literary structure in novels and films. *Love and Death* has two major movements, joined by a third section, or bridge, and framed by a prologue and epilogue. It boasts three mystical dreams, three encounters with death, and three dances, one of which takes place in the prologue, one in the bridge, and one in the epilogue. The prologue includes Boris's introductory remarks to the audience about his plight, and the flashback to his childhood and family. The first half of the film that follows is built like *War and Peace*, as it alternates between Boris's adventures on the battlefield and sequences that describe Sonia's life back home. In the first half of the film the question of love dominates. Sonia speaks of love in sententious phrases stolen from Tolstoy, but love proves to be arbitrary and she manages only to marry a dull herring merchant. Boris seeks Sonia's love, but she loves Ivan, and Boris only manages to get sent to war.

In the second half of the film, death rather than love predominates. Sonia's high-flown discussions of death and moral imperatives are nullified when innocent Boris dies, despite his best intentions, and Sonia, who advocated Napoleon's murder, is saved. The plot to kill Napoleon in the second half of *Love and Death* harks back to Pierre Bezuhov's plan to assassinate Napoleon in the later portions of Tolstoy's novel. Lovers unite and settle into domesticity at the end of *War and Peace;* Allen unites his lovers briefly for domestic comedy in the middle of the film. In a brief moment of respite, Boris achieves fame as a hero despite himself, survives several threats to life momentarily, and

Sonia falls in love with him. In Allen's film, life includes only a few brief happy interludes between unromantic beginnings and inconclusive endings.

Typically, too, Allen's structure resembles a joke. What ultimately happens to Sonia and Boris seems to have little to do with matters of spiritual salvation or the values proposed by Tolstoy. Although Boris questions whether the impersonal bloodshed of war in the film's first half is easier or more justifiable than the more personal one-on-one murder Sonia proposes in the film's second half, the philosophical debates that pepper the film provide no clear solution to this or any other problem.

Remembering Tolstoy, Allen also scatters three dreams in his film, but instead of providing important foreshadowing or significant comment on the action, they are mostly surrealistic nonsense and parody. Rather than leaving the little-man hero with profound insights into himself or his situation, they spoof prophetic literary visions. While Boris appears to get a last-minute reprieve when he is visited by a third mystical vision, an angel of God who promises that the emperor will save him from death, the angel lies and the emperor doesn't come through. In an ironic comment on Pierre Bezuhov's narrow escape from the firing squad in *War and Peace*, D'mitri Karamazov's conviction, redemption, and escape in *The Brothers Karamazov*, and Raskolnikov's limited sentence and salvation in *Crime and Punishment*, Woody Allen conveys his central ideas—that there is a large comic distance between everyday necessities or realities and the grand philosophical or literary solutions to life's problems. All we know is that common sense, humanity, integrity, and the will to survive have a difficult time amid the irrational turns of fate in an absurd world.

Boris also encounters a white-sheeted figure of Death three times, another allusion to Ingmar Bergman's *The Seventh Seal*. In the first, young Boris spies Death and asks about the meaning of life and death, and Death promises to see him again. In the second, Boris observes Death leading away a wine merchant and his mistress, but receives no further enlightenment, and in the third, Death dances Boris away. As in Bergman's film, Death never satisfactorily answers questions. Two dances precede the concluding one. Early in the film, Boris does a clumsy mazurka in which he appears to rupture himself rather than demonstrate acrobatic skill. During the brief interlude in the film's center, Sonia and Boris, now lovers, dance comically through the woods. If the first dance defines Boris's inadequacy as well as his inability to associate himself fully with the rituals that mark the intense bonds between man, family, and Mother Russia in Tolstoy or Dostoevsky, then the shorter dance in the middle of the film is a fleeting moment of play and connection between two people. However comical, it anticipates occasional meaningful moments in later Allen films wherein the hero is briefly content rather than anxious. Boris's eventual death is a pathetic rather than comic element in a new twist to the little man's story; the third dance mediates between pathos and comedy to create an inconclusive ending. Maurice Yacowar describes this finale as a Hasidic dance, part of "a frame of hearty joy" that suggests an "affirmation" of "the immortal continuities of the human spirit at least through art."[8] But Allen's dance is more awkward and hesitant, less committed, joyous, and enthusiastic than the Hasidic version, and his endorsement of art is at least as tentative as his dance.

Then what of love and death? Dead, Boris returns to tell Sonia only that it is a human condition to be befuddled. But as he explains that he has few answers, he also reduces Tolstoy's tedious epilogues with down-to-earth metaphors. "Death," he says, "is worse than the chicken at Tresky's restaurant." The important thing Boris tells us in his most solemn ending tone of voice, "is not to be bitter. If there is a God, I don't think he's evil. The worst thing you can say about him is that he's basically an underachiever." About love, he observes, again in his matter-of-fact way, that "it's not the quantity of your sexual relations that counts, it's the quality. On the other hand, if the quantity drops below once every eight months," he says, "I would definitely look into it.

And with that, Boris follows the white-sheeted figure with a scythe in a more comic dance of death than Ingmar Bergman filmed, but a far less hearty dance than any Hasid ever performed. The film's most memorable image does not dispel convincing evidence that the world is meaningless, and art offers little solace in this film; the little man in his down-to-earth way looks only for small victories—moments of comic antistructure, the fleeting moments of freedom we hesitantly manage to make for ourselves as we long to survive amid our own imposing intellectual edifices and our own well-established filmic conventions.

Annie (Diane Keaton) and Alvy (Woody Allen) have a nervous interchange after their tennis match in *Annie Hall*. *Courtesy of Woody Allen and United Artists.*

5

The Little Man's Screwball Comedy

In his sixth major film, Allen begins in earnest his departure from predominantly funny filmmaking. Allen claims that with each of his successes, his greater command of technique, and the knowledge that he could survive as a filmmaker, he became more "bullish" about expressing his personal concerns.[1] Although Allen had always been moving toward a seriocomic perspective and he had always been an acute social satirist, one more immediate touchstone for the changing mood of his films after *Love and Death* was his acting role in Martin Ritt's *The Front* (1976).

Created by writers and actors blacklisted during the McCarthy era, *The Front* is a serious comedy that deals with problems of commitment and personal integrity during the Communist witch hunts of the 1950s. In Walter Bernstein's script, Allen plays an uncommitted little man, Howard Prince, who fronts for writers who are not allowed to work because of their leftist affiliations. Initially, like the little man of Allen's early films, Prince prefers to remain outside the controversy, but when he is also called to appear before the House Un-American Activities Committee, he finally takes a stand. "I don't recognize the right of this committee to ask me these kinds of questions," he says, and he adds, "Furthermore, you can go fuck yourselves."

Although Ritt's film comes to a happy resolution—the little-man asserts his integrity and wins the girl—the difficulties involved in adopting a clear position in less-clearly defined circumstances may have suggested a number of possibilities to Woody Allen. Allen's involvement in a serio-comic film dealing with the need for commitment and personal integrity, as well as with the human damage left in the wake of a too clearly committed, closed-minded fanaticism, heralds his more recent work. With *Annie Hall* he goes beyond laughs to accentuate a darker side of the dialogic imagination that had remained in the background of his earlier films.

For all their drift toward inconclusiveness, Allen's early films portray oppositions primarily between civilization's "junk" and the guilelessness of the little-man victim. His humility, anxiety, and confusion played their role in dialogues between disorder and the rigidity of closed systems. The little man was often the foolish object of laughter himself, but he also mediated among extremes to retrieve an alternative point of view and to preserve the possibility of escape from absurdity.

Gradually, the humble little man learned to be a more aggressive smart aleck, although he never lost all of his common sense, tentativeness, and innocence. With Allen's adoption of the first-person narrator and a restrospective attempt to understand the events that lead to his execution in *Love and Death*, the persona becomes increasingly more self-aware—a conscious questioner and a searcher—and his innocence becomes more difficult. In *Annie Hall* the narrator's self-consciousness is even more prominent; not just a film critic as in *Play It Again, Sam*, he is now a comic artist like the filmmaker himself, and the sophistication that was located primarily outside the narrator is internalized and has demoralized him to a greater extent than in earlier funnier films. The little man's angst is examined more closely, and it is no longer only funny.

Not only does the narrator become more self-conscious, but the film as a whole becomes more seriously reflexive. Maurice Yacowar acknowledges that the film's many parallels "relate to the idea that art and life are continuous, mutually feeding forces"; the film, he believes, "contemplates death and loss" but "reaffirms the values of life, art, and love."[2] Like Yacowar, Thomas Schatz sees the film's obviously self-referential qualities—the ironic relationships between Allen and his little-man character, the confusions between text and reality underlined by the fact that Allen had been Keaton's lover and mentor in real life, the associative plot structure, and the repeated use of author interruptions and asides to the camera. Schatz concludes that "*Annie Hall* . . . is 'about' how we tell stories, how we remember relationships and our own past, how we impose our rational minds on the happenstance of experience. As such it is a film that virtually demands that the viewer adopt a modernist perspective, a self-conscious attitude toward Allen and his narrative."[3]

Not surprisingly, from Allen's dialogic angle of vision, in *Annie Hall* the nature of self-awareness itself becomes a more obvious part of the problem. The emotional distancing involved, both in the little man's increased self-awareness and its effects upon his search for love and fulfillment, and in the distances created for the spectator watching a defamiliarizing, modernistic self-reflexive film, rather than a classical movie, involve both gains and losses.

What happens in *Annie Hall* is that we experience, more than in earlier Allen films, a feeling for the burden of history, the sophisticated self-consciousness, and the accompanying anxiety that contemporary people carry into their search for love, integrity, and meaning. When, against the background of this self-conscious film and the corresponding pressures of modern-day life, Woody Allen creates a few meaningful human moments of even qualified hope or when he suggests that the searching little man's survival is grounds for some measure of faith, such images must be taken as solace in the face of a mighty fear. Such dread of transience and meaninglessness is the sort that has always frightened our greatest comic minds as they attempted to tear away layer after layer of inauthentic experience to discover something real.

At first viewing, *Annie Hall* may appear to be a departure from Allen's dependence on influences and from his customary densely intertextual and allusive style; however, this film, like all of Allen's work, is best approached along the reflexive lines that Schatz and Yacowar suggest, and as a series of dialogues among antithetical worldviews, set within an intersecting reflexive dialogue between films and about filmmaking. Like *Stardust Memories, Annie Hall* might well be approached through one major resonant allusion within which Allen develops a number of other intertextual dialogues. While romantic comedy generally may have inspired Allen's *Annie Hall*, screwball comedy, particularly, appears to be a focal reference for the film Allen made with Diane Keaton in mind.

Screwball comedies, very popular from the late Depression 1930s well through the years of World War II, are generally regarded as films that aimed at "reconciling the irreconcilable," that dealt with the battle of the sexes and cemented a country threatened by class antagonisms and social discontents. Screwball comedies "created an America of perfect unity: all classes as one, the rural-urban divide breached, love and decency and neighborliness ascendant."[4] While they were laced with snappy dialogue between conflicting personalities with differing lifestyles, and while they focused squarely on a new "consciousness of women,"[5] they ultimately reminded audiences that similarities transcend differences, that uppity women are cute but tameable, and that despite threats to the status quo, the world is a stable and orderly place where traditional values hold and individual integrity is rewarded. Women are temporarily dominant over men in such films as *Bringing Up Baby* (1938), *Adam's Rib* (1949), *Woman of the Year* (1940), and *His Girl Friday* (1940), but men get the edge in time for a conventional happy ending— marriage or reunion. Romances are tested, and despite obstacles, most relationships survive the trial; opposites are united. Of course, these post-1934 Production Code comedies also contain only the most wholesome references to physical sexuality. Couples have romantic or domestic skirmishes, but never discuss serious bedtime problems.

Wacky, chaotic situations characterize screwball comedies, but most of these films are classically structured to suggest an underlying harmony beneath temporary disruption. They follow conventional narrative and dramatic patterns to strict closure; typically, they are symmetrical and balanced, with parallel scenes and subplots; they often obey unities of time and place.

Screwball comedies frequently begin in the city, but couples often grow closer and explore their relationships in country settings, away from the distractions of modern urban life. Nature is regarded positively as a place for lovers to be "natural" and to get to know one another in a simpler, more authentic place.

Although most screwball comedies are primarily classic texts, a surprising number of these comedies contain reflexive references to performance and often spoof saccharine romances and action dramas and films, thereby attempting to offer a more realistic account of romance. These references, however, usually serve only as light puns or as means to render potentially controversial issues, such as changing sex roles, identity problems, disquieting cultural change, or significant individual difference, harmless by defamiliarizing the viewer from the film at crucial moments.[6]

Woody Allen's *Annie Hall* (1977), produced three or four decades after screwball comedy's heyday, echoes the older genre and deals with questions that surfaced in it, but also reflects an intensification of these issues. The older form becomes a backdrop against which to measure cultural change and to describe the contemporary world, where even "newer women" provide men with greater problems; where identities are more confused and lovers (who have histories) have become more neurotic and self-conscious than in a more innocent age; where differences are not always reconcilable; and where opposites cannot be united. The resumption of order after chaos, crucial to screwball comedy, is replaced in *Annie Hall* by such a tenuous resolution that we feel a far less comforting sense of closure. In Allen's dialogic film, human issues cannot be reduced to formula, fixed ideas do not hold, and meaning is found only in evanescent moments of experience. While *Annie Hall* mocks the older genre and the damaging romantic values it entails, however, it also evokes a sense of lost innocence and a longing for the playfulness and naturalness that a self-conscious contemporary perspective makes so difficult to recover. In *Annie Hall*, as in earlier Allen films, Alvy and Annie, as well as the spectators of Allen's film, are either caught in the false expectations aroused by our dreams and romantic film's illusions or are freed from them as we participate in our demystification. Conversely, the film may suggest that sophisticated demystification and a modernistic outlook can itself become a trap.

In *Annie Hall*, Alvy Singer (Woody Allen) sees much of the contemporary world as contradictory, transitory, and unreliable; he is restless, skeptical, and at times paranoid. In such a world, "love fades" or true passion and genuine human connection do not last, and as Alvy says, it is hard to get our heads around that. In this film, Allen's little man is a New York Jewish comedy writer approaching middle age; he is streetwise about urban sophistication, and Annie, his flaky lover from Chippewa Falls, Wisconsin, is a creative innocent. But the relationship has broken up when the story begins, and the film is both an autopsy and a reminiscence. Unlike screwball comedies before it, the film is not concerned with how opposites eventually unite, but with why this important love did not endure. Woven into Alvy's self-conscious quest for answers is a look at the stress that contemporary culture places on romance, and a reflexive examination of the relationship of art to life.

Alvy Singer is a far more self-conscious, complicated, and neurotic character than heroes in earlier screwball films. Originally *Annie Hall* was to be called "Anhedonia" (the inability to experience pleasure), referring to Alvy Singer's depression and his existential angst. Unlike predecessors in earlier screwball comedies, Alvy finds it hard to have fun or to believe in love.

In traditional screwball comedies, heroes seldom aged or had early histories, but we envision their having had secure Andy Hardy childhoods. Alvy's history, on the other hand, is an albatross. In his opening words, Alvy, at forty, reveals his fear of aging, change, and death; yet he tells us that his depression over Annie is unusual because he had a reasonably happy childhood.

Alvy's entire narrative is enveloped in inconclusiveness, however, because he is only a partially reliable narrator. Following
his references to his relatively happy childhood, we see him as
a depressed child who grew up during World War II—this ac-
counts in part for his personality, "which is a little nervous."

Alvy contradicts his initial self-analysis in several other childhood remembrances. He tracks an early depression to his per-
sonalizing the big bang theory that the universe is expanding
and will someday break apart and "that would be the end of
everything." Alvy won't do his homework because "What's the
point?" Thus, Allen traces Alvy's concern with unreliability to
the age of seven, when he experienced full-fledged existential
dread. His innocence is compromised by self-consciousness from
a very early age.

Alvy's is also not the mainstream American family that we
imagine raised Adam Bonner in *Adam's Rib.*[1] Alvy's emasculat-
ing, shrewish mother reduces carrots to shavings as she derides
Alvy for distrusting everyone, and she dismisses Alvy's early
anxieties about the cosmos by screaming in frustration, "What
is that your business? . . . What has the universe got to do with
it? You're here in Brooklyn! Brooklyn is not expanding!" She
and Alvy's father reveal how moral ambiguity has crept into
everyday life as they argue heatedly and comically about whether cleaning women should be allowed to steal. Frank Capra,
George Cukor, and Howard Hawkes never gave their characters
a family so colorful, so New York, so Jewish, or so confusing.

From Alvy's perspective, reemphasized as he interrupts his
own recollections by making an adult appearance within the
scene, days at school evoke further distrust. Incompetent cartoon teachers preside over rigid classrooms filled with dull or
competitive schoolmates who soon lose their innocence, growing up to be methadone addicts and owners of a "profitable
dress company." A rosy-colored filmland childhood is as far from
Alvy's experience as Annie's rural Wisconsin is from his Coney
Island home beneath a roller coaster that shakes his tomato
soup each time it passes.

Adult Alvy's interruption of his own narrative not only emphasizes its subjectivity, but reminds us that we are watching a film. Moreover, his interruption and stream of early memories are only two in a long series of disruptions to classical narrative structure that also serve to violate conventional boundaries between fiction and reality, to indicate Alvy's confusion, and to contrast pointedly with the comforting architecture of traditional screwball film. As Alvy sifts through his associations, so the audience must deal not only with the pieces into which his life has flown, but with Alvy's attempts to make sense of them. The emphasis on self-analysis in a subjective time frame also stresses the contemporary self-consciousness that creates additional pressures on human relationships.

Fragments from Alvy's and Annie's pasts also come to suggest reflexively how film and other media have an impact on modern identity and confusion. Alvy's memories are filled with media interruptions, feature films, cartoons, and references to media theory. Among Alvy's memories is a TV screen that fills the frame, and we see Woody Allen's appearance on the Dick Cavett show. In images drawn from the filmmaker's own history, Allen self-consciously reminds us that the images of experience are too easily confused with experience itself and media plays a more ambivalent role in constructing our hopes and dreams—our personalities—than earlier screwball comedies ever considered.

The influence of visual imagery on contemporary psychology is also highlighted, since Annie and Alvy often go to movies. Two overanxious autograph seekers (no charming locals, these) impose themselves on Alvy's private memories, reminding him of characters from *The Godfather*; they are played by actors who actually had bit parts in Coppola's film. The films Alvy likes are Ingmar Bergman's *Face to Face*, wherein a psychiatrist confronts her own emotional limitations and attempts suicide, and Marcel Ophüls's *The Sorrow and the Pity*, the four-and-a-half-hour documentary dealing with French complicity with Nazism during the Holocaust. These films, which describe contemporary doubts and deal with problems of identity and commitment, contribute to our understanding of Alvy's angst and further distinguish *Annie Hall* from lighthearted screwball romances. Although clearly Allen respects Bergman's and Ophüls's films, in Annie's reluctance to sit through yet another four-hour documentary about Nazism, we come to see that even as screwball comedies may have created overly optimistic illusions, more pessimistic films also reinforce Alvy's negativism. And while Allen's film mediates between the possibilities, it also participates in the very problem it describes.

Allen also analyzes his medium reflexively in a scene where he and Annie wait in line at the New Yorker theater. As Annie and Alvy quarrel, a "Film, T.V., and Media" teacher diverts their attention with a stock critique of Fellini that blames his "self-indulgence" on television. Alvy's sense of inadequacy as Annie grows away from him is counterpointed by the critic's false assurance. In his frustration, Alvy finally redresses the would-be critic for knowing nothing about Marshall McLuhan, who has played a large role in the critic's pontifications. Alvy even produces McLuhan to refute him, but McLuhan's refutation not only undermines the pompous professor, but reinforces the film's dialogic inconclusiveness. "You know nothing of my work," says McLuhan. "You mean, my whole fallacy is wrong." Alvy enjoys the moment of comeuppance with the deflation of the critic's false illusions, but like Allan Felix in *Play It Again, Sam*, he acknowledges the unreliability of his own illusions and once more ironically blurs the distinction between fiction and reality as he sighs, "Boy, if life were only like this."

References to other events from his past further describe Alvy's depressing outlook on life. In *Pursuits of Happiness* Stanley Cavell shows that screwball comedies are Shakespearean-style "old comedies" of remarriage and reunion, hopeful myths of rebirth and renewal.[7] Unlike his screwball relatives, Alvy has been married not once, but twice, and his story reveals not only why those unions remained broken, but the impact of their history on his relationship with Annie, a relationship that echoes the screwball paradigm of achieving one reconciliation, but a relationship that ultimately does not work.

Alvy's depression is also linked to a search for authenticity.

Unlike Capra and Cukor heroes who are eventually rewarded for maintaining their integrity, Alvy is not. He remembers his refusal to leave New York and follow his friend Rob (Tony Roberts), who sells out Shakespeare in the Park to take a TV job in California. Beverly Hills is Alvy's idea of the mindless future-world in *Sleeper*, which suggests how far passivity and optimistic illusions can drive us. To Alvy, California is a metaphor for decadence; people there are "mellow," and Alvy observes that "if I get too mellow, I ripen and then rot." Unqualified by Alvy's sort of skepticism and conscience, the atmosphere in Hollywood (where glib, resolved films are made) is politically dangerous. There people talk about Charlie Chaplin's problems with McCarthyism as "his un-American thing" and they confer awards wholesale; Alvy imagines an award for "greatest fascist dictator, Adolf Hitler." Visiting California, Alvy reluctantly eats alfalfa sprouts and mashed yeast instead of hardshelled lobsters who fight to survive. New York, with all its difficulties, is reality rather than "munchkin land." In *Annie Hall*, as in older screwball comedies, civilization and eros may be antagonists, but in this later film, the lack of authenticity and integrity in contemporary culture has created greater obstacles to intimacy and happiness. And in such a world, Alvy is a malcontent who loses his lover because he cannot adapt to change, rather than a traditional screwball hero who gains a woman and public acclaim for sticking to his principles.

From the onset of their relationship, like screwball couples before them, Annie and Alvy are extreme opposites. Initially, Annie is a crazy, humanizing antitoxin for Alvy's seriousness, and he plays a slow-moving, cautious straight man to her disorderly, kinetic character, not unlike Cary Grant's anthropologist playing off Katharine Hepburn's flighty character in *Bringing Up Baby* (1938). On the way to the tennis court where they first meet, Alvy frets about anti-Semitism. In contrast, during the tennis match the camera catches Annie's spontaneity as she happily flails away at a tennis ball.

Annie is dressed in an unconventional tramplike costume that declares her creative individuality and her independence. The outfit is born out of traditional sex role mergers in earlier screwball situations and costuming; she reminds us of an updated version of Katharine Hepburn in slacks. Her fumbling mannerisms make her a relative of Allen's natural and innocent little men in earlier films, and she presents an androgynous picture that may suggest that despite her apparent lack of ease, she is authentic and complete at the core.

Like other screwball couples, Annie and Alvy come from different cultures and classes. In this case, however, differences are not eventually erased to verify the American melting-pot myth, but remain as an unresolved dialogue and a disquieting sign of our times. Annie's man's tie was a gift from her Grammy Hall in Chippewa Falls; Alvy observes that his Jewish Grammy was too busy getting raped by Cossacks to give him gifts. Annie does not fear death as he does, and she takes risks. She drives through town with an abandon reminiscent of Amanda Bonner's days at the wheel; he is too nervous to own a car. At an Easter dinner in Chippewa Falls with Annie's family, where they serve ham and talk about swap meets and boats, Alvy imagines himself a Hasidic rabbi among Midwestern Wasps. A split screen emphasizes the contrarieties to show Alvy's family at a holiday meal, arguing loudly, eating furiously, and discussing sickness.

Although Alvy's stream of memories destroys conventional chronology, Allen's film does contain a series of parallel scenes, an ironic reminder of the movie's ancestors. We see related sequences scattered about in these memories that indicate a rising and falling movement to the romance. At first Alvy and Annie complement one another. She helps him to rediscover spontaneity and love, and she appreciates his humor and his experienced advice about her singing career. Alvy feels compelled, however, to distrust her innocence as much as Allen's deconstructive film may at first appear to distrust the innocence of screwball comedy's romantic vision. While he admires her, he also eventually denies her "wholeness," her uniqueness. In attempting to change her, he divides her from herself. As screwball heroes often preferred one side of their lovers to another and lectured them on their imperfections, so he teaches Annie his view of reality. She becomes a "newer woman," more self-confident, more self-conscious, and more worldly, but like the absurd alternatives in earlier Allen films, neither Annie as innocent nor Annie as experienced is entirely compatible with her neurotic partner. Annie's very growth contains counterindications—the seeds of the relationships's eventual failure. She finally longs to escape from her reality instructor.

Some recollected moments clearly belong in the early, upward movement of their relationship. Like the screwball couples who disentangled their problems and nurtured their relationships away from the urban sophistication, Alvy and Annie find their way outside the city despite Alvy's doubts about the romance of rural life. He associates the country with dead moths on screens and cult murderers.

In the kitchen at the beachhouse retreat, Annie and Alvy illustrate their ability to transcend adulthood's sex-specific behavior, much as earlier screwball heroes and heroines demonstrated their kitchen compatibility in the face of changing gender roles. Recapturing a sense of childhood innocence and play, in a moment that appears to transcend the film's encapsulating dialogues and the determinate nature of the film as medium, they shoo their lobster dinners toward a pot. Cavell has observed that while screwball comedies seldom involve children or offspring, the characters themselves try to "make room for playfulness in the gravity of adulthood . . . in an attempt to recover innocence."[8]

Such moments are to remember, and Annie takes still photographs of Alvy as she also took photographs of her family to hang about her apartment. While the references to photography tend to defamiliarize and to remind us again that this is a film, and thus to qualify even the film's best moments, Annie's photography, about which she refuses to intellectualize, does not associate her with the slick images that confuse contemporary identity; rather, Annie's photography may also be seen as a contrast presented in the middle of a sophisticated motion picture, as a relatively innocent and human art meant to secure meaningful moments from time. During their first meeting, Alvy said to Annie, "Photography is interesting, you know. . . . The medium enters in as a condition of the art form itself." But Annie's innocence, like Pearl's in *Interiors*, is associated with her simple aesthetic. Annie says, "Well, to me it's all instinctive. I just try to feel it." What begins to emerge in the discussion of Annie's photography is a tenuous and dialogic view of imagery in its relation to the human condition. While Allen casts doubt on his own film and reveals his concern with the dangers inherent in manipulative imagery, he also simultaneously explores the positive possibilities in Annie's authentic kind of photography, which helps us remember good moments, which does battle with time, and which breaks with self-conscious conventions to reach us in a personal way as great "moving" pictures always have.

Later, Annie and Alvy leave the city again, but this time nature offers no escape, for the relationship is in trouble. Initially Annie and Alvy enjoyed making love. He found her "polymorphously perverse," for she responded so readily with every part of her body. In their second visit to the country, however, Alvy forbids Annie to smoke pot to relax, and she cannot achieve intimacy without it. Instead of pot, Alvy puts a corny red light bulb in their bedside lamp "for atmosphere," and in an echo of the earlier scenes, quips that he and Annie could also develop photographs. But in doing so, he comments not only on the state of his romance with Annie, but on the nature of his self-conscious narrative and on Allen's more sophisticated anti-illusionistic film, as opposed to earlier romantic comedy. He suggests reflexively that the emphasis has moved from the metaphor of taking photos like Annie's innocent, spontaneous ones in the early part of their relationship, to a later stage in the photographic process that is more technical and more self-conscious—less natural. *Annie Hall* deconstructs and demystifies the earlier classic romances, but in this dialogue Allen remains as uncertain as he was in his earliest comedies about whether self-conscious filmmaking, anti-illusionism, and demystification are not also part of a backfiring hand-grenade joke such as he made in *Bananas*.

In this second visit to the country, therefore, time and Alvy's tutoring Annie have intervened, and it is not surprising that Annie is as distanced or defamiliarized from Alvy as spectators can be from extremely self-conscious, anti-illusionistic films, and we observe her image leaving her body in the bed even as she and Alvy are going through the motions of making love. Unlike earlier screwball comedies, then, in Alvy's more self-conscious narrative, sexual issues are more complex and sexual intimacy has become a problem. By this time Annie is seeing a psychiatrist on Alvy's advice, and Annie's visit to her therapist is seen on a split screen with Alvy's visit to his therapist. When the therapists ask how often they have sex, Alvy tells his, "Hardly ever. Maybe three times a week," while Annie tells hers: "Constantly. I'd say three times a week."

Although Annie and Alvy break up temporarily when Annie is caught arm in arm with her adult-education professor, they come to miss each other, and like many divorced screwball comedy couples, they reconcile. The difference is that this reconciliation does not last. Annie's moodiness, seen in memories from the last part of their relationship, indicates that she has learned self-consciousness from Alvy and has come to experience his discontent. While she has learned from experience with reading, analysis, adult education, and the films Alvy took her to, her whole background urges escape from the depression that accompanies Alvy's anhedonia. Thus, following a polished nightclub performance, she is flattered by an invitation from Tony Lacey (Paul Simon) to develop her career in California, and she and Alvy agree to end their relationship finally.

While older screwball heroes reestablished order with the authentication of marriage that follows from self-knowledge and change or creation,[9] the lessons the contemporary little man teaches his partner, and the self-knowledge each achieves, produce less satisfying results. Alvy misses Annie and travels to California to propose, but Annie refuses. Back in New York, Alvy tries to deal with his loss through art; he writes a play about his love affair, but adds a happy ending. Art, he observes, is always more perfect than life. But art holds no more lasting meaning than anything else in this film. Woody Allen's reflexive film comments once more on its own construction and depicts a less perfect world. The ending to *Annie Hall* goes well beyond the naïveté of first plays or earlier screwball comedies with happy resolutions.

The important thing about *Annie Hall* is that it is not like the traditional screwball film, which moves forward in a progressive manner to a conclusion that answers questions about disorder and about whether life had meaning with images of renewal and affirmation. After Alvy's long examination and his sifting through his recollections of the confusing affair with Annie, he has no more rational understanding of why the relationship didn't work than before. He lives in circumstances even more reduced than those that challenged his screwball ancestors in the 1930s and 1940s. Change is beyond his control; his world is indeterminate; each forward motion or intimation of progress may contain its own contrariety; and even his best impulses may produce results quite different from those he anticipated. He is just as caught within the world his pessimistic vision, his narrative, and Allen's contemporary self-conscious film have created as the passive spectator of optimistic classic screwball films is caught in the world he has based on traditional romantic illusions.

What, then, is to be saved from this film that duplicates the nervous state of contemporary relationships and reflects the unreal quality of an overly sophisticated world? The film concludes that there are no sure resolutions, no pat answers, just the ongoing process of life itself, some tenuous faith in our instinct to survive, and a filmmaker's refusal to accept either his most pessimistic visions or some easy bromides as an escape from the inconclusiveness of experience. If there is anything one can hold onto, it is the few remembered moments of tenderness, intimacy, and human connection that appear to, but never do quite entirely, escape the envelope of the medium. The conflicts between life's pleasure and pain, between Allen's comic and tragic visions, that have been a running tension throughout this film are perhaps best expressed in two ways at the end of *Annie*

Hall: In the series of images recollecting Annie and Alvy's happiest moments together that survive in Alvy's memory and can be partially reexperienced through film, and in Alvy's closing joke, which provides a good picture of his bittersweet attitude toward life and loss.

A remarkable number of jail scenes occur in screwball comedies such as *Bringing Up Baby, Adam's Rib,* and *His Girl Friday,* but the stars never end up behind bars or even visiting jails in the finale. In his original script, the film was to end with Alvy commenting on life from a jail cell in California, but in an added ending, the imagery is more hopeful.

With the empty restaurant where he met Annie for lunch in the foreground and a busy New York street where life goes busily on seen through a window as the background, with Annie singing "Seems Like Old Times" behind his voice-over, Alvy has left the frame to generalize on his experience. Alvy remembers his good times with Annie in an anecdote. The pain he continues to endure from heartbreaks, he says, is as crazy as the fellow in the old joke who believes he is a chicken. But like the man's family, he observes that we don't alter the absurd situation because "we need the eggs" that love relationships provide.

The threat of time and change, the confusions and contradictions of modern life with its opposing sets of illusions, create far greater obstacles for lovers than they did in older screwball comedies. In an early description of Saul Bellow's work, Robert Alter wrote: "Reality is a multiverse, not a unified system in which fixed principles can be enunciated by those who know the system . . . . There is a tentativeness in the moral exploration of all [his] heroes . . . . [He is] anti-reducing human problems to a formula, a methodology, a technique."[10] So too, Woody Allen distrusts fixed principles, and Alvy's unreliable narrative deconstructs the pillars of his own medium's history, not simply out of disrespect, but out of a complex exploration of both the longing for romance and the dangers inherent in romantic illusions. At the same time, his self-conscious narrative—ultimately, the film itself—also deconstructs, so that we remain either caught or freed by our experience with it. For his ability to capture contemporary concerns in such well-selected detail and with such telling metaphors of meaning and meaninglessness, Woody Allen's *Annie Hall* received four Academy Awards and international critical recognition for being one of the best films of our times. In terms of his development as a filmmaker, this contemporary screwball film—with its reflexive, dialogic comedy and its pathos—is the gateway to Allen's later, most mature and significant work.

Hoping for a reconciliation, Eve (Geraldine Page) receives only a polite kiss from her estranged husband, Arthur (E. G. Marshall). Eve's control and her pain as well as the distance she creates between people are emphasized in this shot from *Interiors. Courtesy of Woody Allen and United Artists.*

6

Beyond Allegory

Interiors (1978) is Woody Allen's first full-length noncomic film. Allen wrote and directed but did not act in his seventh major movie because of the comic associations his appearance might evoke. The film received mixed reviews from American critics: while some reviewers appreciated the risks Allen was taking and admired his growing technical expertise, others rejected the film as too imitative, too negative, or too allegorical. Although Allen probably did not intend it so, *Interiors* is indebted to Ingmar Bergman's films, especially *Cries and Whispers* (1972); however, it is made in Allen's own idiom. And *Interiors* is not merely negative or simply allegorical but is a complex series of inconclusive dialogues. Several noncomedic characters now express the little soul's growing self-consciousness and his anxieties; they participate in the search for meaning that resided in the little men of the earliest comedies. Other characters recall the unselfconscious innocence and naturalness of Allen's earlier little men. As in all Allen's films, the characters in *Interiors* have debates with themselves and with each other.

Like *Cries and Whispers*, *Interiors* deals with three sisters, who may be "part of a single soul."[1] Both *Cries and Whispers* and *Interiors* are about "frustration, ... the yearning for faith, and physical companionship."[2] Allen's work, like Bergman's, considers the effects of emotional distance, coldness, and indifference on the quality of human life. Both Bergman's and Allen's films contrast bravery (defined as active confrontation with life and the meaning of death) with escape or the inability to deal with such fundamental issues of existence. In spite of suffering and despair in each film, "love is the grace offering the . . . answer to life's misery and transience."[3] However, Bergman's and Allen's films both suggest that such grace is achieved only in fleeting moments of communion and reconciliation.

While *Interiors* is influenced by Bergman's films, it is a "less chilling" American relative. Allen told Roger Ebert that *Interiors* "doesn't have that Swedish sort of cold cerebral guilt. . . . It comes more out of the tradition of American family dramas."[4] Although *Interiors* is the most solemn of Allen's films, Penelope Gilliatt wisely observed that it is still rooted in a comic perspective, "and it echoes."[5] Like all of Allen's work, *Interiors* converses with influences in order to explore its own concerns, to draw attention to the means of its own construction and to question the relationship between fiction/film and life. It deals both with hopelessness and with hope.

Interiors portrays an upper-middle-class New England family, its stresses and dissolution. Eve (Geraldine Page), a decorator, prides herself on the tasteful modern interiors she creates. Without warning, at breakfast one day, Eve's husband, Arthur (E. G. Marshall), upsets Eve's orderly world when he tells his wife and grown daughters that he wants a trial separation. Eve, whose history of apparent control and serenity has been blemished periodically by an accompanying emotional fragility, has a nervous breakdown shortly after the announcement.

Despite her daughters' attempts to lend support, when Arthur's continued reluctance to return home threatens her well-made plans, Eve attempts suicide. Although she recovers and tries to make a new life for herself, she still cannot accept the separation. When Arthur finally destroys her faith in reconciliation and marries Pearl (Maureen Stapleton), Eve deliberately walks into the ocean and kills herself. Just as one family member's death is the locus for an exploration of family psychology in Bergman's *Cries and Whispers*, Allen's restrospective film looks into the effects of Eve's personality on the rest of the family—especially on the three daughters. Renata (Diane Keaton), a successful poet, is married to Frederick (Richard Jordan), an unsuccessful novelist; Flyn (Kristin Griffith), an actress, works in films and TV. Joey (Marybeth Hurt) lives with Mike (Sam Waterston), a political filmmaker, and cannot discover what to do with her life.

The interiors of the film's title refer to the sterile, beautiful home and the ambience that Eve creates for her family. The formal white, pale gray, and beige rooms that Eve designs with such care are form without content. As Maurice Yacowar has pointed out, they are, ironically, merely "exteriors,"[6] devoid of passion, love, and tolerance for human imperfection. The title of the film also refers to the interiors, or painful mental landscapes, of the family members Eve helped to fashion. More important, *Interiors* deals with the difficulty of recovery from the spiritual sickness that lies at the heart of a desensitized contemporary society, enticed by a series of solutions to human problems that are ultimately unresponsive to human needs.

The tension between contemporary sophistication and the search for innocence, love, and authenticity, which has been a problem throughout Allen's films, is worked out primarily in the contrast between Eve and Pearl, and opposition that may be indebted to Bergman's interest in the schism between spirit and body as an essential modern malady, and more particularly, to the contrast in *Cries and Whispers* between Maria and Karin's coldness and Anna's compassion. Eve, named after the first woman in *Genesis*, is a mother, not of the earth, but of a fragile aestheticism—a dehumanizing and destructive belief in formal beauty. Her separation forces her exile from an inverted Eden. She is banished from her perfect world and driven into an inconstant environment that she is not equipped to handle.

Arthur's opening description of his life with Eve is a telling summary: "It was all so perfect, so ordered. Looking back, of course, it was rigid. . . . She'd created a world around us . . . where everything had its place. . . . It was like an ice palace." Eve's creations are the more solemn descendants of those orderly settings in which Allen's comic little-man figures created a delightful disorder in earlier films. The sparsely furnished family beach house that Eve designed, the bare floors and clean white surfaces of her carefully arranged home in the city after her separation, or the ultramodern apartment she meticulously planned for Joey and Mike, all reflect Eve's intolerance for irregularity. Form rather than function dominates Eve's vision. Despite the four-hundred dollar price tag that is beyond Mike and Joey's means, Eve asks them to buy a "unique" vase for their foyer; and she moves a lamp Mike finds more useful in the living room back to the bedroom, because, she says, "We should stick with my beiges and my earth tones." Human needs and comforts are secondary to a fanatic aesthetic fantasy.

For Eve, art is protection against menacing surprises. She creates her husband and children as well as the rooms in which they dwell. As Renata says, "She put Dad through law school and she financed the start of his practice. . . . It was like he was her creation." Eve spends her time obsessively rearranging vases of cut flowers in her bare apartment once she can no longer manipulate people. That control is Eve's protection not only against minor disruptions, but against the fear of the greatest unforeseen contingency—death. Her attitude toward art is religious. As Allen put it in an interview for *Take One*," Dealing with vases and things, that doesn't mean anything. . . . You have a sense of immortality, that your work will live on after you, which is nonsense. Art is like the intellectual's Catholicism, it's the promise of an afterlife, but of course, it's fake—you're only doing it because *you* want to do it."[7]

Eve wears "ice-gray" suits, stately beige robes, gowns of black velvet, with white clerical collars. Her severely tailored clothes are undisturbed by lively designs or bright colors. High necklines and a coiffure centrally parted and pinned up tightly on her head in a cone-shaped chignon complete a picture of dignified austerity. Originally, Allen planned that Eve's rigidity should be associated with a more "religious character"; she was, he said, "to have believed in Christ and be very involved with that, and my feeling about that sort of involvement is that it's crazy. . . . Renata comes to realize in the movie, if it's successful, that the only thing anyone has any chance with is human relationships."[8] The Eve who emerged in *Interiors* was not as extreme in her Christianity as Allen's original conception, but she haunts cathedrals and chooses to discuss reconciliation with Arthur in a large, empty church. Late at night, a lonely Eve turns to fundamentalist programming so prolific on American radio and television. Eve is both a creator of and created by a culture that supports her extremism. Her religiosity and her aestheticism serve as unstable shelters from life's difficulties and from the threat of insanity or death that lurks just beneath her calm exteriors.

Eve emphasizes her desire to insulate herself by closing car windows and asking Mike to shut out the city sounds that upset her delicately tuned sensibilities. When she attempts suicide for the first time in the film on camera, she seals windows with an aesthetically appropriate black electrician's tape, but she is forced to finish the job with makeshift white adhesive strips meant for bandaging wounds. Her houses—her works of art— are extensions of her injured psyche, and the world outside intrudes to bring Eve pain and illness that she can only escape by trying to keep it out altogether and by retreating finally into death.

Eve's construct of reality is so inflexible and built so precariously that it cannot stand the unsettling intrusion of divorce. When Arthur tells Eve that they should finalize their separation, she breaks the stillness of the cathedral where they are talking and, with sudden uncontrolled hysteria, smashes the red votive candles that celebrate formal beauty and order. As Eve runs screaming from the church, she reveals the chaos and pain just beneath her cool surfaces. Ultimately Eve becomes a pathetic figure who, like Maria and Karin in *Cries and Whispers*, suffers from the emptiness of the world she has created.

Eve's opposite is Pearl, whom Arthur meets on the beaches of Greece. Arthur's second wife and the daughters' new mother is a "precious Pearl," the lively sign, as in Hawthorne's *The Scarlet Letter*, of joy and grace amid gloom and spiritual sickness. Allen's very American Pearl is a warm, down-to-earth character, closely related to Allen's earlier comic persona; she makes mistakes, and her spontaneity brings an unsettling, yet saving, disorder into the family's confining lives. At her wedding, Pearl, taken up by the rhythms of swing, dances into one of Eve's vases perched on a buffet. As she sends it crashing to the ground, Joey yells, "Jesus Christ, be careful." But Pearl's accidental destruction of Eve's fragile idols contrasts with Eve's frenzied smashing of the votive candles in the church, and signals the toppling of Eve's obsessively ordered world.

Pearl would rather bask unashamedly in the sun than visit cathedrals. She wears loud red dresses with open necklines and prints in primary colors that flush with life amid Eve's pale settings. Her dark hair is curled and loose. She is plumpish, or zaftig, rather than fashionably slender like Eve. Pearl is from Florida; she was married twice, to a jeweler and to an orthodontist. She loves popular music and dances at her wedding. Pearl worries about moving into Eve's barren beach-house retreat because it is so far away from everything, and because with all her belongings, she says, it might come to look like a warehouse. She tells Arthur to stop worrying about what he eats; she chatters openly about her personal life, and she invites communication rather than inhibiting it, as do Eve and her daughters.

Unlike Eve, Pearl is associated with primitive mysteries and magic, rather than with a religion that encourages escapism on late-night TV or finds its home in the empty pews of giant churches. Pearl is a social creature who tells fortunes and does card tricks; she is interested in voodoo and collects African fertility statues with big hips and breasts. If Eve is linked to sterility and death, Pearl is linked to fertility and life; she lets Arthur nuzzle her in public; she loves sirloin steaks, blood-rare.

Eve is primarily framed in long and extreme-long shots that are indebted to Bergman's style and that capture her vulnerability in the lonely spaces that she makes. Allen structures Eve's scenes so that she appears to be part of a posed arrangement. When she tries to commit suicide, the camera draws back to reveal her placed like a conventional model on a couch in the middle of a balanced composition. Close shots of Eve usually dwell upon her attempts to control anguish, and when she appears with other characters, the proxemics reflect the distance she breeds between people; she or those she converses with may leave the frame in the midst of a conversation. Pearl, on the other hand, is usually portrayed in medium shots and in the company of several figures. The compositions are less formal, the figures more relaxed. Pearl sprawls comfortably on a couch with Mike as she does card tricks. While Eve usually moves slowly and deliberately through the frame, Pearl moves with spontaneity, energy, and life.

Pearl is related to Allen's idea of the true innocent, and the authentic, natural person who, like the early little-man figures and like the early Annie in *Annie Hall,* suggests an antidote for dehumanization, but her virtue is not without qualifications. Joey calls her a vulgarian. She has a son who sells paintings of clowns on black velvet in the lobby of Caesar's Palace in Las Vegas. As Allen told Ira Halberstadt, "I don't know which philosopher it was that wrote that the natural person, the brave person, the good person, will always be perceived as a vulgarian by the other people. And this is what I think is true with Maureen [Pearl]. Maureen is far more natural and flexible and decent than all of them, but she'll always be perceived that way, as a vulgarian. Of course, she probably is a little vulgar, but I want people to be on her side. . . ."[9]

The first shots of Arthur in the film herald his choice of Pearl over Eve. With his back to the carefully designed office Eve made for him, and anticipating a better life, he faces a window that overlooks a busy New York skyline. For Arthur, Pearl is a second chance, fresh air after life in closed rooms. He urges his daughters to accept Pearl because "She's affectionate . . . full of energy, and demonstrative and open." As Penelope Gilliatt observed, Pearl "seems exempt from guilt, and this exemption is one of the innocences celebrated by this film."[10]

The clear contrast between Pearl's innocent openness and Eve's defensiveness is what led some critics to dismiss *Interiors* as an uncomplicated allegory. Jack Kroll, usually an Allen fan, wrote that Allen "creates a blatantly simple cleavage between 'art' and 'life.'"[11] While Allen does focus on the contrast between

Eve's deadening aestheticism and Pearl's life-embracing naturalness, his film ultimately presents a more complex set of possibilities. *Interiors* is complicated not only by an intimate portrait of Eve's pain and some sympathy for her appreciation of beauty, which evokes compassion in the audience and softens the allegorical prominence of her character, but Allen closely observes the confused lives of Eve's offspring. Our reactions to Flyn, Renata, and Joey create dialogues beyond the dichotomy of Eve and Pearl to give the film greater depth, breadth, and inconclusiveness.

Rather than merely presenting a blatant cleavage between art and life, Allen's film demonstrates the intimate and complex relationship between life and its filmic representation. Allen attempts to construct a more richly textured, dialogic representation of relationships. He presents an essential contemporary dichotomy, and he simultaneously presents evidence that exposes the limitations of reductionist descriptions of human problems and the fallacy in "well-made" films with comfortable resolutions. Consequently, his reflexive film comments not only on opposing cultural codes, but on its own nature and construction.

The self-conscious questions Allen raises are suggested as Pearl discusses a recent play with Joey, Mike, Renata, and Frederick at dinner. Disputing the complicated meanings of the play, which Frederick has described as "pessimistic to the point of futility," Joey summarizes one side of the issue when she observes that the writer "argued both sides so brilliantly you didn't know who was right." To which Pearl responds: "I didn't get that. . . . To me it wasn't such a big deal. One guy was a squealer, the other guy wasn't. I liked the guy that wasn't." Frederick laughs and says, "Well, it was a little more complex than that, don't you think?" But Pearl insists: "Why? You like the squealer? Did I miss something?" When Joey asks, "How do you figure out the right thing to do? How do you know?" Pearl innocently replies: "You just know . . . you feel it. I mean . . . you just don't squeal."

Joey's reactions to the play reflect her greater self-awareness and intellectual curiosity as well as her resulting anxiety and indecisiveness. Her inquiry is related to a question that Mike, the political filmmaker, had posed earlier in *Interiors* as he worked on a movie about Mao Tse-tung that criticized Mao's homiletic style. Earlier Mike had said into his dictaphone, "An example [of Mao's homilies] would be 'The hardest thing is to act properly throughout one's whole life'" and Mike adds, "What the hell does that mean?" Because they are more self-aware, more intellectually sophisticated than Pearl, Mike and Joey, Renata and Frederick perceive more complex sets of alternatives. Throughout much of the film, they are seen "pinned and wriggling on the wall," as afraid "to eat a peach" as T. S. Eliot's Prufrock caught amid a proliferation of contemporary choices and contradictions.

While Allen sees Pearl as a lucky natural who has something to teach Eve's family about confronting life, about self-trust and compassion, his film admits that such naturalness can involve vulgarization, and more significantly, that most thinking people do not enjoy such a comfortable relationship with their instincts, but suffer from the sorts of internal dialogues that characterize Joey's view of the play and Mike's reluctance to accept Mao's homilies. Thus, while *Interiors* criticizes formalism devoid of human connection and expresses a contemporary longing for Pearl's naturalness and wholeness, the film does not rest on any easy resolution, nor is it merely an allegory. In the discussion of the play, Allen wonders about subjective perceptions and how people's lives and predispositions determine their responses to art, to morality, to commitment, and to action. In the film as a whole, he tempers a simple faith in Pearl's innocence as a antidote to the family's spiritual illness with a detailed exploration of the sisters' confused lives and with an ambivalent conclusion that resists facile explication.

Each of the daughters embodies a category of character that has grown out of the original little-man persona of the earlier films. Renata and Joey, and to a lesser extent Flyn, have been inspired by their mother's love for beauty and art, but they are wounded, frustrated searchers for solutions to the problem of retaining integrity or authenticity in a world where the naturalness that characterizes Pearl is difficult to recover.

Flyn is perhaps the least self-aware of the three women, but she, like the others, is a victim of Eve's obsessions. Flyn, according to Allen, is "the person who avoids the issue by dehumanizing herself."[12] She is associated with the Hollywood world of false and desensitizing images that Allen criticized directly in *Annie Hall* and indirectly in *Sleeper* and a number of other earlier films. A movie star, who is viewed as a sex object and who plays insignificant roles in glossy productions, Flyn fears that she has only a few good years left before her "youth will be frozen on old celluloid for TV movies."

Like a passive spectator, Flyn has internalized her Hollywood image and lives in a world of appearances. Anticipating seeing Flyn at a birthday party for Eve, Frederick laments that he will have to listen to Flyn's talk about her clothes and her weight. Flyn flirts with Frederick; and finally, drunk, he tries to rape her in one of the several terrifying moments in the film where a character's interior frustrations erupt into angry and aggressive outward revolt at the promises and denials of his life. Frederick tells her, "You're always flirting with me. . . . You like to be looked at. . . . You don't exist . . . except in somebody else's eyes." Flyn's sense of herself is so confused with the images to which she conforms that she performs off camera as she might on camera, with stock reactions or barely any emotion at all. Her responses to her mother's pain and the dissolution of the family are distant and superficial. She escapes a disturbing sense of inauthenticity with cocaine.

We do, however, have brief glimpses of Flyn's potential for genuine feeling and authenticity. On the beach with Renata, Flyn is responsive and momentarily self-discerning as she muses about the inauthentic roles she is forced to play. The girls put their arms around each other and walk together for a shared moment that provides some respite from the distances and distrust typical of Eve's family. Like Alvy Singer's ability to trust his feelings in *Annie Hall*, Flyn's ability to enjoy love is a buried potential that appears occasionally when someone shows her affection. Such captured moments of connection echo other brief scenes of reconciliation and communication between the sisters in *Cries and Whispers*.

Renata, the most successful of the three daughters, is Eve's favorite because she is a recognized poet and because she married a novelist; however, Renata has reached a crisis in her marriage and in her career. She feels her mother's pain acutely, and she is reluctant to tell Eve the truth about her relationship with Arthur. Renata fears for Eve's mental health and self-destructive qualities because she sees some of her mother reflected in her own emotional fragility and her own growing desperation despite her apparent success and her apparent strength.

Renata tells her psychiatrist that she has not been able to write for a year and has been preoccupied with her own mortality. She senses futility about her work. "I mean, just what am I striving to create anyway? I mean, to what end? . . . I mean . . . do I really care if a handful of my poems are read after I'm gone forever?" Renata confesses that she cannot "shake . . . the real implication of dying. It's terrifying. The intimacy of it embarrasses me." Renata's distrust of her own work and her wrestling with the questions of whether art is meaning enough further underline the reflexive quality of Allen's film. Allen said, "Renata speaks for me, without question. She articulates all my personal concerns."[13]

Renata's frustrations with her life and her fear of death and meaninglessness appear forcefully in visual and verbal imagery. Alone at her desk, Renata is no longer able to find words to express her dread. She experiences a moment of angst and alienation, which Allen renders in visual images as precisely as he has always captured contemporary speech patterns. From the opening moments in the film, where five windows contrast with five vases on the mantel, one for each member of Eve's family, Allen has consistently used windows as a motif for insight and to suggest an opening into the world beyond Eve's confining interiors. Thus, Eve closes windows, Arthur's window over New York has no frame about it, Joey as well as Renata look through windows as they try to grasp the meaning of their lives, and all three daughters face a window in the film's final moments.

Renata's breathing becomes labored as she tries to see

through a window of her study, her view of the sky obstructed by a thorny maze of intertwining branches. She tells Frederick, "It was as if I had a sudden . . . clear vision where everything seems . . . sort of awful and predatory. "While Eve can never understand or fully communicate the anxiety that is heightened by the impending divorce, Renata is a more open, articulate, and self-analytical spokesperson for her mother's impotent struggle with transience, confusion, and death.

Although Renata and Frederick discuss their problems more openly than Eve and Arthur, Renata's success and the manner in which she manages to "turn out" work, have children and run her home presents problems for her marriage. When he attempts to rape Flyn, Frederick says, "It's been such a long time since I made love to a woman I didn't feel inferior to." Renata gets the accolades from critics that Frederick no longer receives, and although she reminds him that he should be interested in the quality of his book rather than the reviews, Frederick voices another equally real concern for the artist. "I don't care about fine work! I don't wanna wait twenty-five years to be appreciated. I wanna be able to knock somebody over now!"

Frederick, an insecure artist at the mercy of reviewers' perceptions of his work, further reflects the obstacles that stand in the way of attaining integrity. He reinforces Renata's own growing realization that immortality through art is not meaningful or satisfying enough, but unlike Renata or Joey, he turns to immediate feedback and to the clichés of his profession, dwells on self-pity, and drinks to avoid despair; he becomes a teacher and reviewer to make money, and his bitterness is generalized commentary on the psychology of some angry reviewers who show their personal disappointments in poisonous public interpretations of others' work. While Frederick is not two-dimensional or unsympathetic, his attempts to resolve his difficulties with his work are not courageous. His struggle and lack of courage is what Mao's homily ("The hardest thing is to act properly throughout one's whole life") may be all about.

Although Renata loses patience with Frederick, like Flyn, she is also capable of expressing love. She attempts to offer solace to Eve, even though she wants much more to avoid her. Like

Joey, and the sisters in Bergman's film, she is capable of remembering her childhood with her sisters; she puts her arms around Flyn and is able to express a need for her; and following a major fight with Frederick, she tells him that she wants to "help . . . not hurt." Renata surely does not succeed in reaching a resolution to her problems, but as she questions herself and continues her attempts to write, she is both a sign of the heavy burden that contemporary sophistication lays upon the sensitive artist, and a sigh of courage, as she begins to engage fearful issues of human existence.

Like Flyn and Renata, Joey, the third sister, is also wounded by Eve's coldness. Joey has held a series of jobs in which she tried to "express herself," but she lacks Flyn's and Renata's talent. Like Frederick and Flyn, she is dependent on others' approval. She seeks to satisfy her mother's ideals without having the qualifications to succeed. Allen believed Joey was the central character in the film. She is "that middle ground sort of person that really is screwed. They do question life, they are sensitive and intelligent and all of that, and they have no talent. They know they don't want to work in an office, they know they don't want to just junk their lives being a housewife raising kids or a guy working for an insurance company. But they're not going to be Nureyev and they're not gonna be Michelangelo, so they're in bad shape."[14]

Joey has trouble making commitments not only in work, but in other areas of her life. She lives with, but avoids marriage to, Mike. She is tossed between her mother's sense of the beautiful, which she can appreciate, and Mike's concern with political solutions and political art. She cannot be part of Mike's political activities because she understands that she is too self-centered. She also seems to grasp Renata's objection to Mike's utilitarianism, which values lives of thousands of people over the life of a single person, a view that Renata calls "killing for an abstraction." Although Joey sometimes thinks that what she needs is to settle down and have a family, when she finds out that she is pregnant, her first response is anger, and she talks about abortion because having a child "is so irrevocable."

Although Joey is both attracted to and repulsed by her mother, of the three daughters, she finds it hardest to accept Pearl, who threatens to cut Joey free of Eve's influence. Joey is the first to accuse Pearl of vulgarity. Although it is her mother she seems concerned for, Joey's own personality is threatened. She warns Arthur that Pearl may be a gold digger; she refuses to dance with Pearl at the wedding, and when Pearl breaks her mother's vase, it is Joey who screams at her for her clumsiness, in an echo of Eve's unforgiving voice. While Joey is afraid of becoming her own person, she also fears the loss of her father, whose love for her is tied to the absence of love in his relationship with Eve.

Like Renata and Flyn, however, Joey also sometimes breaks through her anger and frustration to indicate her potential for recovering genuine love and warmth. She attempts to support Eve, and she repeatedly tries to come closer to Renata, whose rejection of Joey is based on Arthur's favoritism. Most significantly, in a tender moment following a stormy encounter with Eve and a fight with Mike, she reaches for Mike in bed and awakens him with a kiss that brings them together in one of the film's most hopeful moments. Finally, too, it is Joey who bravely tells her mother about her shortcomings, but tempers her insights with love. In doing so, she comes to an understanding about her reactions to her mother, but she also begins in earnest to sever herself from Eve's influence. This is an initial, difficult step in her movement toward a new mother and the renewal Pearl represents. Talking to Eve following the wedding, Joey says, "You're not just a sick woman. That would be too easy. The truth is . . . there's been perverseness—and willfulness of attitude—in many of the things you've done. At the center of—of a sick psyche, there is a sick spirit. But I love you. And we have no other choice but to forgive each other." Allen foreshadows the possibility that Joey will turn from Eve to Pearl as Joey calls to her mother, and Pearl, who is also in the shadows but has not seen Eve, answers, "Yes?" When Joey asks, "What?" Pearl replies, "You said 'Mother,' and I said 'Yes.'"

Joey is finally seen as one of the most courageous figures in the film. She, who has the hardest time making a commitment and acting on it, makes a brave attempt to save her mother from drowning. While Flyn, Renata, Frederick, and Arthur sleep, and despite her conflicting emotions about Eve, Joey rushes into the water and risks her own life. The ocean takes Eve's life but affirms continuity through Joey's rebirth. If Joey is at first drawn after her mother toward despair and toward death, she also begins to commit herself to living. Mike pulls Joey from her baptism in the waves, and Pearl resuscitates her with "the kiss of life." As Joey takes her first breath in a new life apart from Eve, she reaches for Pearl's hand and grasps it firmly. Then, she embraces Mike alone on the sand to confirm the importance of human relationships and love. Although this literary moment threatens to upset the film's dialogic balance and lend credence to allegorical readings, the emphasis in the scene is on Joey's ability to act prior to her beginning to develop a relationship with Pearl. "The real act of courage for me," Allen said, "is the guy who acts in spite of an almost paralyzing fear."[15]

The final sequences of the film recapitulate and summarize the film's oppositions. The family's difficulties remain unresolved, but the family may yet have the opportunity for a better life. Before Eve's funeral Pearl helps Arthur attach his suspenders—a small, comfortable gesture that indicates she will continue to help him recover from Eve's death, but Arthur's guilt and pain are also in evidence. Each of the daughters drops a white rose, Eve's favorite flower, on her casket. The rose, which was associated earlier with Eve's false, cloistered innocence, her rigid sense of purity in line and form, and her death in life, now also suggests the possibility of grace. The flowers remain an ambivalent sign, embodying both Eve's cold formalism and Allen's hope for recovery of authentic innocence.

The final sequences of the film also underline the contradictions that characterize *Interiors* as a whole. Allen hints at affirmation. The camera lingers on Flyn's tears and what may be genuine grief at her mother's death, a display of emotion that makes her appear less beautiful in a conventional sense, but that intimates that she may remain capable of penetrating the encrustation of Hollywood imagery and of feeling authentic human connection. Renata and Joey respond to their mother's death with more than grief: in a moment of reconciliation, they hug one another after years of distrust and distance. Allen said, "My feeling . . . is that Joey is going to have a calmer life than her mother. There is some feeling between her and Keaton, though Keaton isn't quite ready yet for a rapprochement." And he added, "I think Joey will feel the influence of Pearl."[16]

The final shots of the film recall the family in earlier days. Writing in a notebook similar to Agnes's diary in *Cries and Whispers*, in which she remembers a brief interlude of joy and peace among her sisters, Joey records a memory of Eve decorating a beautiful Christmas tree for her family. The image suggests that with Eve's death, there is a chance that her better moments will have their impact, that with time, forgiveness is possible; but in the same instant it is clear that the daughters will not easily escape the negative qualities of Eve's influence or their damaging past. The last image of the film is, therefore, appropriately noncommital. Dressed in mourning black, the three daughters stand before a window overlooking the beach in a classically arranged composition. Joey says, without any easily interpreted inflection, "The water's so calm." And Renata replies, "Yes."

Woody Allen's *Interiors* is a film that is neither futilely ambiguous nor simply pessimistic or optimistic. It is not merely an allegory. *Interiors* is a solemn film, related to the work of Bergman and other contemporary European filmmakers—it popularizes and translates their work into American contexts—but like other Allen films, it carries Allen's identifying mark and mood. It is more hopeful even with its severe qualifications. It deals with Allen's specific concerns about art and filmmaking in relation to life. The film conveys a longing for a humane and honest art and a more humane and honest life. It reflects hope for self-understanding, personal integrity, and authenticity beyond self-delusion, repression, and empty ideology. But in his portrayal of Renata, Flyn, and even Joey, he also demonstrates that not everyone can easily be as open and authentic and as uncomplicated as Pearl; and even Pearl is less than a perfect ideal.

In *Interiors*, Allen bravely commits himself to an experiment with "serious" filmmaking, and his film even appears to make a commitment to the values embodied in Pearl instead of Eve, but any commitment in *Interiors* is qualified by a series of dialogues, not only within and between the characters, but between the reflexive film and itself. On several levels, then, *Interiors* explores the lesson in Mao's homily at the same time that it questions the oversimplification lodged in any aphoristic summing up of the human condition. Like Allen's earlier films, *Interiors* reflects not only a hope for renewed innocence and authenticity in the face of the burden of contemporary sophistication, but Allen's understanding of how difficult it is for a spiritually wounded society to disentangle itself from the confines of its own false images and ideologies and to achieve a more personally satisfying, more meaningful existence. Although *Interiors* is a first effort at wholly "serious" filmmaking and suffers occasionally from its own determined solemnity and self-conscious practiced style, in *Interiors*, Allen makes a valiant effort to express the difficult relationship between his characters' inner and outer worlds, between individual psychology and social ideology, and between artistic conflict, cultural conflict, and creative process. *Interiors*, like all recent Allen films, is an exploration and not a conclusion. The filmmaker does not sacrifice the complexities and difficulties—the disorderly human clutter—of actual living to provide simplistic resolutions, but, on the other hand, he does not deny the possibility that for brave moments ambiguity can be overcome.

A "Tow Away Zone" sign in the foreground and a dachshund named Waffles create a dialogue with the late-night romantic mood as Isaac Davis (Woody Allen) and Mary Wilkes (Diane Keaton) begin a precarious relationship in *Manhattan. Courtesy of Woody Allen and United Artists.*

7

Between Bridges

Manhattan (1979) begins with an arresting montage that identifies the urban locale (57th Street, Orchard Street, Washington
Square, the Staten Island Ferry, Yankee Stadium). *Rhapsody in
Blue* rises to a crescendo, capped by an extended explosion of
fireworks above the Manhattan skyline. Over this romantic, yet
playfully parodic, display, a writer names Isaac Davis (Woody
Allen) struggles to create a unifying vision for his first novel and
to furnish a perspective for Allen's eighth major film. Should his
viewpoint be angry? celebratory? polemical? Is New York a romantic city that still "pulsates to the great tunes of George
Gershwin," or is it "a metaphor for the decay of contemporary
culture," characterized by the "lack of individual integrity"?

The romantic Gershwin melody, the opening montage, and
the black-and-white cinematography remind us of the 1940s,
when a curiously naive mixture of New York musicals and films
noir expressed the innocence of our most utopian dreams along-
side our growing disillusionment. Isaac's tentativeness, his
search for the right language to express his contradictory feelings, draws attention to the film as exploration rather than resolution and to its nature as a fictional construction. Isaac's
voice-over together with the montage, and the score helps (in
Allen's words) "to vibrate several themes in the picture: the
passing of time; the poignancy of where the city's gone, the fact
that, in a certain sense, Isaac's living in the past when things
seemed better to him."[1]

As in other Allen films, *Manhattan*'s classic references serve as a backdrop for an exploration of contemporary concerns. In musicals, "the modern metropolis is at once the promised land and proving ground for amateur performers. . . . The American success ethic generally is associated with New York City."[2] In even the early film noir, "Man has been inexplicably uprooted from those values . . . that offer him meaning and stability, and in the almost exclusively urban landscape of film noir . . . he is struggling for a foothold in a maze of right and wrong. . . . Nothing—especially woman—is stable, nothing is dependable."[3] The contradictory allusions in *Manhattan*'s prologue set up a serio-comic mood and introduce oppositions between innocence and sophistication, integrity and betrayal, a longing for hope and a fear of hopelessness is postmodern times.

Manhattan is the story of a television comedy writer, Isaac Davis (Woody Allen), who seeks personal integrity in his work and who tries to find a meaningful relationship with a woman amid the confusions of contemporary life and mores. At the film's outset, Isaac is involved with Tracy (Mariel Hemingway), a seventeen-year-old high school student. Twice divorced and still recovering from his last marriage, forty-two-year-old Isaac has trouble believing that his relationship with Tracy is anything but a passing winter-spring affair. He distrusts it even as he enjoys it, and so he is drawn, as Allen's little-men always are, to alternatives.

His best friend, a literature teacher and writer, Yale Pollack (Michael Murphy), has an attractive, loyal wife, Emily (Anne Byrne), whom he claims to love, but whom he betrays when he meets free-lance journalist Mary Wilke (Diane Keaton). Although Isaac does not like Mary at first, after Yale and Mary end their affair, Isaac goes out with Mary and eventually rejects Tracy for her. After Mary and Isaac, Yale and Emily double-date, however, Yale and Mary take up their relationship once more, Yale leaves Emily, and Mary rejects Isaac. Disillusioned, Isaac ruminates on life's meaning and rediscovers Tracy among his most valued experiences. He races across Manhattan to see her, but finds Tracy about to leave for six months of theatrical study in London. Although he declares his love and asks her not to go, she does not change her plans. A close shot of Isaac's reaction ends the film and summarizes his doubts and hopes in a memorable visual synecdoche.

The joined qualities of innocence and anxiety that characterized Allen's little man in the comedies continue to move toward disjunction in *Manhattan,* so that the little man is a more seriously disturbed reflection of the effects of a sophisticated culture on sensitive people; and innocence in its purest expression is found in a female character. In *Manhattan,* even more than in *Interiors* or *Annie Hall,* a female is an obvious and idealized version of innocence. As in *Interiors,* Allen retains vestiges of an earlier pattern in which a natural female character assists a disillusioned character to find himself or herself; but in *Interiors, Annie Hall,* and especially in *Manhattan,* the results of that redemptive relationship are less conclusive than Allan Felix's education with Linda Christie as a tutor in *Play It Again, Sam.*

As Allen moved away from predominantly comic features, his films began to deal more obviously with the ethical polarities in contemporary life. The pervasive instability and deception against which earlier film heroes attempted to retain a code of conduct in films noir such as *The Maltese Falcon* (1941) is related to the little man's attempt to define and retain integrity amid change and moral laxity in New York. *Manhattan* deals with "civilization's junk": TV shows without substance, artists who compromise with economic pressures, unpleasant living conditions, indifference, superficiality, rudeness, and betrayal are central issues in the New York where Isaac Davis tries to live properly and honestly. "There's no center to the culture," Allen said. "We have this opulent relatively well-educated culture, and yet we see a great city like New York deteriorate. We see people lose themselves in drugs because they don't deal with their sense of spiritual emptiness. I intend *Manhattan* to be a metaphor for everything wrong with our culture."[4]

While Allen continues to explore the ethical issues that concern him, in *Manhattan* he also takes a more serious and intense look at human feelings and relationships. He told Natalie Gittelson that in *Manhattan* he developed what he had learned in making *Interiors*. "There," he said, "I was trying to deal with heavy emotions, heavy confrontations. . . . Each time, I'm attempting to express more and more feelings."[5] Thus, while Allen appears to be a harsh critic of moral insensitivity, and his films of this period sometimes resemble modern morality plays on first viewing, in *Manhattan* as in *Interiors*, he is not simply a self-righteous moralist. He mocks as well as understands the imperfect corrupted figures in these films, and he sympathizes even as he makes fun of those characters who are not natural innocents, but who struggle bravely, caught between sophisticated conditions and an older (or newer) dream that moral clarity and authenticity may yet be possibilities in an unstable world.

Such paradoxes, conveyed through characterization and dramatic conflict in Allen's film, are also closely related to reflexive issues—to the nature and purpose of art and filmmaking. Not only are most of the main characters artists or concerned with art, but an argument between Yale and Isaac in an early sequence in *Manhattan* suggests the reflexive part of the dialogue. Yale says, "I think the essence of art is to provide a kind of working through the situation for people . . . so that you can get in touch with feelings that you didn't know you had, really." But Isaac says talent is little more than luck and that the important thing in life is making brave decisions and acting courageously. Thus, Isaac does not view art as privileged; the problems for artists are the problems of life more generally, and his concern, unlike Yale's, is with the difficulty of achieving personal integrity in creativity as in life. Later, he will also argue that the way to handle Nazis is with bricks and bats instead of with "biting satire."

The conflict between ambiguity and certainty, between moral relativity and ethical assurance, between getting in touch with problems and taking a stand in life and in art, between the attractions of sophistication and the longing for innocence give rise to a larger dialogue regarding the prospects for the human condition in the face of those conflicts. Ultimately, those dialogues give structure to the film, which becomes a metaphor for the emotional tug-of-war that is life in the late 1970s. Isaac Davis is an older Alvy Singer. At forty-two he is one of Allen's midlife attempts to deal with aging in his films. Not only is Isaac recovering from his second divorce, but his second wife, Jill (Meryl Streep), took their son and left Isaac for an attractive woman. While Isaac accuses Jill of being promiscuous and immoral, she has a satisfying relationship with her new mate; and Mary tells Isaac of research that proves children *can* be raised successfully by two women. However, together with other partner-switching in the film, Jill and Isaac's relationship also emphasizes the instability of contemporary coupling.

Jill publishes an exposé of her life with Isaac that she plans to turn into a movie. From her point of view, the book is honest, but honesty is no simple term in this problematic film, and Yale sees the difficulty with Jill's sort of exposé when he says that "gossip is the new pornography." On the other hand, Jill's book does suggest that Isaac, for all his integrity, is far from being only an outsider to the blemished world around him. He refuses to acknowledge to Jill that he tried to run over her lover with a car, and, according to the book, Isaac was "given to fits of rage, Jewish, liberal paranoia, male chauvinism, self-righteous misanthropy, and nihilistic moods of despair. He had complaints about life but never any solutions."

The question of honesty reappears throughout *Manhattan*. Thus Mary Wilke prides herself on her frankness but lies to Isaac because of her love for Yale. And Isaac also contrasts his perception of Mary's husband, Jeremiah (Wallace Shawn), with Mary's. Mary talks about Jeremiah as a "devastating" "dominating" "genius" who "opened her up sexually." Yet when Isaac and Mary bump into balding, squat Jeremiah, this "great ladies' man" turns out to be "a little homunculus." As Isaac sums it up, "It's amazing how subjective all that stuff is." The disparity in perception contributes to our sense that all certainty is precarious, and that makes taking an honest stand or making a commitment no simple matter.

Much more than earlier little-man figures, Isaac has been

around, but as with Alvy Singer of *Annie Hall* and Allan Felix of *Play It Again, Sam*, we see signs of a basically good character whose innocence is buried within a sophisticated facade. In a reflexive joke during the film's first sequence, Isaac smokes a cigarette, like a tough initiated film noir male should, but he doesn't inhale it because it causes cancer, and the familiar code comes to emphasize both the attractions of sophistication as well as his difference from the fast-track world he lives in. Isaac is a television writer, and like the blemished heroes who still try to maintain a code of personal integrity in films noir, his potential for integrity appears early in the movie when he quits his TV job because he finds the canned show "Human Beings, Wow" "empty" and "antiseptic". Isaac objects not only to bad television writing, but to the drugs with which the directors avoid facing the show's banality. Isaac decides, instead, to write his first novel, but economic pressures make his decision difficult; and the moral little man becomes anxious about whether, ironically, he can maintain two alimonies and child support.

Isaac also frets over his relationship with Tracy (he's going with a girl who still does homework). Although Ike and Tracy have similar tastes and enjoy each other, Isaac has problems making commitments. From her sophisticated vantage point, Mary also fuels Ike's concerns, hinting that his affair "with the little girl" is abnormal. Responding to Tracy and Isaac's relationship, Natalie Gittelson observed that "*Manhattan* testifies with eloquence and candor that Allen may have a soft spot in his heart for young, young women. But there is little of Humbert (*Lolita*) Humbert here. Although sex is by no means devalued, the real attraction lies between kindred spirits. The older Allen grows the more he seems to value innocence in women—not sexual innocence, but that shiningness of soul that age so often tarnishes."[6] Even clothed in blue jeans, casual shirt, and sweater, Tracy is as pristine as Mark Twain's Victorian ideal, Joan of Arc. So young, so unformed, so uncorrupted is Tracy that even while we are asked to believe in her, we are forced to admit that she may be more romantic fantasy or elusive ideal than obtainable reality.

She is not unlike the girl next door of musical or romantic comedy or the redeeming "good girl" operating on the fringes of a corrupted film noir world. The antithesis of the duplicitous femme fatale, she "offers the possibility of integration for the alienated, lost man. . . . She gives love, understanding . . . asks very little in return . . . and is generally visually passive and static."[7] The camera repeatedly captures Tracy's beauty in carefully composed close shots and long takes that emphasize Mariel Hemingway's classic features. Tracy is associated throughout the film with a relaxed pace that contrasts with the frenetic quality of Manhattan's sophisticated life.

Tracy is a younger version of the early Annie in *Annie Hall* and a relative of Pearl in *Interiors*. Although Tracy is bright and sensitive, she lacks the immobilizing and schizophrenic self-consciousness and sophistication of the older Manhattanites. Tracy has a camera Isaac gave her, and like Annie in *Annie Hall*, she thinks photography is "neat" and "lots of fun." Like the early Annie, Tracy is linked through still photography to a simpler, more innocent world, to less complicated technology, to cinema's roots, to stable images, and to captured memories. But as the camera is also a reflexive image, we are also forced to wonder whether Tracy is also just a kind of fiction, the incarnation of Isaac's longing, an unrealistic, unobtainable ideal.

During one visit, Tracy climbs a shadowy spiral staircase culled from film noir, but the setting belongs to Isaac, not to her; in fact, he attempts to preserve her innocence by discouraging her from moving in with him. Tracy wants to be an actress, but she has not yet become an experienced "performer." As she climbs the staircase, Isaac promises to take her to see a Veronica Lake movie, and she jokes with him about her familiarity with 1940s movie queens like Lake and Rita Hayworth. In fact, Tracy resembles these stars, who Isaac associates with an earlier time; the camera emphasizes Tracy's long hair falling over one eye (Lake and Hayworth style) in the film's conclusion, when Tracy is on her way to theater arts school and Isaac is in danger of losing her.

Scenes with Tracy are comfortable. She and Isaac shop together for groceries at Dean and Deluca's Food Mart, eat pizza at John's; they enjoy W. C. Fields's movies and share Chinese food from cartons. She is a natural in bed and delights in sex. Given her choice of entertainment for an evening, Tracy chooses a New York musical or girl-next-door convention—a romantic horse-and-buggy ride in Central Park that reminds Isaac of his prom night. "I don't think it's corny," she says. "I think it's fun." She prompts Ike to look at the clear night sky full of stars, to admit he's crazy about her, and to tell her that she is "God's answer to Job." "You would've ended . . . all argument between them," Ike says. "He would've pointed to you and said . . . 'I do a lot of terrible things, but I can also make one of these.'"

Their breakup at an old-fashioned soda fountain both calls into question the illusions associated with Tracy and underlines her genuineness, as the setting evokes images of more innocent times and of earlier, more innocent films. And Tracy's definition of love there is fitting in its straightforward simplicity. "We have laughs together," she tells Ike. "I care about you. Your concerns are my concerns. We have great sex." She also gives Isaac a harmonica, an uncomplicated musical instrument, because she is "trying to open up that side" of him, to put him in touch with a more innocent self that he cannot bring himself to believe in. Isaac, however, confesses that he is capable of betrayal and rejects Tracy in a moving scene that Mariel Hemingway plays with conviction and restraint.

The cause of the breakup is not only Ike's uncertainty about going with a younger girl but his strange attraction for the very sophistication that repels him. Mary is a modern New York woman with a subtle beauty and the cerebral quality that first offends Ike. She represents an alternative to Isaac's discomfort with his sentimental longing for a simpler, older set of romantic ideals. Although the contrasts are not as sharp as between Eve and Pearl in *Interiors*, Mary is set against Tracy in several ways. While Tracy, like Pearl, is satisfied enjoying art without analyzing it, Mary evaluates in the voguish jargon that Allen spoofs in earlier films. At the Guggenheim Museum, Mary and Yale are caught up in seeing "negative capability" and in using the word

derivative in a derogatory fashion to proclaim their sophistication. Together, Mary and Yale compile a list of artists and phi-
losophers who belong in "the academy of the overrated"—
among them Isaac's (and Allen's) favorites.

Although initially Mary is unsympathetic, Allen complicates
Mary's personality. He portrays her vulnerability and shows her
with Ike laughing at her own jargon; Ike has wonderful moments with her and she comes to seem charming and appealing.
Like the swiftly changing surfaces of contemporary life, our
evaluation of Mary shifts several times throughout the film.
Even while we come to understand and like her, we are fore-
warned about the dangers in this high-strung and neurotic representative of modernity.

Mary is associated with images of instability and change. Ike
meets Mary for the second time at an ERA benefit at the Museum of Modern Art, where Bella Abzug makes a brief and sympathetic appearance; but unlike Tracy, the uncomplicated high
school student who has never been in analysis, Mary calls her
analyst "Donnie" and ministers to his problems on the telephone. She is also a free-lance writer, willing to do film noveli-
zations because there's good money in them. When Ike finally
goes out with Mary, we watch buildings being torn down as Ike
laments changes that are altering New York. We see Mary and
Ike portrayed on or against bridges, near "tow away zone" signs,
and in moving cars. Ike and Mary first become friends on a romantic midnight stroll, but traffic lights and signs ("Don't
Walk" and "One Way") seem to carry warnings. Mary's dog is
called Waffles, to suggest her indecisiveness and its dangers for
Isaac.

Unlike Isaac's comfortable times in bed with Tracy, he sus-
pects that self-conscious Mary reacts more mechanically. While
Tracy and Isaac agree that they love W. C. Fields's films, Mary
and Ike argue over Inagaki's *Chushuingura* and Dovzhenko's
Earth. The only gift Mary gives Isaac is a framed picture she
buys in Nyack, but unlike the simple harmonica from Tracy that
Ike treasures, he quickly throws Mary's gift into a convenient
garbage can. And when Ike and Mary take a romantic boat ride

in Central Park Lake, Ike reaches into the water and dredges up enough muck to make the perfect moonlight bay romance too murky for comfort.

A Sunday walk in the sunshine becomes a rain-drenched run in an electrical storm, and although Isaac later notes that Mary was sexy in that scene, she is finally a less-satisfying memory than Tracy riding through Central Park or sipping a soda. While Tracy and Isaac sit beneath the stars in an old-fashioned carriage drawn by a horse, Mary and Isaac's romance takes them to the planetarium, where outer space is brought down to earth for more careful observation. This mise-en-scène underlines one of the film's themes, expressed in Isaac's observation that people in sophisticated Manhattan are so concerned with their neuroses and personal problems that they miss the cosmic issues, and it also contrasts with more innocent moon-June settings.[8] The couple, for all their romantic whisperings, are like shadowy aliens in a glorious, but artificial cosmos that also draws attention to the self-conscious techniques of contemporary cinema such as *Manhattan*. The backdrop includes a rocky replica of the moon pictured with its craters close up. While it is awesome in its own way, when we are able to see it in its precise details, it is not the romantic old devil moon beaming over Central Park in the clear night air.

In the planetarium sequence, the mooned rings of Saturn are first seen close up as a wide diagonal black line between two white spaces. A related pattern appears in a painting on the wall of Isaac's apartment during Mary's first visit and in a raquetball court scene where Isaac tries to hit a space between two lines on the wall. Similarly, when Mary and Isaac double-date with Yale and Emily, the camera moves from two shots of the couples to three shots in which we see Yale first between Emily and Mary, and then Mary between Isaac and Yale. These image patterns echo the betwixt-and-between states in which the characters find themselves and suggest the care with which Allen has come to use visual imagery to underscore his dialogues.

Although Yale encourages Isaac to write his novel and applauds his best friend's departure from TV, Yale's ability to constantly rationalize and to make "minor" compromises identifies him with Mary, and with a contemporary inconstancy and a crippled sense of integrity. As he walks through film noir shadows into patches of sidewalk illuminated by neon lights, early in the film, he confesses his duplicity to Ike, excusing his deception with Mary because he has only had a few small affairs before. He buys a sports car instead of using the money for the book or journal that he has been planning to publish, he lies to Emily, and finally, he betrays Isaac. Isaac pursues Mary only after Yale has broken with her and has encouraged Ike to ask her out. But Yale secretly phones Mary even while Isaac is in the next room, and he takes her out behind his closest friend's back.

Isaac and Mary's relationship breaks up just after he has had a particularly harrowing encounter with Jill. Mary reveals her fickleness and lies to Isaac about the extent of her encounters with Yale while she and Isaac were still a pair. Like the Buchanans in *The Great Gatsby,* Yale and Mary's "carelessnesses" leave Ike badly hurt, and his reaction to their betrayal is expressed precisely in the language of physical shock. It is as though he has been hit by a car. "I'm stunned," he says. "Somebody should throw a blanket over me."

Although Ike tells Mary that he cannot express anger, and indeed Allen's little man has never been able to express anger directly on the screen, in *Manhattan* Allen extends the range of emotions he portrays. Isaac's anger leads him to Yale's classroom and a no-holds-barred discussion about betrayal, personal integrity, and moral relativity. Isaac berates Yale for leaving Emily for Mary, whom he calls "the winner of the Zelda Fitzgerald Emotional Maturity Award." He criticizes Yale for changing his mind all the time and for not telling him about the rekindled relationship with Mary. Yale defends himself, protesting that Isaac is "so self-righteous. . . . We're just human beings, you know. . . . You just can't live the way you do, you know. It's all so perfect." But Ike tells Yale that small lies lead to greater social and political immorality: "You're too easy on yourself. . . . You rationalize everything. . . . You cheat a little bit on Emily, and you play around the truth a little with me . . . and the next thing you know, you're in front of a Senate committee . . . informing on your friends."

Behind them, in the classroom where they talk, are a primate and a human skeleton that raise questions about moral and social progress despite present-day sophistication. The more comic edge to the serious discussion is not only in the primate skeleton's resemblance to Isaac, but in the hint of a larger absurdity that qualifies the significance of Ike's stand at the same time he is taking it. Ike tries to face up to the implications of death rather than avoiding them, but like Yorick's skull in *Hamlet*, the skeletons become a grotesquely humorous commentary on time, change, and meaninglessness that threatens to make Ike's impassioned commitment to a moral position and to any certainty, for that matter, ludicrous.

However, even as the skeletons mock Ike's stance, they also underline thoughts about integrity and moral consistency that can be taken seriously. As Ike puts it, in a series of statements that are filled with good lessons as well as subverting ironies: "You know, someday we're gonna . . . be like him [the skeleton]! I mean . . . he was probably one of the beautiful people . . . and . . . this is what happens to us! . . . It's very important to have . . . some kind of personal integrity. You know, I'll be hanging in a classroom one day. And . . . I wanna make sure when I . . . thin out that I'm . . . well thought of!"

Although the worlds in which the hero lives and works may be dislocated and uncertain, and although desire is seldom fulfilled in film noir, such films assume "that to every puzzle there is a key through which a complex but coherent pattern will emerge within seemingly anarchic events."[9] While the hero may not necessarily enjoy an upbeat conclusion to his adventures, he is usually vindicated for his integrity and constancy. Similarly, the less-complicated Pollyannaish resolutions of New York musicals assume a conventional reunion of lovers or other happy ending, often following a grand finale or production number. Allen's film alludes to both these possibilities and to resolutions in more recent films as well, but the conclusion of Allen's film reemphasizes flux rather than the certainty Isaac longs for.

Thus, a summary discussion Isaac has with Emily further

underlines the extent to which he is misunderstood, and how even the most apparently guiltless figures in this film are accomplices in the betrayals. Emily admits her complicity as she confesses that she knew of Yale's affairs but believed marriage required compromises. Ike tells her he is "just a noncompromiser" and that "it's always a big mistake to . . . look the other way . . . 'cause you always wind up paying for it in the end anyhow . . . but then, . . . you know. I'm . . . living in the past." After this statement, however, Ike looks confused when Emily tells him that she was angry at him because if he hadn't introduced Mary to Yale the whole thing might never have happened. Ike only nods his head in sad surprise at yet another misperception that is his reward for attempting to be honest.

Although Isaac has chastised Yale for changing his mind, in the last sequences of the film Ike comes to change his. He rediscovers the center of innocence he seeks in Tracy, attempts to recover it and to repair their relationship. But time is at work here, too, and we are left with a question as to whether such innocence or stability in the midst of a sophisticated world remains a viable possibility, or whether it is already, or has always been, an impossible dream. *Manhattan*, like *Annie Hall* and *Interiors*, is a film in which the need for certainty and commitment is never clearer, but the possibility of achieving such meaning seems always to be receding into the past.

Settled on the couch of his apartment, recording his ideas for a story into a dictaphone, Ike contemplates a plot about people in Manhattan who are always creating "unnecessary neurotic problems," which, though real, prevent them from confronting "more solvable, terrifying problems about . . . the universe." Like little-men in other Allen films, Isaac appears to reach a hopeful resolution as he concludes that his story should be optimistic. He asks himself why life is worth living and mentions his favorite things. Among a list that includes Groucho Marx, Willie Mays, Swedish movies, Flaubert's *Sentimental Education*, and Cezanne's apples and pears, he discovers Tracy's face. When he cannot reach her by phone, he begins his long run across town to her house.

Isaac's race through Manhattan, with Gershwin's triumphant

"Strike Up the Band" for accompaniment, reminds us of Dustin Hoffman's race to the church in Mike Nichols's landmark film of the sixties, *The Graduate* (1967). During the 1960s, Nichols's film epitomized a desperate, but renewed, optimism in the face of cynicism and duplicity. Hoffman's search for authenticity amid suburban affluence and its values resulted in a happy ending that left Mr. and Mrs. Robinson and all they stood for before an empty altar, while Dustin Hoffman escaped with his innocent bride. The fact that Anne Byrne, Hoffman's then recently divorced wife, played Emily in *Manhattan*, may be yet another indirect reference to the same film. Additional references, however, are to the affirmative endings in New York musicals. Isaac's big production number, however, his exciting and climactic run across town, ends in a different, less certain conclusion, more suitable to a film of the 1970s.

Isaac arrives at Tracy's apartment building just as she is about to leave for London to study acting. He sees her through a glass door brushing her long hair as if she is already only a reflection, a framed memory, and the music behind them changes to Gershwin's painfully romantic "But Not for Me." Although he tells her he loves her and asks her to stay because he desperately wishes to hold back time and preserve innocence from corruption as Hoffman did in Nichols's film, Tracy tells him that he has come too late. She offers him a consolation that he finds hard to believe after his recent experiences. "Not everybody gets corrupted," she says. "Look, you have to have a little faith in people." With *Rhapsody in Blue* in the background, the camera moves in for a close look at Isaac's reaction to Tracy's words. Caught in his face is the fear of change, of having already lost Tracy and all she represents—yet a continuing longing for innocence and meaning may be there, too; the image expresses a perfect liminality that echoes all the doubts and hopes of Allen's film. In Ike's reactions, Allen captures an uncertainty and a pathos that stops short of sentimentality.

As a finale, while the music swells, the film pictures the Manhattan skyline in the early morning, then as the sun sets, and finally, at night—buildings and bridges bright with lights.

Isaac's city is "the human condition in giant parenthesis formed by the George Washington and Brooklyn Bridges."[10] Whether the innocence the little man longs for can survive in the face of time and instability, whether personal integrity can triumph amid sophisticated arguments for moral relativity, whether honesty and authenticity are definable in the face of subjectivity, and whether books or films that espouse such commitment and integrity are possible to take seriously are unanswered questions. What remains is New York in all its corruption and all its romantic promise. What remains is Isaac, named both ironically and as a sign of hope, after Abraham's son, whom a benevolent or capricious God was all too willing to kill, but who was finally spared. Isaac is the little-man victim and survivor, the hero and fool, the artist who attempts to be honest. The indeterminate future of his city, his unresolved life, his unfinished book, and the inconclusive film that conveys his story and ours are Woody Allen's *Manhattan*.

Finding himself amid grotesque travelers on a dingy train, Sandy Bates (Woody Allen) asks his conductor why he is not riding in a train of happier people on the next track (*Stardust Memories*). *Courtesy of Woody Allen and United Artists.*

8

8½ or 9½

While *Manhattan* won rave reviews, *Stardust Memories* (1980) was received with far less enthusiasm. Critics objected to "intentional obfuscation"[1] in a film that violated classic filmic conventions to a greater extent than any of Allen's earlier work. Pauline Kael asked, *"What* is going on in this movie?"[2] Janet Maslin regarded the little-man main character as "the film's most daring invention," but she found "its attitude toward him . . . incomplete."[3] And Stephen Schiff said the film was "a whiff of nostalgia gone rancid. . . . [It] doesn't probe, doesn't risk. . . . It never searches beyond *8½*; it hides behind it."[4]

Nonetheless, Allen called *Stardust Memories* his favorite film.[5] He believed that he had made "a very good picture," but that "many people took it wrong."[6] Vincent Canby agreed. While acknowledging that the film sometimes appears "to be going off in a dozen different directions at once," Canby found "the effect . . . exhilarating." *Stardust Memories* "isn't a steal," he wrote, "because it is complete in itself, with a life of its own." Canby recognized that *Stardust Memories* alluded to Fellini in order "to illuminate Mr. Allen's own concerns."[7]

Despite the negative reviews, *Stardust Memories* is a remarkable film. It is a watershed for Allen's continuing interest in metafictional style and one of his most effective inquiries into the nature of film viewing and filmmaking. More than earlier Allen films, *Stardust Memories* forces viewers to be engaged spectators—to be aware of the film as construction and to become conscious of audiences' participation in creating their film experiences.

Although the little man had been gradually becoming a less humble, more self-conscious, and more blemished central figure, in *Stardust Memories,* Allen drives his inquiries further. In presenting a still less appealing little-man, who often feels alienated from fans, Allen threatens to cut audiences away from their familiar lines of identification with the main character and to leave viewers with additional uncertainty. In *Stardust Memories* Allen experiments with departures from conventional use of narrative time and space, resolution in form, and classic patterns of spectator-character empathy. Like Allen's other recent films, *Stardust Memories* is "incomplete" and inconclusive.

Stardust Memories is either Allen's "8½" or his "9½," depending on how you count his major films produced by 1980. "8½" also suggests the incompleteness of the gestation period of a film; as we watch it, *Stardust Memories* is in the process of being born. "9½" indicates that Allen's film is about a sophisticated world beyond ripeness, and it emphasizes the way the film goes beyond Fellini's *8½* to explore Allen's personal vision. Both possibilities are typical of the shifting interpretations to which the film lends itself.

Guido Anselmi, the main character in Fellini's *8½,* is a representative modern man and artist. He is a film director who cannot complete the film he is making because he cannot find a satisfactory meaning, and he explores his own life for answers. Despite his past success, he finds himself overwhelmed by problems he cannot resolve—the demands of the film industry, his alienation from his wife, his church, and his family, his history. He worries about artistic and sexual impotency as he confronts middle age. In the same way, *Stardust Memories* is about Sandy Bates, a divorced film director in midlife who is also having problems finding meaning and completing a film. His story, like Guido's, is a series of juxtaposed moments from his personal fantasies, his personal life, and the film he is making. As in *8½,* the transitions among these segments of experience are associational rather than chronological or logical, and since *Stardust*

Memories is a film about making a film, it is impossible for spectators to distinguish with confidence between scenes from the film made by the main character/director and those outside it, or to distinguish the action in the film Bates is making from the life he personally lives. Since Allen, like Fellini, is a film director, and *Stardust Memories*, like *8½*, contains autobiographical references, it also converges with Allen's life outside his art, creating yet another dimension of drama and meaning.

Although Sandy's success, like Allen's, is built upon his reputation as a comic filmmaker, he no longer wants to make comedies with happy endings because he believes that comedy cannot convey the pain and misery of contemporary life. *Stardust Memories* begins with Sandy's original, wholly pessimistic ending for his film; what follows is a series of recollections and experiences—dialogues between Sandy and himself and between Sandy and others—that either justify that ending or argue for less pessimistic alternatives.

In trying to bring his film to a satisfactory close, Sandy's problem is not only that he must resolve an array of aesthetic and philosophical issues, but also that he must satisfy the commercial demands of filmmaking. He has difficulties with audiences and fans, with his secretary, his accountant, his taxes, his producers, his writers, with publicity people, and with studio executives. His personal life is integrally related to his troublesome creative life. He personally worries about aging and death, about cosmic entropy, about human suffering, and about family responsibilities. Like so many of Allen's little men, Sandy also finds it hard to love, to achieve lasting relationships and satisfying intimacy. Like Alvy Singer in *Annie Hall*, he attempts, with Dorrie (Charlotte Rampling), to deal with the lingering memory of their unsuccessful affair, and he cannot find the ideal woman among other romantic possibilities—neither his current lover, Isobel (Marie-Christine Barrault), nor a new interest, Daisy (Jessica Harper), who reminds him of Dorrie.

Much of the film is set either in Sandy's apartment or at the Stardust Hotel, where Sandy reluctantly appears at a weekend film festival similar to those sponsored by film critic Judith

Crist at Tarrytown, New York. At that weekend, fans see his old films and interrogate him about his life and work. The Stardust Hotel scenes are interspersed with scenes from Sandy's old films, from his new unfinished one, from his childhood memories, and from his love affairs. All of these become part of the film he is making as we watch.

Aside from the parallels between Allen's Sandy and Fellini's Guido, there are situational and structural parallels as well. For example, $8\frac{1}{2}$'s opening fantasy sequence finds a frightened Guido caught in his automobile in a tunnel, surrounded by indifferent motorists. *Stardust Memories* opens with the original ending to Sandy's film, a fantasy where he is trapped in a subway car. The entrapment in the train, like Guido's entrapment in the tunnel in $8\frac{1}{2}$, carries comic-serious intimations of powerlessness. *Stardust Memories*'s beginning (the original ending of Sandy's film) alludes not only to Fellini's beginning, but to one of the proposed endings to $8\frac{1}{2}$ that Fellini decided not to use: a happy, triumphant scene in a train where all the people in Guido's life have gathered, dressed in innocent white.[8]

In Sandy's film ending there are two trains. In one train, which Sandy sees across from the one he's in, beautiful, happy people, all in white, are holding Academy Awards and they're having a wonderful time. In Sandy's dingy subway car, haunted looks and tears reflect his fellow travelers' misery, and their stern-faced conductor looks like the Grim Reaper. Sandy is perplexed: why should he be on the sad train and not on the other? He tries desperately to leave, but in comical little-man fashion he gets tied up in emergency brake cords. Amid comic and pathetic images, we are left uncertain whether Allen is asking serious questions about positive and negative views of life, whether he is making fun of Fellini, or whether he is mocking Sandy's self-indulgent depiction of his own despair.

Unlike either Fellini's discarded triumphant ending or the transcendent finale that actually ends $8\frac{1}{2}$, Sandy Bates's original ending is blatantly negative. Both trains end up in a junkyard. There are visual puns in the junkyard scene as there are elsewhere in the film. In Fellini's opening, Guido escapes from the stifling tunnel and floats out over the cars and into the sky, only to find that he is attached to earth by a long rope. In Sandy's first ending (and our beginning), flying birds provide an illusion of freedom; then, the camera booms down to reveal the passengers from both trains approaching a huge junk pile from both sides of the frame. The birds are only gulls hovering over garbage.

The next sequence finds us in a projection room where film executives, much like Guido's associates in 8½, express their dissatisfaction with Sandy's pessimistic ending. They object to the "pretentious"quality of Sandy's new, "serious" work and decry its poor prospects in a marketplace where audiences do not want to look at reality too closely. The dissatisfied executives eventually try to tack a Hollywood-style ending on Sandy's work, a spectacular scene in the clouds where a big band is playing and all the people from both trains in the opening sequence are united in a grand affirmative resolution labeled "Jazz Heaven." This proposed ending, which parodies conventional unrealistic Hollywood finales, is totally unacceptable to Sandy. Not only does he find it silly, but he insists that it violates the point of his film—that "no one is saved."

In the projection-room scene, as in other sequences in Allen's film, the comfortable boundaries of conventional film language are interrupted, not only by the emphasis on the film within a film, but by other blurrings of art and life. The producers in Sandy's movie echo critics of Allen's films, and Allen casts his own manager and producer, Jack Rollins, as well as United Artists executive Andy Albeck to play these executives. Such art/life confusions are reinforced later by the presence of film critic Judith Crist, who appears in a cabaret scene.

Other defamiliarizing techniques also underscore Sandy Bates's confused state of mind. Sandy's apartment is decorated with lamps that resemble theatrical spotlights, and with blow-ups of frames from Marx Brothers films, but the decor includes horrifying newspaper photos of domestic and international tragedy as well. During times when his love affair with Dorrie goes well, Groucho appears in the frame. When Dorrie and

Sandy quarrel over her jealousy and she recalls her flirtations with her father, the walls display posters of a newspaper that headlines incest between a father and child and a photo denoting a violent struggle. Early in the film, when a depressed Sandy tells his producers that he no longer wishes to make comic films, the apartment wall is covered by the shocking Pulitzer Prize photo portraying a civilian being shot in the head at close range during the Tet offensive. The mise-en-scène both imitates and mocks Godardian self-conscious, anti-illusionistic political filmmaking at the same time that it emphasizes and mocks Sandy's conflicting views of life in relation to the movie he is making.

Much of Sandy's depression is related to the demands of his public life. Although he has won public acclaim, he takes little joy in notoriety. In *8½*, the producers, colleagues, and fans who impose themselves on Guido's rest cure at a sanitarium enter the frame from both sides, and are often seen in wide-angle, grotesque subjective shots to accentuate Guido's sense of entrapment. *Stardust Memories* imitates that style. The Stardust Hotel sequence opens with demanding fans crowding Sandy into corners of the screen or entering the composition from both sides to enclose him within a tightly framed space. Similarly, subjective shots and reaction shots in wide-range perspectives emphasize Sandy's confinement. In addition, the pace of the fan scenes at the Stardust Hotel is frenetic, and the film slows down to lingering long takes only in the sequences when Sandy is with a woman or alone in a moment of quiet escape. Audiences of Allen's film are called upon to establish distance between themselves and Sandy, and to question their roles vis-à-vis charismatic public figures and media-produced heroes.

Guido's and Sandy's midlife crises also involve fears of aging and death. Fellini defines Guido's fears in close shots of elderly people during the sanitarium sequences; in Guido's fantasies of his aging parents; in his relationship with his middle-aged friend Mario, and Mario's young amour; and in his problems with Concucchio, an aging director. Sandy's fear of aging is reflected through his concern with mortality in the early train sequence; in the importance of his friend Nat Bernstein's sudden death, which haunts him; and in a later sequence where he meets Charlotte Ames, a woman who once played his mother in an earlier film, but whom he can hardly recognize because she has had cosmetic surgery to hide her age.

Both directors seek respite from such fears. In Fellini's film, beaches and water are associated most frequently with healing. Although Allen has sometimes used beaches as settings for moments of meaningful experience and intimacy, in *Stardust Memories* this pattern of imagery is less predictable. The beach, which fades off into a hazy dreamlike horizon all around the Stardust Hotel, offers no comfort to Sandy, who associates beaches with childhood recollections of old hotels with faded awnings. On the other hand, the beach is the timeless setting for a fantasy in which the child Sandy receives a much-wanted gift—an elephant from Dorrie, and an adult Sandy imagines a good moment with Dorrie in which she, like Tracy in *Manhattan*, presents him with a musical instrument; however, he also receives *The Way of Zen* and a pocket watch, suggestions that spiritual unrest and time circumscribe even his most positive moments.

Such ambivalence is typical: In both *8½* and *Stardust Memories*, the director/protagonists also search for understanding and meaning among childhood remembrances. Such memories offer a potential refuge from adult problems; however, the images of childhood innocence and their connection with artistic potency are funnier and even more ambiguous in Allen's particular idiom than in Fellini's. Guido escapes to several negative fantasies of childhood guilt and punishment from parents and priests, but more frequently he remembers comfort and security, a sense of wholeness missing in his adult life.

In *Stardust Memories*, Sandy escapes from frustrations and entrapment into childhood memories on several occasions. The first time, he escapes from demanding fans at the hotel by imagining himself in a magician's cape that permits him to fly straight up and out of the frame; thus he metaphorically and literally escapes from the film. In Fellini's film, the childhood memory of Guido's mother's bathing him and putting him to bed is one of his most positive fantasies; however, Sandy's flight also involves an escape *from* his mother, suggesting, as in *Annie Hall*, that his childhood history provides little comfort and is not the source for affirmative artistic inspiration.

In *8½*, the childhood bathing fantasy is also linked to young Guido's faith in magic and to the later appearance of a magician figure, who eventually leads Guido to the aesthetic resolution in the final scenes of *8½*. In *Stardust Memories*, when he is particularly frustrated or lonely, Sandy recalls images of himself as a magician. He pictures himself as a child performing in a cabaret where he has gone for beer with Daisy and her boyfriend Jack (a college professor who reductionistically explains all comedy as latent homosexuality or deep-seated hostility). For Guido, childhood eventually becomes a key to artistic recovery; for Sandy, childhood memories offer moments of escape and evoke a longing for innocence, but no more; they cannot be tapped for adult solutions.

Another childhood memory figures in Sandy's visit to his sister with Isobel, where the two women look at an old photograph of Sandy fighting during a Hebrew School play, because he resented Abraham's willingness to sacrifice Isaac. This image is related in a comic manner to Guido's recollections of his punitive Catholic upbringing. Both directors' recollections define sources of adult frustration and guilt. The austere Catholic atmosphere emphasizes fear and public humiliation. But Sandy's recollection is far more comic, far more in keeping with the sort of contrast between Jews and Gentiles that Allen drew earlier in *Annie Hall:* the undercranked Jewish scene is more frenetic, quarrelsome, and confused. Sandy fills his fast-motion scenes with people comically having a lively go at one another; there is a lot of body contact and little distance or austerity.

Neither the awesome quality of Catholic mysteries and the extreme repression and guilt associated with them nor the miraculous aesthetic equivalent to Catholic salvation that ends Fellini's film is evident in Allen's or Sandy's resolutions to their films. A magician leads Guido to a mystical recovery of childhood spontaneity, innocence, and artistic potency at the end of

8½; but magic in Sandy's film is treated less sentimentally, more comically. Sandy remains confused and cannot find transcendent solutions. While he may be a creative magician working in film, that experience carries no final satisfaction for his or the world's ills, and while he can manipulate time in art, that magic does not necessarily extend to life.

Both Guido and Sandy also seek relief through other fantasies. Guido seeks solace through a revenge fantasy near the end of *8½,* when he is forced to listen to a writer's pretentious intellectual advice. With a gesture, Guido lifts Carini, the critic, from his seat and happily hangs him. Sandy's film contains two revenge fantasies. When one of Sandy's fans makes pretentious comments about Sandy's films, he is nabbed from behind and removed forcibly from the frame by a hairy "hostility creature." That same hairy beast appears in an earlier fantasy resulting from Sandy's anger when he returns to his hotel room and finds a young female fan in his bed, prepared to "make it" with him. The film cuts to Sandy's old movies and a chase scene in the snow where a voice-over announces that Sidney Finkelstein's hostility has escaped. Mounties, a psychiatrist, Sidney (Sandy Bates), and a pack of dogs discover the bodies of Sidney's schoolteachers, his brother, his ex-wife, and her alimony lawyer, and finally we see Sidney's mother, about to be hurled to the ground by the hostility monster. Removal of the critic in *8½* may necessarily precede Guido's magical, nonintellectual reconciliation with figures from his past. The hostility sequences in Sandy's films also treat troublemakers comically, but while the revenge fantasies describe how a filmmaker may express his personal hostilities through his work, they help to explain only that Sandy's hostilities, even worked out in films, are not easily dismissed, and his endings may reflect this lack of resolution.

Stardust Memories also alludes to *8½* in Sandy's search for meaning in his relationships with women; his artistic problems are related to his romantic confusions. In *8½,* Guido is caught between two women, Luisa, his wife (Anouk Aimee), and Carla, his mistress (Sandra Milo). Guido's ideal and his escape from the conflict between his wife and his mistress is Claudia, the woman in white who may save his film; she is a symbol of order, sincerity, and innocence. She appears in a series of fantasies, often during the height of Guido's frustration, and she provides him with a momentary hope for escape from his artistic impotence and fragmented self-perception. In her seductive and nurturing way, she evokes in mature form the innocent childhood that Guido remembers when women loved and cared for him and when the world seemed complete.

In Guido's male chauvinist fantasies there is no insoluble conflict. In one such dream, for example, Guido pictures himself as an adult bathed and served as in his childhood by a harem including his wife, his mistress, and all the other women he has known. Similarly, after Luisa harasses him because she knows he is seeing Carla, Guido imagines a fairy-tale relationship between his wife and mistress in which they stop their competition and become close friends, both devoted to his needs.

Like Guido, Sandy is constantly distracted by his memories of love for an actress, in this case, Dorrie. Less idealized than Guido's redeeming Claudia, but still beautiful, Dorrie appears in a white slip to Sandy, much as Claudia once appeared to Guido, and Sandy's joyful memories of Dorrie, such as when Sandy chased a pigeon from his apartment, resemble the playfully innocent moments at the height of Alvy's romance with Annie Hall. Dorrie also once dabbled in photography, and so she reminds us of Tracy in *Manhattan*, as well as the early Annie.

But unlike Guido's Claudia, Isaac Davis's Tracy, or the early Annie Hall, Dorrie means trouble. She also resembles the later Annie, Isaac's Mary, and the daughters of Eve in *Interiors*, who suffer from insecurity and personality disorders. Her interest in photography is a passing fancy and she is into "graphics." Tony, Sandy's friend, describes Dorrie as being wonderful only two days of each month and a complete mess the other twenty-eight. She takes lithium, she has depressions, she is paranoid and jealous. Therefore, while Guido has recurrent pleasant memories of his lady in white, Sandy often remembers his Dorrie in a white hospital gown following her nervous breakdown. His longest recollection of her—during her stay in a sanitarium—represents a significant departure from Guido's vision of Claudia and the potential innocence she represents. Sandy's memory of the last time he saw Dorrie is depicted through a series of close shots of her in her sanitarium bed. He recalls her haunted face through unsettling jump cuts, repeated images accompanied by reiterated dialogue, in which she expresses her longing for Sandy but explains that she cannot stand closeness, in which she brags of her attractiveness but seems pathologically insecure. In a film that alludes to the robust style of 8½, this scene, which presents a disquieting drama of spiritual malaise and confused identities, intrudes to describe Sandy's painful reservations about idealism and romance.

Sandy's Isobel resembles Guido's wife, Luisa. Far less self-conscious than Dorrie, Isobel is a warm, natural French woman. Sandy calls Isobel and asks her to come to the Stardust Hotel, just as Guido called Luisa to join him in 8½. Isobel, like Luisa, is an attractive and steadying influence, but she has two demanding children and does facial exercises to keep her skin taut as she anticipates middle age. When she tells Sandy she has just left her husband, he becomes as unsettled as Alvy Singer was when Annie wanted to move into his apartment. Sandy reveals his doubts about a romantic life with Isobel as he escapes into memories of Dorrie, who is more exciting and unstable, and as he pursues Daisy, who reminds him of Dorrie. Thus, Sandy's strategies for avoiding commitment to Isobel are much like Guido's attempts to avoid Luisa. Claudia and Carla offer Guido fantasies of innocence and of forbidden experience—a chance to escape time and responsibility.

The third woman in Sandy's life, Daisy, offers a momentary escape from his memories of Dorrie and from his ambivalence about Isobel; but Daisy, like Dorrie, suffers from neuroses: she is obsessed about her weight, sees a psychiatrist, has commitment problems, and worries about an unresolved lesbian relationship. Although she is sexy and reminds Sandy of Dorrie's "haunted" quality, Sandy's prospects for salvation in a long-term affiliation with her are as shaky as the reference in her name and her occupation. Like Daisy in *The Great Gatsby*, she is associated with contemporary ennui, and she means as much trouble as the restless classical violinist played by Charlotte Rampling (Dorrie) in *Georgy Girl.*

So none of the women in Sandy's life provides the perfect relationship—the relationship that will recover the meaning, the intimacy, and the innocence that Allen's heroes always long for, and which for Guido was embodied in the elusive Claudia. Sandy's problem is especially obvious in a comic fantasy quite different from Guido's dream of Luisa and Carla's reconciliation. In Sandy's fantasy from one of his films, he plays a Frankensteinian doctor who tries to create the perfect woman from two different women who bear some characteristics of both Dorrie and Isobel, but once he has created the perfect woman, he only finds that he is attracted to the woman who now contains the worst characteristics of both patients. Like the opposing worlds, neither of which offered meaning to the heroes of earlier Allen films, and like almost everything else in *Stardust Memories*, Sandy's women together represent an unresolved, unresolvable dilemma. However, in this later film there is even less comfortable mediation than in the earlier Allen comedies. No woman in Sandy's life finally offers easy salvation.

In both *8½* and *Stardust Memories*, the directors' films also have a vague science-fiction, space-travel motif, which in both seems to provide another image of escape from their troubled worlds. In *8½*, Guido builds a huge scaffolding for a spaceship that is part of the original planned ending for his film, while in *Stardust Memories*, Dorrie first appears and meets Sandy on his set amid a structure that resembles Guido's scaffold. In *Stardust Memories*, the space theme, which suggests some parodic allusions to the popularity of George Lucas's and Steven Spielberg's special-effects films, is also exploited in a long sequence near the end of Sandy's movie.

Sandy and Daisy, having gone for a ride and run out of gas, find themselves in a field where a group of people are waiting for UFOs to land. This UFO segment of the film may well have been inspired by a humorous essay Allen originally wrote for the *New Yorker* and which he collected in his third book of writings,

Side Effects, published in the same year that *Stardust Memories* was released. The UFO sequence also makes several visual references to the last scene in *8½,* which provided a sign of unity after confusion and fragmentation. But although Sandy enjoys several moments of closeness with Daisy in the UFO scene, not even his close encounter with some visiting space creatures provides answers, and Sandy remains frustrated in his search for both personal meaning and social solutions.

The final sequences of both *8½* and *Stardust Memories* are perhaps most crucial in distinguishing Allen's effects from Fellini's. Guido's film, like Sandy's, has several possible endings. In *8½,* Guido goes to a press conference, is harassed by reporters, fans, and photographers, just as Sandy is in the Stardust Hotel sequence and in the later UFO scenes. In one ending, frustrated by the questions he cannot or does not want to answer, Guido crawls under a table to hide and then takes out a gun and shoots himself.

In a more positive alternative ending to *8½,* the one that actually concludes the film, Guido lives and is reconciled with the warring factions in his life. That final sequence returns to the beginning of the film with Guido in a line of cars, not in a tunnel, but moving across the open beach to the movie set and scaffolding. Guido is led there by the magician, Maurice, who seems to help the director reunite with his magic or imaginative talent and creativity that defies rational explanation. In the final scene, all the people who have been in Guido's film, in his fantasies, in his personal life, and in his childhood memories, descend from the scaffolding and dance around a circus ring in a ritual directed by Guido with a megaphone. Guido accepts his role as a director and joins the dance led by circus clowns who follow a boy in white, a figure assumed to be the young Guido. As Ted Perry writes: "The jail of self opens to a world of spatial horizons and human community. . . . What the viewer knows . . . is that . . . a filmic space which was formerly subject to internal implosions and external manipulations has now been given wholeness. . . . The epiphany is then an affirmation and celebration, however simple, of unity, of spontaneity, of freedom, of innocence. . . . The boy inside the man [Guido] has been freed and restored, not by design, deliberation or development, but by an act of grace."[9]

Several alternative endings to the original pessimistic one that began Sandy's film are also affirmative, yet different from Fellini's, and the final moments of Allen's film are far less unifying and optimistic. This lack of reconciliation leaves *Stardust Memories* standing, much more than *8½*, as a testimony to the difficulties of resolution, and to the problems that plague an artist trying to bring order to his life and aesthetic order to his film in postmodern circumstances. Like *Interiors, Stardust Memories* opposes a wholly pessimistic perspective with a more hopeful perspective, but then, ultimately, places even its apparent resolution within an inconclusive frame.

In one of Sandy's endings in *Stardust Memories*, Sandy is shot by a fan—a variation on Guido's suicide attempt in *8½*. Earlier, Sandy had told Dorrie in comic terms that suicide was not really a middle-class option. In his family his mother was too busy running chickens through a deflavoring machine to think about taking her life. With that, Sandy rejects suicide as a possibility. However, in this ending Sandy's death provides an opportunity for the director to ponder the meaning of life and death. When Sandy's spirit, appearing before fans at the Stardust Hotel again, is told that his work will live after him, he observes that he would trade an Oscar for "one more second of life." As in *Annie Hall*, life remains more important than art, and Sandy, like other little men before him, finds no salvation in artistic immortality.

Then, in the person of the "late great Sandy Bates," Sandy discusses his love affair with Dorrie and its unhappy ending, but he recalls that while he was on the operating table following the shooting, suddenly life became "very authentic," and as he sought something that would make life meaningful, a memory came to him. The camera cuts to Sandy sitting in his apartment with Dorrie on a fine spring day, listening to Louis Armstrong's record of "Stardust." Sandy's voice-over continues as the static camera, in a long slow take that contrasts with the frenetic pace of much of the rest of the fragmented film, catches Dorrie's face as she lies on the floor looking up at him. Sandy recalls how for a moment "everything seemed to come together perfectly." "It's funny," he says, "that . . . simple little moment of contact moved me in a very, very profound way."

In the audience, however, Sandy's fans have three different reactions: one yells that he's a "cop-out artist," one finds Sandy's moment of meaning "beautiful," and another asks, "Why do all comedians turn out to be sentimental bores." In Allen's film, unlike Fellini's, even when Sandy produces a captured moment of unity and a happy ending, the divided audience is part of that ending and provides a comment on the involvement of the spectator and his or her selective perception. The audience makes even that convincing moment of meaning a question, rather than a satisfying resolution.

From this dream sequence Sandy's film moves to another possible concluding scene. In the hospital his "murder" is explained away as a fainting spell and a hallucination. As he awakens, although Isobel is ministering to him, he calls for Dorrie, and Isobel leaves him. When Sandy tries to follow her, all his status as a celebrity does him no good, for in his car police discover a pistol for which he has no license. Once again, just as in *Take the Money and Run*, *Love and Death*, and *Annie Hall*, the little man finds himself in jail, a metaphor that implies a sense of entrapment that cannot suddenly be made to disappear as in *8½*.

In the next sequence—and in yet another possible ending—Isobel and her children are on their way to the railroad station with Sandy in pursuit. When he catches up to her, he tells her that he loves her and explains that the weekend's experiences have made him feel so different that he has a new idea for the conclusion of his film. "We're . . . on a train and . . . there are many sad people on it, you know? And I have no idea where it's headin'. . . . But it's not as terrible as I originally thought it was because . . . you know, we like each other . . . and . . . we have some laughs, and there's a lot of closeness, and the whole thing is a lot easier to take." Sandy explains that his new ending is "good sentimental" and that in his new ending Isobel loves him because she realizes that he's "not evil or anything, you know? Just sort of floundering around . . . just searching, okay?" To complete this version of the film's conclusion, the camera cuts to an exterior shot of the couple embracing through the window as the train pulls out, an echo of, as well as a response to, the opening train sequence, which was Sandy's original depressing finale.

While Sandy's revised endings—the recollected moments with Dorrie, the embrace with Isobel on the moving train that could be going anywhere—are meaningful, authentic moments in which salvation may remain at least a possibility, these endings are surely not the wholehearted reconciliation afforded by Guido's direction of his entire history around the circus ring. Sandy Bates's affirmative endings are more personal, more down-to-earth and less transcendental, than Guido's. Sandy does not join a circle. He is not reconciled with all of his past. He does not recover childhood innocence. He does not achieve an epiphany where the world comes together through the magic of the artist's aesthetic ordering. He cannot hope to satisfy everyone—not all of his audience, nor all of his friends, his colleagues, or his family. Instead, Sandy's endings, like Allen's idea of filmmaking, are smaller, but no less significant. Allen once told Gene Siskel, "Finally, through the course of searching his own soul, at the end of the film—this is what I had hoped to show—he [Sandy] came to the conclusion that there are just some moments in life—that's all you have in life are moments, not your artistic achievements, not your material goods, not your fame or your money—just some moments, maybe with another person, . . . those little moments that are wonderful."[10]

None of Sandy's endings is like Guido's grand spectacular triumph; there are only briefly caught moments surrounded by the knowledge that time still circumscribes our lives, that misery and death remain realities, that authenticity is constantly threatened by mutability. Although they are powerful, these captured, remembered moments seem more fragile and more tentative. They are related to, yet quite different from, Guido's transcendental and magical epiphany.

To complicate matters more, however, the last moments of *Stardust Memories* carry the art/life, dream/reality issue beyond even these interpretations. As Sandy's film appears to end with the alternative train sequence, the lights go on and we are again in the Stardust auditorium. The actresses who played Daisy and Isobel have dropped their roles. They discuss Sandy's tendency to clinch too long in love scenes; the actress who played Dorrie *does* worry about her weight. The fans, too, leave the theater with their varied reactions to what they have seen. The last of these is an elderly couple, who complain that they prefer an old-fashioned melodrama with a plot.

Finally, Sandy walks to the front of the empty theater and picks up his sunglasses, which, like Guido's, are icons of notoriety and a mask that preserves the director's mystery and identity. In Fellini's film, Guido's donning his sunglasses also typically signals that a fantasy sequence will follow. Sandy implies that he has been a member of the film's audience as well as its director and main character. He lingers before the now empty white screen that dominates the frame; and then, putting on the sunglasses so as to further confuse the fantasy from the "reality," he leaves the auditorium as the lights are gradually dimmed so that our screen fades to black.

These final moments of *Stardust Memories* are a poignant comment on the artist's relationship to his work and his world. They tell us that in this film there is no conclusive triumph of the artistic imagination over disorder; there is only the artist who continues, perhaps always futilely, trying to make some sense of things. The aesthetic satisfactions that Guido and Fellini celebrate in the unifying dance around the circus ring, and Sandy's smaller, captured moments, must both be set beside the single figure of the director who comes face-to-face only with himself and a two-dimensional white screen. In the filmmaker's last moments, he finds himself not joyfully at one with his world, but very much alone and still puzzled before the indeterminate blankness. The meaning of his acts, the authenticity of his work, and the significance of the images we have seen present more open-ended questions than in any of Allen's earlier efforts. The intersecting optimistic and pessimistic images we have observed are left as unresolved possibilities—as dialogues. One of Allen's least appreciated reflexive efforts is one of the best summations of his concern about the probability for attaining meaning in the face of contemporary fragmentation, alienation, and instability. As a mature artist, he confronts himself, his audiences, his critics, and his medium, and he deconstructs them all, even to the very last frames of his film.

Dulcy Ford (Julie Hagerty), Ariel Weymouth (Mia Farrow, partially hidden), Dr. Jordan Maxwell (Tony Roberts), Leopold (José Ferrer), Andrew Hobbes (Woody Allen), and Adrian Hobbes (Mary Steenburgen) make their way through the woods to a picnic in *A Midsummer Night's Sex Comedy. Courtesy of Woody Allen and Warner Bros.*

9

Recapturing Lost Moments

Woody Allen's *A Midsummer Night's Sex Comedy* (1982) suffered the misfortune of being released during the same summer as Steven Spielberg's special-effects blockbuster *E.T.* and the long-awaited film version of the Broadway musical spectacle *Annie*. In American theaters, Allen's small summer movie enjoyed a short unappreciated run; critics were less than lukewarm about Allen's painterly film. Some observed Allen's debt to Ingmar Bergman, but dismissed the film as "a crib job"; others, more perceptively, noticed that the film gave the impression "of someone speaking fluently but formally in a language not his own."[1] Most did not look closely enough at the film's intertextual, dialogic style to catch the many resonances that make this beautiful comedy one of Allen's most visually complex metafilmic experiments.

A Midsummer Night's Sex Comedy takes place during a two-day period shortly after the turn of the century. Leopold (José Ferrer), a renowned university professor, arrogantly extols civilization over primitivism, and scientific rationalism over the mysterious and unseen. He is about to be married to lovely Ariel Weymouth (Mia Farrow), a woman much younger than he, in a quiet weekend ceremony at the country home of Leopold's cousin Adrian Hobbes (Mary Steenburgen). Adrian is married to Andrew (Woody Allen), a stockbroker by trade and an inventor of whimsical gadgets by avocation. Andrew believes in more than meets the eye, and he builds machines to embody his faith. Joining these couples for the weekend are Andrew's best friend, play-boy Dr. Maxwell Jordan (Tony Roberts), and his hastily acquired lover, Nurse Dulcy Ford (Julie Hagerty).

The three couples play badminton, picnic, fish, and hunt for butterflies in the meadows and woods. They switch partners, they rendezvous and miss planned rendezvous in an expanded bedroom farce. Adrian and Andrew have sexual problems, and Andrew recognizes Ariel as a former girlfriend with whom he missed an earlier opportunity to make love and for whom he still carries a torch. Maxwell also comes to love Ariel; and Leo-pold, admitting to a surprising animal lust for Dulcy, asks her to make love with him in a last moment of sexual freedom on the night before his marriage. Partners change, relationships are threatened by betrayal, and for a time all is disorder. Jealousies between Adrian and Ariel, Maxwell, Andrew, and Leopold threaten to disrupt the pastoral mood; however, eventually much is resolved. Andrew discovers that he and Ariel cannot relive lost moments. Maxwell solves the Hobbeses' lovemaking problems when he tells Andrew of a brief affair he had with Ad-rian and thus relieves Adrian's guilt at the deception. Maxwell and Ariel's relationship shows promise when Leopold dies while in the throes of passion with Dulcy, but Andrew's invention, a "spirit ball," reveals that Leopold's essence lives on in a woods filled with lights of those people who were caught by time in similar ecstasies. Leopold becomes the proof that his own the-ories are too limited. Dulcy is independent, bright, and pretty enough to find other interests. Order is restored, and this appar-ently "classical" film ends as it began, with the triumphant strains of Mendelssohn's Wedding March.

Woody Allen sets his summer comedy in 1906, the year after Einstein published his first papers on relativity, the year that Cezanne died and some believe the modern age began in ear-nest. Initially, the film's leisurely pace and country setting suggest that the rapidity of contemporary life has not yet over-whelmed people: machines are still wonderful novelties rather than pollutants, invention is an individual, magical, creative act rather than a corporate enterprise. It is a time when motion pictures are being born and before they have become significant shapers of human personality, when still photography and impressionist painting are interrelated arts—both responses to an era of transition that stands between an innocent world and a more sophisticated world to come.

Although *A Midsummer Night's Sex Comedy* is, in Allen's own phrase, "hopefully funny"[2] and celebrates love over death on a narrative level, time and change menace the captured moment. Beneath its pastoral settings, romantic reunions, and magical solutions lies an additional story. Allen portrays a relatively stable world but threatens that world and his dominant classical/realistic discourse with intertextual comparisons and counterpoints. This film is not simply sentimental or nostalgic melodrama; it is yet another variation on Allen's favorite concerns. He captures our longing for stability and wholeness—for the satisfaction of desire and the validation of the artistic imagination that typify most illusionistic comedian comedy; however, his reflexive references, together with the film's surfaces, also convey life's limitations and the limitations of his medium. The result is an inconclusive text.

A Midsummer Night's Sex Comedy sets up an accessible dialogue on the narrative surface and an additional conversation or dialogue between surface narrative and intertextual allusions. Amid its comedy of errors, the film's narrative deals with our inability to recognize or grasp fleeting instances of opportunity that might alter history and free us from time as a determinate system, but it ultimately offers happy compromise in the realization that life as it turned out may be the best way after all. More important, it also offers a release from time, and a celebration of filmmaking—in the magical immortality finally granted Leopold through the lens of Andrew's spirit ball, or prototype projector. Interwoven into the narrative, for all its happy endings and inconsequential romances, however, are filmic quotations that heighten the issues that have been conveyed in small comedic contexts on the narrative level, and that amplify the issues to provide a reflexive subtext and a postmodern commentary on classical resolutions and unitary worldviews.

In *A Midsummer Night's Sex Comedy,* the references are most obviously to Shakespeare's *A Midsummer Night's Dream* and less obviously to Max Reinhardt's film version of Shakespeare's play (1935). Allen also refers to Ingmar Bergman's *Smiles of a Summer Night* (1955) and most prominently to the films of Jean Renoir, especially *Une Partie de campagne* (*A Day in the Country,* 1936), *La Regle du jeu* (*The Rules of the Game,* 1939), and *Le Dejeuner sur l'herbe* (*Picnic on the Grass,* 1960). Together, these references help to make the mixture of comedic overtones and disquieting undertones that produce *A Midsummer Night's Sex Comedy's* richest effects.

Max Reinhardt's film of *A Midsummer Night's Dream,* based on the director's earlier 1905 theatrical success with Shakespeare's play in Berlin, has obvious dramatic parallels with Allen's summer movie. Both films portray couples who fall in love with the wrong people; partners switch, but eventually harmony is recovered. Both works deal with contrasts between the unseen and the seen, the natural and civilized worlds. Allen probably took delight in Reinhardt's magical fairyland atmosphere, and in the film's gnomish comedy, and he played with these to achieve his own ends; thus, Andrew Hobbes's early comic attempts to fly with the help of parachute silk on his arms and a clumsy flying machine resemble Oberon's fairy band waving their gauzy wings. And Allen alludes to Reinhardt again with a whimsical series of animal shots that establish the pastoral atmosphere. Unlike Reinhardt's romantic forest, however, Allen's includes a lumbering tortoise and a skunk, and curiously also recalls a series of animal shots culled from the hunt sequence in Renoir's *Rules of the Game.*

While *A Midsummer Night's Sex Comedy* recalls the lighter fantastic sequences in Reinhardt's film, Reinhardt's 1935 production is also remembered for other reasons. Reinhardt made his movie while fascism was garnering power in prewar Europe, and Allen may also have been attracted by strange traces of German expressionism in Reinhardt's work—the frightening portrayal of a powerful Oberon, the occasional macabre faces among the fairy king's retinue, the hysterical quality in Puck's voice—all of which give Reinhardt's Shakespearean forest a sinister edge. Such moments, which may have signified a warning of times to come, create a tension with the imaginative comic surfaces, a tension not unrelated to the quality Allen's film produces primarily through filmic allusions that both complement and contrast with his dominant discourse or plot.

Ingmar Bergman's *Smiles of a Summer Night* is also related to *A Midsummer Night's Sex Comedy*, both in its story and in its themes. Like Reinhardt's film, Bergman's helps to underline Allen's comedy as well as his more serious interests. Bergman's main character, Frederick Egerman, is a cousin to Allen's Leopold, and like Leopold, he is treated both sympathetically and critically. Egerman is a stiff, middle-aged businessman—initially self-deceiving and self-important—who has difficulty committing himself to love with the right woman. By the film's end, he, like Leopold, has endured several humiliations, including the loss of his youthful wife to young Henrik Egerman. Eventually, he comes to appreciate the older, wiser actress Desiree, a more suitable companion. Like *A Midsummer Night's Sex Comedy*, Bergman's film deals with three sets of partners who jeopardize their relationships with clandestine affairs and betrayals before regularity reemerges at the film's conclusion.

Allen's film also shares with Bergman's a concern for innocence and experience—naturalness and sophistication, idealized love and compromise, as well as the related issues of change, time's tyranny, and death. *Smiles of a Summer Night*, like so many of Bergman's films, contrasts natural relationships between innocent characters who enjoy open sexuality, like Frid, the Groom, and Petra, the maid, with the convoluted relationships of the more sophisticated characters like Frederick and Henrik Egerman, the Malcolms, and Desiree Armfeldt. Similarly, Allen explores the contrast between Leopold's sophistication and his natural instincts. Leopold's rigid views and his university classroom settings are opposed to lively sexual play in the meadows and forests. In a brief comic allusion to Edenic innocence and the consequences of experience, Andrew shows Leopold, his rival for Ariel's affections, his apple-paring machine, providing a reflection on a similar scene in *Smiles of a Summer Night*, in which Count Malcolm carefully pares an apple as a challenge to his rival, Frederick Egerman.

Allen also borrows and adapts Bergman's Russian roulette scene in which Frederick's supposed death at the hands of his rival for Desiree and Charlotte Malcolm turns out to be a false alarm because Count Malcolm has used blanks in his gun. In *A Midsummer Night's Sex Comedy*, Maxwell Jordan apparently tries to kill himself with a pistol in Andrew's workshop, but just grazes his temple; later, he is actually hit, but again not fatally, by jealous Leopold's arrow. In Allen's film, as in Bergman's, the sudden disruptive awareness of death provides moments of enlightenment that lead to proper unions and reunions, but the near deaths also give both films an anxious edge that qualifies the comedy of the lovers' shenanigans and draws attention to closed systems and to our mortality.

Bergman's film includes repeated close shots of an intricately carved clock on which several moving figures, including a medieval representation of death, provide a further comment on life's transience. In this comedy of affairs between youth and age, Desiree also plays the guitar and sings "Freut euch des lebens, weil noch das lämpchen glüt," warning her companions "to enjoy life as long as their little lamps are still glowing." In Allen's film, Andrew is skeptical at first of Maxwell's suggestions that affairs are permissable because one must "seize life" since you "only live once." Maxwell advises Andrew to "gather ye rosebuds while ye may" and underlines his admonition with solemn images of the suffering and sudden death that he observes as a doctor in the hospital. Later Andrew laments not having grasped an earlier significant moment in his life when he and Ariel did not take advantage of their sexual attraction to each other to discover if they were in love.

While in Bergman's film Henrik and Frederick's young wife, Anne Egerman, do grasp the moment, make love, and run away together, and while Frederick himself has an opportunity to correct an earlier mistake of not committing himself to Desiree, in Allen's film the resolutions are handled more problematically.

Andrew attempts to relive that important lost opportunity with Ariel, but the couple find that they cannot recapture time and lost innocence. Their experience emphasizes the evanescence of such moments and the instability of experience and raises unanswered questions about whether it is best to seize opportunities and act while one can. Although order is restored in Allen's film—Andrew ends up happy again with Adrian and Ariel ends up with Maxwell—history in Allen's film cannot be altered. The characters and the audience are left with the sad understanding that important moments occur when we are most innocent and least self-conscious and that ironically such youthful moments cannot be relived once time has passed and we have gained enough sophistication to sense their importance. Ultimately, we come to realize that even the moments that Allen captures from earlier films can never be remade or perceived in precisely the manner in which they first appeared, but are themselves altered by time and sophisticated perception.

A Midsummer Night's Sex Comedy is also indebted to Jean Renoir's *Picnic on the Grass*, *A Day in the Country*, and *Rules of the Game*. Allen's film is an extension in his idiom of Renoir's concerns. And Leopold in *A Midsummer Night's Sex Comedy* is related to Professor Etienne Alexis in Renoir's *Picnic on the Grass*, which may be seen as an extended treatment of themes touched upon in the shorter *A Day In the Country*. Alexis, a scientist and politician, is to be married to a rigid, sophisticated woman. During a picnic, a Pan-like goatherd creates a magical wind that blows away carefully laid plans and sends Alexis into the arms of a sexy country woman, Nanette, who teaches him the joys of nature, spontaneity, and love. Although he loses Nanette for a time, just as Allen's Andrew loses Ariel, Alexis rediscovers her on his wedding day, and unlike Andrew and Ariel's unsatisfying attempts to recover their lost moments, Alexis marries Nanette rather than his intended.

Renoir's film suggests that even sophisticated people are still in part satyrs, and that their natural inclinations are only repressed in the face of modern obligations. He leaves room for a rediscovery of naturalness within the constraints of civilization.

Nanette and the goatherd with his strange panpipes imply that the magical and natural are ultimately supreme and that it is a mistake to accept entirely the limits of modern empiricism. As Andre Bazin writes: "It is as if Renoir, annoyed or frightened by the sinister character of technocratic society and its standardized notions of happiness, was seeking through the healthy, vigorous reproach of an almost farcical fantasy to restore a taste for the joys and charms of life. It is not surprising, then, that the veneer of entertainment should cover the most serious of purposes."[3] Allen's film may be, in part, a response to similar fears and hopes, but its dialogues make its conclusions far less ascertainable.

Renoir's earlier *A Day in the Country,* adapted from Guy de Maupassant's short story *A Country Excursion,* like Allen's film, is set in the early years of the century and deals with the problem of missed opportunities and time's passing. During a weekend trip to the country with her parents and future husband, Anatole, Henriette Dufours meets a local adventurer, Henri, who seduces her while her father and Anatole are fishing. At the end of the film, years have gone by, and Henriette, now married unhappily to Anatole, returns to the river banks and meets Henri for a few emotional moments before she returns to Anatole. Although Renoir's river has become only a brook in Allen's film, Renoir's movie, like Allen's, deals with the freedom associated with nature as opposed to the restrictions of sophisticated daily life, as well as with the changes that occur in the characters' lives with the passage of time. Bazin points out the issues that may have drawn Allen's attention to *A Day in the Country* when he notes that "in no other film has Renoir more openly presented ... the conflict between the Apollonian world and the Dionysian world, between the fixed framework of existence and the irresistible movement of life, between the theater set built once and for all and the changing, forever moving production which animates it; in short, between order and disorder."[4]

A Midsummer Night's Sex Comedy alludes to the style and themes of Renoir's films mimicking not only impressionistic techniques and compositions generally, but imitating specific

Renoir scenes. To underline their interests, both Allen and Renoir explore aesthetic conflicts that concerned the impressionist painters. Both Renoir and Allen develop the tensions between closed, balanced, or framed compositions and more open compositions, where much appears to be going on beyond the frame; however, as we remember his more specific interwoven references, even some of Allen's open frames appear more staged, more formal than Renoir's own painterly creations. In Allen's film we are seldom completely unaware of the camera or of the composer behind it. This quality is evident, for instance, in several shots where Allen's use of deep focus presents scenes imitated at such a distance that moving figures appear to form a vaguely familiar and almost static tableau. While the lighting and the ambience remind us of both Jean and Pierre-Auguste Renoir's impressionism and the deep focus alludes to one of Jean Renoir's favorite techniques, Allen and Gordon Willis's deep-focus compositions also create frames with a great deal of negative space rather than the variety of motion on several planes that is typical of Jean Renoir's depth-of-focus style. The effect is to remember, but to qualify or work variations on, Renoir's manner. Allen creates a sense of remembered images twice, rather than once, removed from impressionist paintings. Allen's film reminds us that we are seeing images of images of images, and that the original vision and beauty of Renoir's father's paintings, as well as of Renoir's own vision and films, are vulnerable to time and to increased self-consciousness. Like Renoir, however, Allen seems to comprehend and to exploit the threshold, or liminal, quality of impressionistic style.

From the perspective of the late twentieth century, accustomed to greater abstractionism, the impressionists may appear to be the last romantics. Impressionist paintings appear to be among the last portrayals of nature seen whole by artists who were still in harmony with it. At the same time, the impressionists' interest in empiricism and surfaces, in the captured moment, in the changes that even a short time and different light effects could have upon a subject, as well as their experimentation with a technique that dissected the image with short brush strokes, looks forward to a newer world—dynamic, transient, and far more fragmentary. Arnold Hauser notes that "the do- minion of the moment over permanence and continuity, the feeling that every phenomenon is a fleeting and never-to-be re- peated constellation, . . . a river into which 'one cannot step twice,' is the simplest formula to which impressionism can be reduced. Every impressionistic picture is the deposit of a mo- ment in the *perpetuum mobile* of existence, the representation of a precarious, unstable balance in the play of contending forces."[5]

A Midsummer Night's Sex Comedy's impressionistic style is, therefore, an integral reference to the evanescence of the mo- ment and to the transitional, threshold quality of the apparently innocent times Allen portrays as occurring on the brink of a more sophisticated era. It refers as well to his themes of the un- seen and the seen, the natural or innocent and the sophisticated, freedom and restriction. His choice of style is related to his con- cern with subjectivity, restlessness, and transience, and con- versely to his longing for captured moments, a romantic affirmation, and a sense of stability.

Allen links style, plot, theme, and self-conscious interest in his art, not only through the film's painterly quality and its allu- sions to older films, but through other self-reflexive images. Old- fashioned box cameras appear prominently in many sequences, and Andrew's spirit ball is a prototype of a moving picture pro- jector, a magic lantern with which he hopes to look into the past and future as well as capture the present. The emphasis on pho- tography and early filmmaking is appropriate to 1906, when photography and painting enjoyed a close relationship and filmmaking was in its infancy. The relationship between the two media underlines a moment in time when realism and roman- ticism, art and artifice, objective observation and subjective perception were not so much in conflict as they are today. The references to cameras, however, also defamiliarize the audience from the film and help to stress the transitional nature of the moment, which threatens at any time to divide man and nature, machine and art, subjectivity and objectivity, mimesis and fan- tasy into opposing camps.

Moreover, while the references to cameras, which attempt to capture moments, may be interpreted as a positive description of photography and filmmaking's role in the fight against time, at the same time (given the inability of the characters to recapture and relive important moments within Allen's own film, Allen's inability to revisit the precise moods of earlier films he alludes to, and the disagreements the characters in Allen's film have over whom or what the spirit ball is portraying) the references to apparatus become symptoms of the filmmaker's problems and his doubt. Such images may also emphasize his own comic absurdity—the artificiality and the limitations of his medium. The cameras, like Andrew's inventions, thus help to give the long captured moment that is *A Midsummer Night's Sex Comedy* its remarkable fragility and depth.

A Midsummer Night's Sex Comedy also makes some disturbing allusions to Jean Renoir's problematic comedy *Rules of the Game*. *Rules of the Game*, like *A Midsummer Night's Sex Comedy*, is a film about switching love partners during a weekend in the country. In *Rules of the Game*, the mix-ups occur during a hunting party at the home of Marquis Robert de La Chesnaye and his wife, Christine. Like *Sex Comedy*, it is a film that appears to be a classically arranged comedy of manners, but it has been interpreted as a precarious moment of farce before a storm, a film with comedic surfaces that is actually about self-deception and instability that prefigure a disordered world to come. The film was produced in 1939 as Hitler's Army overran Czechoslovakia, and when Renoir was asked, "Did you . . . discover later all those things in *La Regle du Jeu* which make one feel the approach of the war?" he replied, "I didn't tell myself, 'It's absolutely necessary to express this or that in this film because we are going to have war.' . . . My work was impregnated with it, despite myself."[6] Renoir also said that in *Rules of the Game* his desire was "to show a rich, complex society where—to use a historic phrase—we are dancing on a volcano."[7] According to David A. Cook, "*La Regle du Jeu* is ultimately concerned with social breakdown and cultural decadence at a particularly critical moment in European history."[8]

The little-man character in *A Midsummer Night's Sex Comedy*, who tries to fly, bears some resemblance to Andre Jurieu, who heroically pilots his plane across the Atlantic in only twenty-three hours because of his love for de La Chesnaye's wife, and whose sense of integrity and romantic vulnerability eventually lead to his pathetic death in a case of mistaken identity. But Andrew, played by Allen, also resembles Octave, the mediator between lovers, played by director Renoir; and Robert de La Chesnaye, who like Allen's little-man inventor, delights in music boxes and other clockwork toys. Allen also makes reference to Renoir when Maxwell looks through a telescope to observe Ariel and Andrew playing in a meadow and Leopold observes Maxwell through a spy glass stealing a kiss from Ariel. In *Rules of the Game*, Christine sees her husband through a telescope kissing his mistress and misinterprets their goodbye embrace for a clandestine moment of intimacy. Her interpretation leads Christine, a careless flirt much like Ariel in Allen's film, into her own set of betrayals, culminating in the death of the romantic flyer. In both films, such distanced observation involves subjective interpretation, which may lead to misinterpretations or multiple interpretations. In Allen's film, the interest in subjectivity refers self-referentially to how audiences respond to cinema, and it is also a symptom of modern uncertainty.

In *A Midsummer Night's Sex Comedy*, each of the characters interprets the images projected by the spirit ball differently. Leopold believes he sees Andrew and Ariel in the spirit ball's projections, so he goes out with blood in his eye and mistakenly hits Maxwell with an arrow meant for Andrew. The issues raised here have surfaced in Allen's films before: compare the audience's mixed reactions to Sandy Bates's *Stardust Memories*, Isaac Davis's questions about Mary's perception of her former husband in *Manhattan*, and Alvy's attack on the film critic's arrogant interpretations of Fellini in *Annie Hall*. It is enough to make us wary of monologic assumptions about reality or of imposing meanings—even as tentative as the ones this book develops—on Allen's films.

Although he continued to be concerned with single couples,

beginning with *Interiors* Allen also began to make films that concentrated on group interaction. In these films, his interest in several couples or an extended family may result from his desire to stress the interweave of social contexts in which human relationships exist and the universality of romantic entanglements, deceptions, and betrayals as they operate within a complex of associated characters, none of whom now represents the pure natural or innocent figure, whom Allen made the center of films like *Manhattan*. In *A Midsummer Night's Sex Comedy*, as in *Stardust Memories*, no single woman, such as Pearl in *Interiors* or Tracy in *Manhattan*, is an emblem of the innocence Allen's little man seeks. In *A Midsummer Night's Sex Comedy*, as in *Rules of the Game*, the characters are treated sympathetically, but even the most apparently innocent or potentially innocent turns out to be capable of betrayals and lies.

Andrew has a regular job as a Wall Street stockbroker, which permits him (like Allen as comic filmmaker?) to deal with people's investments "until there is nothing left." Nevertheless, he embodies some of the romantic hope that was embodied in little-man characters in the early comedies. Although he has sexual problems and his attempts to fly or soar above his world all land him in the brook (associated with passing time), he has faith in unseen worlds and his Rube Goldberg–like inventions testify to his very human fallibility, his creativity, and his perseverance. His inventions mediate between the empirical and unseen worlds, and he believes in love. His name also suggests the film's tensions. He may be named for Merry Andrew, the playful comic spirit and prankster, while his last name is Hobbes, perhaps a reference to rationalist philosopher Thomas Hobbes. Hobbes, whose view of human nature had a cynical edge, associated laughter with the desire for power and with moments of triumph in which we realize our superiority over others less fortunate and over ourselves in less fortunate moments. Hobbes believed in laughter as a didactic tool, but he also worried that such laughter of superiority, arising out of others' defects, might be morally damaging. Andrew represents a persistent, though blemished, hope in fantasy and magic, inventiveness and creativity, however clumsy or unsuccessful he may ultimately be. Blemished he is, however, for even in the earlier more innocent time of this film, Allen's characters lie and betray one another in a contemporary fashion. Although Andrew chooses to help Maxwell win Ariel early in the film, carrying her to the appointed rendezvous on his flying bicycle, he falls into the brook, as he will later fall from transcendent heights to ordinary human deception. He lies to his wife, Adrian, not once but many times, about his feelings for Ariel and about their meetings.

While Mia Farrow's Ariel looks like an adorable ingenue in innocent white lace dresses, appearances are deceptive. She is a woman of the world. At the time Andrew first met her, she had left a convent school to sleep with half the men in Europe. She is willing eventually to betray her fiancé to be with not just one man, but two men. Wide-eyed Dulcy Ford also talks in a whispery little voice, but she is a "new woman," an expert in sexual technique, and she carries contraceptives with her to weekend trysts as a matter of course. Secret meetings in the forest with older men are not new to her, and she easily agrees to betray Maxwell and Ariel for a quick last-night fling with Leopold, because he is "elegant."

Dr. Maxwell Jordan is a confessed playboy who does not initially believe in commitment and who sees marriage as "the death of hope." When he is drawn to Ariel because of "the way she smells," he betrays his best friend, his weekend date, and Leopold. He is not above sleeping with his best friend's wife. Leopold, who appears to be the most straitlaced and prudish of the lot, turns out to have a colorful sexual past, to love the taste of blood, to be capable of ripping a woman's clothes from her back in the heat of sudden passion, and to deceive his wife-to-be. Most tellingly, Adrian, Andrew's wife, seems to be an innocent character throughout most of the film. She appears to be befuddled by Andrew's apparent disloyalty, she seems to know nothing of premarital or extramarital sex, and she seeks counseling in how to make love; but she, too, it finally turns out, has lied by omission and has betrayed Andrew to sleep with Maxwell—an echo of the betrayal between closest friends in *Manhattan*.

Although these deceptions are treated lightly on the face of the film, in *A Midsummer Night's Sex Comedy* innocence is mixed with betrayals and sophisticated experience in such a way as to make the characters, for all their Victorian semblances, appear to be contemporary as well as turn-of-the-century. They are characters who are all involved in nervous romances, and they act out of familiar slippery contemporary mores and have contemporary problems trying to make up their minds whom to love. Although the couples eventually resolve their problems into what appears to be happily-ever-after relationships, as in *Rules of the Game*, the partner switching, betrayals, and temporary alliances look ahead to an era when intimacy and stability are harder to achieve and authentic lasting relationships are harder to find—a less reliable world is just around the corner of the big gray house where Andrew and Adrian live. It has already corrupted the pastoral moment, for we view that moment made by a filmmaker in our times from a contemporary perspective.

Like Renoir's film, Allen's presents a well-ordered set of games that conceals serious issues. In its allusions to Renoir, Allen's film looks ahead to our time when innocent and not-so-innocent lies and deceptions become the ordinary rules of life—the conventions of acquiescence and social survival—and where these symptoms of social instability and moral uncertainty may have profound psychological and political consequences. Indeed, Allen's film suggests that our dreams of an ideal and innocent past may have contained blemishes even from their inception.

Woody Allen may not envision a world war just beyond *A Midsummer Night's Sex Comedy*, but in this film, as in *Zelig* (made at the same time), the filmic references strike disquieting notes not unlike the vague threat that Renoir evoked in *Rules of the Game* and Max Reinhardt's *A Midsummer Night's Dream* anticipated in its more macabre moments. It is not coincidence, perhaps, that both directors expatriated to the United States in the face of Hitler's ascendancy to power in Germany. While Allen, like Renoir, shows compassion for his characters and moments of love between them as some indication of hope in a confusing world, *A Midsummer Night's Sex Comedy*'s references to *Rules of the Game* create anxiety beneath a farcical surface. Gavin Lambert has observed that Renoir's characters in *Rules of the Game* are "a party of lively, easygoing, unprincipled people. They are not vindictive or pathological; if not rich, they are still elegant and charming. Their 'sin' is something much less obviously abnormal. It consists of having no values at all, of always evading the important issues."[9] Like the characters in *Manhattan* who are blamed for a similar false or careless innocence, the figures in *A Midsummer Night's Sex Comedy* are typical of characters in Allen's films of the late seventies and eighties. The characters in Renoir's *Rules of the Game* are their ancestors, and they, in turn, are ours.

Allen's concentration on visual style and on making a beautiful film, the film's mixture of tones, and its subtler humor make *A Midsummer Night's Sex Comedy* characteristic of Allen's filmmaking in the eighties. The whole of *A Midsummer Night's Sex Comedy* is like Andrew's attempts to relive a past moment with Ariel. It is a captured moment that turns out to be less perfect than conventional memories of the Victorian American countryside tend to be. While the magic lantern projects Leopold's spirit immortal in the forest and suggests the triumph of filmmaking and the imagination, the film on a reflexive level is less conclusive. The filmmaker cannot reproduce the real or the filmic past with assurance; he tries to capture the innocent instant, but his world intrudes; he tries to deal in truths, but he is always the dealer in illusions. As in *Stardust Memories*, both the filmmaker who writes his film and the spectators who read it are victims of the Heisenbergian uncertainty principle; they change what is observed even as they observe and create. In view of the influences and intertexts with which the narrative converses, neither art nor the imagination offers salvation; the medium remains filled with possibilities or determinate; the narrative solutions remain wishes.

The film sits on the brink of modernism, looking backward toward innocence and authenticity and forward toward a sophisticated, fragmented world where personal integrity and a sense of place within the natural order are less available. Amid its comedic surfaces, its joy, its magic, its tender moments of connection, it also contains what Arnold Hauser, in discussing middle-class society of the late nineteenth and early twentieth centuries describes as "the marks of insecurity and the omens of dissolution."[10]

A Midsummer Night's Sex Comedy is an earnest comedy that has not yet come into its own. It is, like all of Allen's more recent films, a funny but profound exploration of ambiguities, a delicately balanced metafictional mixture of reality and artifice, belief and doubt. In its concern with lost time and lost innocence *A Midsummer Night's Sex Comedy* recollects the mood of *Annie Hall*'s and *Manhattan*'s endings and develops an elegiac tone Allen continues to explore in *Zelig, Broadway Danny Rose,* and *The Purple Rose of Cairo.*

Chameleon man Leonard Zelig (Woody Allen) is almost indistinguishable from Calvin Coolidge and Herbert Hoover as he stands between them in *Zelig*. *Courtesy of Woody Allen and Warner Bros.*

10

The Little Man
Becomes a Legend

Zelig (1983), among the best-received of Allen's movies after *Annie Hall*, has been widely celebrated for its humor and its charm. Characteristically for the post–*Annie Hall* productions, however, *Zelig* also displays a saddened mood that at once interacts with and subverts the film's comic surface to produce an inconclusive and dialogic text. Like several of Allen's other films, it deals with an awakening little man and includes hopeful captured moments of human connection; however, the happy cure for the little man's problems does not necessarily forecast as certain a resolution for the world beyond the darkened theater and the film experience. The little man in *Zelig* remains involved in questions that are central to all of Allen's films—whether identity and personal integrity can survive oppressively dehumanizing and exploitative social circumstances; whether it is possible to find an authentic self in a world where illusion and reality are confused and where truth always appears to be unreliable and self-contradictory. *Zelig* also involves a reflexive dialogue regarding the nature and validity of its own language and medium.

Zelig is a pseudodocumentary that attempts to explain the story of Leonard Zelig, a fictitious historical figure portrayed as a strange phenomenon of the 1920s and 1930s. Allen said that he wanted to use the documentary form because "One doesn't want to see this character's private life; one's more interested in the phenomenon and how it relates to culture. Otherwise it would just be the pathetic story of a neurotic."[1] Clearly an American "product" whose story is presented as part of Jazz Age mythology, Zelig is a sensation akin to flagpole sitters, an innocent version of the "great imposter," a nonautonomous chameleon-man. His desperate need to be liked not only makes him change his point of view to fit his surroundings but makes him change physically. In the presence of baseball players, he becomes one; among criminals, he is a criminal. Among Negroes he becomes black, among Indians, Indian; and among fat people he weighs two hundred pounds. Zelig is reptilian, a lizard, in the sense that his malady is like a reptile's skin, a protective coloring or shield against the pain of disapproval and rejection.

Zelig becomes a case study for Manhattan Hospital's doctors, who cannot agree on a diagnosis and who argue about how to treat him. Their solutions are impersonal and ignore his particular human needs. The film emphasizes the exploitation of the little man not only by indifferent doctors, but also by his greedy sister and her husband, Martin Geist (German and Yiddish for *ghost*), by advertisers, by Hollywood, and by the sensation-consuming public. Only Dr. Eudora Fletcher (Mia Farrow), a psychiatrist, believes that Leonard Zelig's problems are psychological and cares personally for her patient. Initially, even her motives are questionable: she has professional ambitions and hopes to make history caring for Zelig's special "disease." Gradually, however, and despite several setbacks, Eudora comes to love Zelig, cures him, and marries him. In the process she manages to give something of herself to him, and as he imitates her love, he eventually grows strong enough to gain an independent identity.

It is easy for the audience to identify with Leonard Zelig. In this film, as in *Broadway Danny Rose* (1984) and *The Purple Rose of Cairo* (1985), which follow it, the little man (or woman) seems to be more closely related to the relatively innocent and unselfconscious character of Allen's early comedies, rather than the more self-conscious little men of *Manhattan* or *Stardust Memories*. Like Allen's earliest characters, Leonard Zelig invites our empathy and identification because he is so childlike, so unfulfilled in his desire for love and security. Indeed, his sickness, the way in which he *becomes* others to fulfill his needs, metaphorically suggests a comic version of the empathic dream-state relationships frequently experienced between the spectator and filmic illusions in classical cinema. The little man in this film is also *zelig*—"blessed" or "lucky"[2]—in the sense that despite deadening odds he actually makes a human connection and affirms a human identity. As in classical romantic comedy, he marries. Therefore, his narrative satisfies the audience's immediate empathic needs because they identify with his unfulfilled desires (expressed in countercultural behavior) and because their sense of community and traditional values are eventually satisfied through his recovery and assimilation into the dominant culture.

In *Zelig*, however, the little man, for all his innocence and lack of sophistication, is more inconsistent than a traditional illusionistic hero; he has moments of corruption that subvert the spectator's expectations and interrupt empathic connections. When, for instance, Zelig kicks his golf ball into the cup, reminding us of Jordan Baker in *The Great Gatsby*, he appears to indicate, like characters in more recent Allen films, that even he, the outsider, is compromised by the dominant culture's moral laxity. Zelig's story is also told through a myriad of defamiliarizing reflexive frames and is cast in an elegiac tone; while we take pleasure in Leonard Zelig's cure, we may also experience acutely the ironies in its portrayal.

In her review of *Zelig*, Pauline Kael astutely observed that the film's main character appeared to be a fading image.[3] Much of the film's poignancy and Chaplinesque quality derive from the little man's presentation as a memory or legend. The little man's story embodies the spectator's search for renewal—the recapturing of a dream of childhood's spontaneity, innocent enjoyments, a unified sense of self—at the same time that it involves a pattern of awakening the spectator from a passive acceptance of that story and the unconditional hope it appears to embody. As portions of *Zelig's* style and structure are defamiliarizing and run counter to the film's own narrative, exposing its fictionality, it invites spectators to question their relationship to all films, both illusionistic and nonillusionistic, and to the corresponding social codes films reflect. As a result, even as we become aware of the fiction and the medium in which *Zelig's* "successful" narrative is told, *Zelig's* image seems in danger of being lost forever, a memory perhaps, not of real human potential but of images of human potential that we once believed attainable in a more naive age. We recognize that the image passes through our dreams in the flickering lights and shadows of a movie made of old movies retrieved from the flux of time. More than in Allen's earlier films, we sense the relentless movement of time, the burden of history, the transience of experience, the possible futility of the quest for authenticity, and the loss of innocence that are central to his films in the 1980s.

To achieve this duality, Allen continues in *Zelig* to experiment with, and to extend his use of, reflexive devices. As early as the *Clockwork Orange* allusions in *Sleeper* and the later allusions to *8½* in *Stardust Memories*, Allen experimented with intertextual references to films that were themselves well known for their self-consciousness and reflexive resonances. Such references not only defined his particular concerns by paralleling them, but were doubly defamiliarizing inasmuch as they were themselves works that elicited anti-illusionistic responses, thereby demanding greater critical distance or awareness from the spectator and making reality still more difficult to distinguish from fiction. In *Zelig*, Allen's references to Orson Welles's *Citizen Kane* (1941) and Chris Marker's *La Jetée* (1962) are two of the most important intertextual keys to understanding the film's techniques and best dialogic effects.

References to *Citizen Kane* are more obvious than those to *La Jetée*, for among the film clips that make up Zelig's tale, Allen scatters references to San Simeon, to William Randolph Hearst, and to Marion Davies, who inspired Kane's story. Through the interplay of realistic, pseudorealistic, and expressionistic techniques, *Zelig*, Like Welles's film, comments reflexively on the nature of its own medium, on time, and on memory. Using newsreels, interviews, intersecting times, and contradictory personal perspectives, both films question whether truth is ascertainable through any means. Kane is never knowable because his story is a package of opposing images (some of them doctored or falsified as in *Zelig*) told through the prism of several narrators. But Kane never physically changes or is changed by movie special-effects trickery. This insubstantiality and inauthenticity is in Allen's film driven to its comic (yet perhaps more ominous) extreme, so that Zelig's physical transformation is a reminder that the issues that pervaded Welles's film still persist—that, in fact, they have been exacerbated rather than resolved in the forty-plus years that separate the two works.

Also like *Citizen Kane*, *Zelig* explains the roots of its protagonist's malady in psychological terms that have broad implications. Like Charles Foster Kane's childhood, Leonard Zelig's is unromantic; unlike Kane's, but like Alvy Singer's or Sandy Bates's, it is urban, Jewish, and funny—Leonard is the son of Morris Zelig, "about whom little is known, but whose role as Puck in the orthodox version of *A Midsummer Night's Dream* was coolly received," (a comically defamiliarizing reference to the critical reception of Allen's own *A Midsummer Night's Sex Comedy*). Leonard's parents took the part of his anti-Semitic tormenters, and his father's deathbed legacy to his son was the reminder that life is "a meaningless nightmare of suffering," and that he should save string. Allen parodies the rejection and arrested development that helped to fashion Kane's pathological need for approval and longing for love unsatisfied in childhood. Even in parody, however, Allen's film expresses the same concern as Welles's for the burden that personal history and the loss of innocence place on the individual's quest for a satisfying identity. The fact that Leonard Zelig survives his father's pessimistic view of the world is, on one level, encouraging.

There are, of course, political, social, and economic givens that both *Citizen Kane* and *Zelig* work into their dialogic deconstructions. For instance, although neither is primarily a political film, both use as a premise the naïveté of the public and the contradictions in special-interest groups. As Charles Foster Kane exploits and is exploited by his involvement in the media and the political and social currents that surround him, as though he were a kind of cipher for fanatics at both ends of the political spectrum, so Leonard Zelig is regarded as unfair to labor because he can hold down five jobs and is at once "a triple threat to the Ku Klux Klan" because he is a Jew who can transform himself into an Indian or a black.

Like *Citizen Kane*, *Zelig* is also a self-conscious investigation of the legitimacy of the media, of the validity of public taste, and of the liabilities of being a celebrity. In *Citizen Kane*, we witness Kane's rapid rise to power and prominence. We see the outcome in his later years, when he is pictured as a captive of his own earlier longing for love and public approval. Similarly, Leonard Zelig falls prey to his need for love and is exploited more directly by society, by self-important doctors, advertising hype, exploitation by hucksters, and his sister's economic ambitions. Like Charles Foster Kane secluded and confined in a wheelchair behind the high fences of Xanadu, Leonard Zelig is confined in police wagons and straitjackets, hidden within the imprisoning walls of hospitals. His sister removes him from those walls only to exhibit him within a fenced enclosure (much as we, the public, see Kane behind his) as a freak.

Both men are victimized by a cold and fickle society. Just as Thatcher's coldhearted rearing of Kane placed economic priorities ahead of human understanding, so the Manhattan Hospital doctors' ruthless treatment of the patient's condition suggests the dangers inherent in positivist or scientific, solutions to human problems and in the substitution of intellectual power for that longed-for emotional fulfillment, which seems so impossible to attain. *Zelig* thus leads us to question not only the illusions that manipulate and trap us but the misapplied scientific remedies of society—even in deconstructive films resembling *Zelig*. Intellectual self-awareness can be as self-defeating as passive empathy or escape, inasmuch as self-consciousness can destroy not only false illusions, but our ability to dream better dreams and to trust in useful empathy and authentic human connection. Therefore, *Zelig* is not totally pessimistic: it may also appear to hold out hope for a perspective that "would transcend the sterile dichotomy of realism and modernism alike."[4] When Saul Bellow observes in the film that Zelig's insanity—his illness, in effect—drew attention to and produced its own cure, he is saying that Zelig's ability to transform himself gave him the very identity he lacked—even if that identity was a spurious one. Therefore, even while making a self-conscious film that deconstructs itself as a means of criticizing transparent cinematic ideals, *Zelig* maintains a dialogue with traditional ideals that realistic-illusionistic cinema creates and sustains. Like Dr. Fletcher's more personal approach seen beside the extremes of the other doctors' depersonalized and contradictory diagnoses, Allen's film itself mediates between extremes in both its form and its style; and while maintaining its skepticism and inconclusiveness, it also takes a humane point of view.

There is a technical kind of deconstruction, too. Like *Citizen Kane*, but to a far greater extent, *Zelig* self-consciously destroys the chronology and the dogmatic single perspective of traditional dominant narrative film—with a rich intersection of times, narrators, and points of view. *Citizen Kane* made film history by presenting Kane's story as an overlapping series of retrospective interpretations of his life, representing contradictory perspectives. These narratives are in turn interrupted by doctored newsreel footage, which alludes to real-life historical events and persons. It is finally possible to follow the film's narrative line, yet ultimately *Citizen Kane* misleads, much as Gothic or detective films do, by developing a deceiving line of inquiry that promises eventually to explicate the life of a man whose life was, after all, finally perhaps unknowable, either to an observer or to himself. These intersecting perspectives, which depict Kane at different ages, are themselves presented from the dual perspectives of youth and age; therefore, they produce what William Johnson sees as the portrayal of "the struggle between tradition and progress, old and new, order and disorder," a "stereoscopical . . . fusing together" that creates "a poignant vision of Kane's loss" that gives an "almost tangible presence to the passing of time."[5]

Allens' *Zelig* not only incorporates, but exaggerates, Welles's techniques with an outrageous pastiche drawn from history, literature, old film clips, imitations of traditional film genres and conventions, interviews, and interpretations. While *Citizen Kane* includes a number of variations in viewpoints and several shifts in time frames, *Zelig* includes even more variations. In the film's "present tense," we see the primary frame for the narrative—the pseudodocumentary within which everything else in the film is conveyed. In including a voice-over narrator for the primary documentary frame, Allen spoofs the disembodied voice that many such documentaries incorporate to provide an apparently objective, single-perspective presentation of a history that is actually pluralistic, selective, antihistorical, indeterminate, and— in this case, ironically—fictional.

Within the pseudodocumentary frame, color usually signifies present tense (following the technique of Alain Resnais's *Night and Fog* [1955]), while the historical compilation in past tense is marked by black-and-white cinematography on grainy, aged film stock. In present tense we hear Zelig's history from an aging Eudora Fletcher, her middle-aged sister, and her cousin, all of whom were immediately involved in Zelig's story. We also hear from eyewitnesses who observed, in less intimate circumstances, Zelig and the culture in which he lived: Bricktop, owner of a French nightclub in the 1920s who comments on Zelig's (and Allen's?) popularity in France; a former waiter at a Chicago speakeasy, a former SS officer, and two reporters (who add to the confusion as they confess that while they customarily exaggerated the truth to attract readers, no such exaggeration was necessary in Zelig's case). All present testimony to substantiate portions of Zelig's story, in a cinema-verité fashion such as Allen first exploited and parodied in *Take the Money and Run*.

In addition, the present-tense portion of the frame documentary also includes a variety of interpretations of Zelig's cultural and aesthetic significance. As in *Stardust Memories*, but here more neutrally, Allen anticipates critical interpretations of his film. Allen has luminaries such as Saul Bellow, Susan Sontag, Irving Howe, Bruno Bettelheim, and John Morton Bloom appear on screen to interpret Zelig's significance throughout the documentary capsule. While each personage defines Zelig's significance from his or her particular social/historical/psychoanalytical/literary/aesthetic perspective, making the commentary appear real, we are also defamiliarized from the film by the knowledge that these are real-life people playing themselves and pretending to interpret an imaginary character within a fictional context—and all on the problem of identity. These figures may have legitimate insights to explain the Zelig phenomenon; yet together, their insights, not unlike the pluralistic testimony in *Citizen Kane*, testify only to the subjectivity and unreliability of intellectual formulations about history, culture, and art. Even like this present book, these attempts to offer an explanation are part of the problem.

To further enrich the dialogic process, within the primary documentary frame exist additional past-tense frames. The primary documentary includes past-tense eyewitnesses who participated either directly or indirectly in Zelig's life and times, ranging from men on the street who merely wanted to be like Zelig, to individuals like Eudora Fletcher's mother, who destroys conventional success myths as she is interviewed about her famous daughter's attempts to cure Zelig. Such juxtapositions further undermine the lines that distinguish history and fact from fiction, particularly as they show the contrast between the general public's view of celebrity and the behind-the-scenes reality. These views are reinforced by additional "historical" data within the past-tense frames of the present-tense documentary: Movietone, Pathe, and Nazi-German newsreels, each with their own voice-over narrators, eyewitness testimony, clips of Zelig's life; headlines and newspaper reports about Zelig; brief images of Zelig's hospital records; shots of families listening intently, as though to fireside chats, for news of Zelig's exploits on the radio; and actual film clips from the 1920s and 1930s that show literary figures such as F. Scott Fitzgerald writing about Zelig in yet another frame device—his diary.

In addition, the primary frame includes within its past-tense frames a series of clips doctored to include Zelig playing among Hollywood celebrities, whose lives are not so unlike Zelig's own, or Zelig changing into his various personalities. Because these clips are doctored, such bits of documentation, which would ordinarily make Zelig's story more realistic and credible, serve in a defamiliarizing manner to remind us that manipulation of truth in visual media today has become far more sophisticated. Computer-aided digital remaking of photographs, for instance, makes visual representation dangerously and comically unreliable.[6]

These clips of Hollywood social affairs that include Zelig and Eudora break down the separation between reality and fiction further as they add to our sense of Zelig's story as part of a larger myth and commentary upon our culture. Reference is also made to Charles Lindbergh, Clara Bow, Charlie Chaplin, Marion Davies, Fanny Brice—all celebrities whose success was qualified by tragedy and betrayal. Each presents us with a case of potential innocence victimized by a fickle public and by the publicity that accompanies fame. Zelig's personal history involves a betrayal by family and public such as Jean Harlow suffered and paternity suits such as those brought against Chaplin at the height of his popularity.

Zelig's life is also a collage of references to the literature of the lost generation. Zelig's sister's death involves a love triangle, and her betrayal of Martin Geist for a bullfighter reminds us of Hemingway's tale of post–World War I disillusionment, *The Sun Also Rises*. Likewise, the appearance of F. Scott Fitzgerald; the brief allusion to the lack of personal integrity of Jordan Baker, a character in Fitgerald's novel; innocent Zelig's own betrayal by the public and his family, those closest to him—these all echo the campy but real tragedy in *The Great Gatsby*, which appears to be a frequently cited reference for Allen's sense of the world. Such literary allusions underline the film's larger issues still further—they draw attention to the role-playing that is required by public figures, the exploitation and betrayal of talent, the film's nature as fictional, intertextual, pluralistic dialogue, the transient quality of life, and ultimately, the sense of waste or lost innocence with which (in part) the film leaves us.

There is even a final fillip of reflexivity in the inclusion within the primary present-tense frame of an even more obvious past-tense allusion to cinema itself—"The Changing Man," supposedly a slick Hollywood film of Zelig's story within his own. Moreover, the white-room sessions involving a too-obviously hidden camera and other apparatus to help create psychiatric history further blur the distinctions between illusion and life and question the authenticity of both illusionistic and so-called anti-illusionistic film.

Yet despite all of *Zelig's* warnings about the dangers in an uncritical, passive spectatorship, Allen also injects moments that appear to briefly transcend his own medium—moving moments captured on film that speak more hopefully about the possibilities for a survival of innocence and for the existence of a love born out of genuine human connection rather than false dreams. To understand how such moments take on their effects and their complex role within the anti-illusionistic frames, it is necessary to look at the importance of several allusions Allen makes in *Zelig* to Chris Marker's reflexive film about film, memory, war, and love, *La Jetée*.

Marker's *La Jetée*, is a kinestatic fiction made almost entirely of still photographs that are edited to make the images appear to be progressing or moving. It is the story of a man whom we see at the film's onset on a *jetée*, or pier, at Paris's Orly airfield as a child and whose preoccupation with the passing scene is interrupted by sudden violence. The accompanying voice-over tells us that the Orly scene is a pre–World War III memory. A nuclear holocaust destroys the world as the child knew it, and we find him next as an adult in a series of underground caves resembling concentration camps, where some experimenters have established an oppressive leadership over survivors. These doctors are attempting to find a way to escape their predicament—to sustain life despite the aftermath of the holocaust—by using prisoners' memories to find a way into the future where other generations may provide help. Because of a vivid memory he retains of a woman's face from the scene on the jetée at Orly, he is selected to undergo a series of memory experiments that will send him first back to the past and then, it is hoped, forward to the future and the solution the scientists seek.

Constrained, masked, and injected with chemicals, the man manages to reach the past and to establish a special relationship with the woman he remembers. The backward journey is depicted through static images, except for one moment of "transfigurative" movement in which he sees the woman's eyes move. Bruce Kawin suggests that "the hero's love has allowed him to enter the being of the beloved or of love itself, to escape analysis for intuition, *perhaps* to transcend the system. But it is only a perhaps because this remains a film, and the movement is simply the more rapid succession of stills. Marker gives us and the characters the impressions of a romantic apotheosis—however understated, which is, of course, why it is so powerful—without actually letting anyone out of the Medusan trap."[7] Therefore, even that moment of respite from stasis can remain only a moment.

The hero eventually manages to reach the future and to bring back what the doctors want. But when the people of the future invite him to join them, he declines in favor of a return to the past and to the woman of his memories. Thus, in the film's last sequence the man finds himself again on the jetée at Orly where he sees the woman and moves toward her. Then he witnesses again the violence that began his tale—it is his own murder at the hands of the doctors, who have followed him into the past. The narrator sums up the film with the observation that "one cannot escape time." Kawin believes that this might be rephrased to read "One cannot escape from film."

It is not just the image track that arrests him, but the whole medium of sound film, which is itself a symbol for the activity of consciousness and narration as well as for the nature of time. This is not just a reflexive paradox in which a character in an artwork finds himself unable to escape from the laws and nature of the medium; it is that, of course, but . . . it is also an essay on the limits of mortal consciousness and on the relations between pol-itics and transcendence, an essay on the nature of the romantic temperament in a world that seems always to be on the verge of war. It is about the attempt of the loving consciousness to reclaim the sane world of happiness and commitment in the face of . . . controlling and destructive forces.[8]

Kawin's words are appropriate for most of Allen's later films, but especially for *Zelig*. In fact, *Zelig*, which surely presents a far lighter, comic facade than *La Jetée*, also contains a particularly arresting series of static photographs resembling Marker's. These surface most obviously during the part of the film where Zelig is being interrogated and examined by doctors and where Eudora Fletcher first attempts to hypnotize him. The allusion to *La Jetée* is even more explicit in a brief scene in the hospital, where a doctor accompanying Eudora appears to be wearing complicated optical apparatus similar to that worn by the om-inous voyeurs of memory who experiment on the man in Mark-er's film.

But *Zelig*'s narrative is not dominated by Marker's technique. Allen supplements Marker's many still photos with film clips from old silents where movement appears speeded up, frenetic, and artificial. Combined with the static quality of the stills, such a sense of motion further draws our attention to the medium we are viewing and to its dialogic apparatus. After Eudora Fletch-er's love begins to cure Zelig, however, these particular tech-niques diminish: there are fewer haunted images of Zelig alone in the still frame or captured in deep-focus shots while unrelat-ed activity goes on between him and the camera. Similarly, the frenetic quality of anonymous crowds and traffic passing over the screen gives way to more frequent two-shots of Zelig and Eudora—intimate, human scenes in which neither stasis nor fre-netic movement dominates. Such scenes parallel other captured moments of human communication throughout Allen's films.

In contrast to those more mechanical images in which we are

clearly aware of the camera, the images of Eudora and Zelig in love seem ad-libbed—spontaneous rather than contrived, playful rather than self-conscious. Even where the camera is evident and the two play to it, the images have the amateurish, innocent home-movie air of the film's last sequence. Among the most memorable of these moments is a car-washing scene, where Eudora helps Zelig (who is learning to be himself by reexperiencing the developmental stages of childhood in a more supportive atmosphere than he previously knew) aim his "hose" in a proper way. Similarly, a scene in which Zelig pins a brooch (with the price tag still attached) on Eudora's coat, a scene in which he sits alone with her on a bench in the garden of her country house, and a scene in which he tries to dance without inhibition are all moments that appear genuine, funny, human—"good sentimental" occasions. These moments contain their own dialogues and conditions, yet in the weight of emphasis, they contrast with both the streamlined pseudo–love scenes of the Hollywood version of Zelig's life and the more defamiliarizing images, the stasis or frenetically artificial quality of the rest of the self-conscious documentary that circumscribes them.

Near the film's climax, after Zelig's original recovery is followed by a relapse and subsequent disappearance, we get the impression, too, that Allen's little man, caught within the static conventions and imitative roles he had adopted once more, slowly awakens, moves, and lives again. Dr. Eudora Fletcher, who has grown to love him, and who has searched the world to find him, comes upon him at a Nazi rally. Zelig, in his zeal for acceptance, has become a Nazi officer and has a place on the platform where Hitler is giving a speech. Fletcher tries to gain Zelig's attention across the mesmerized spectators and over Hitler's ravings. In a series of crosscuts between Fletcher and Zelig, we watch Zelig's gradual recognition of his mentor and his increasing animation as he remembers and imitates her. Like the woman in *La Jetée*, he appears to awaken from his motionless acquiescence; he waves excitedly and jumps up and down behind Hitler to create a disruption amid the fascists, who represent the epitome of closed systems and suggest the protofascist nature of passive audiences drugged by their false illusions.

As Saul Bellow says in one of the contemporary interviews in the film: "But then it really made sense. It made all the sense in the world, because although he wanted to be loved, he craved to be loved, there was also something in him that desired immersion in the mass and anonymity, and fascism offered Zelig that kind of opportunity so that he could make something anonymous of himself by belonging to this vast movement." But as the little man awakens and is reminded of the empathy and love he shared with Eudora, he destroys the deadening stasis and sameness and causes havoc for the fascists. In this, he reminds us of the spontaneity and disorder that playful little men of Allen's earlier comedies created among military formations, within geometric gardens, and in well-organized parades.

In both an aesthetic and a political sense, those moments make us respond, much as did the temporary moment of movement amid stasis in Marker's *La Jetée*. Such moments represent a brief recovery of innocence, a celebration of individual intuition over closed social, political, and philosophical systems, and over positivist analysis. They represent a cry of aesthetic rebellion and an insistence on freedom in the face of the overwhelming dehumanizing pressures that life seems to present to us.

Yet even that strong cry is conditional, since Zelig's entire narrative is fictional and unreliable. Moreover, the last images of Zelig and his bride, even as (and because) they are portrayed in the amateurish and artless manner of old-fashioned flickering, grainy black-and-white home movies, are fading figures, receding memories. Our sense of the ephemeral nature of such "authentic" humanity is accentuated by the unedited long take and the deep-focus composition in which Zelig and his bride gradually move deeper into the background of the frame, before they hug and kiss and then slowly disappear behind the house. The camera lingers over the empty scene much as the camera lingered over the empty restaurant near the end of *Annie Hall*, after Alvy and Annie had already left the screen. At the same time that we witness one of the film's most poignant images of connection, we have a strong sense that despite the conventional "crawler" that ends *Zelig* and describes the couple's future beyond the film, we may have lost something—that Zelig's image—perhaps only the memory of an image—is fading in the course of time and within the constraints of its articulation. Like receding images of Chaplin's little tramp moving down a long road, the last image we have of Zelig is inconclusive. He both escapes and remains caught within the film, half fiction, half real, a memory, a legend. The hope for a cure remains only a "perhaps."

Robert Stam notes that the "challenge" for reflexive films today "is to crystallize and actualize utopian hopes even while exposing their degraded expression. . . . The most successful reflexive texts conserve both diegesis and identification, but undermine them from within. . . . Unafraid of pleasure, the thrust of their interrupted spectacle is fundamentally comic, not in the sense of provoking hilarity, but in the sense of maintaining a socialized distance between the desiring subject and the text. They articulate the play of desire and the pleasure principle *and* the obstacles to their realization."[9] *Zelig* expresses our dreams of desire and deconstructs them. In refusing to lead us back into empty optimism while depicting the value of authentic feeling, Allen's film moves us both intellectually and affectively: *Zelig* is one of Allen's most explicit warnings about fascism and one of his most complex and successful inquiries into the comedy and tragedy of the human condition.

Woody Allen performs a demanding role as "living legend" Broadway Danny Rose. *Courtesy of Woody Allen and Orion Pictures.*

11

Allen's Rose Period

Following Woody Allen's own manner, it may be appropriate both in a serious and in an ironic fashion to deal with *Broadway Danny Rose* (1984) and *The Purple Rose of Cairo* (1985) as representatives of Allen's "rose period." The rose images in these films' titles underline the inconclusive nature of Allen's texts. Picasso's rose period was not merely a time when his paintings took on shades of rose and pink, but signaled his maturing vision and style. This was the period, too, when images of the carnival or circus, the harlequins, appeared most prominently in his work.[1] Allen's films of this period are characterized by the poetic economy of their dialogic imagery and narrative constructions, by a rose-colored quality that evokes sunset times and memories of a lost past, and by carnival figures in the surface structure of the narratives. At the same time, the atmosphere of the archetypal carnival—the inversion and subversion of traditional codes and relationships—occurs on the deeper structural level of these films.

The rose image also bears a rich heritage of intertextual significance from a history of literary, filmic, mythological, and biblical texts. Roses are beautiful flowers with thorns; they combine invitations to delight with the threat of pain. They are religious and sexual signs, associated in both Western and Eastern mythologies and folktales with sacrifice, martyrdom, and death as well as with continuity and renewal. White roses are ambivalent images of genuine romantic impulse and of lost or corrupted innocence in director Jack Clayton's films, most notably *The Great Gatsby,* to which Allen so frequently alludes.[2] Moreover, roses appeared in Allen's *Interiors,* where they were also ambivalent signifiers of limitations and possibilities, especially in that film's ending. White roses have signified innocence, and in heraldic tradition they are also the sign of pretenders to the throne. Purple roses are associated with dignity and royalty, and in Christian mythology they are associated with crucifixion and rebirth. Roses are associated with the mother of Christ and with Cecilia, one of the most innocent martyred saints in Christian literature.

In *Broadway Danny Rose* and *The Purple Rose of Cairo,* the appearance of the term *rose* in both titles may indicate that Allen is not only using all of the heroic allusions associated with it, but may also be mocking the heroic pretensions associated with the term, since the little-man heroes of both films are a far cry from saints or kings—yet are, in their way, embarked on their own kinds of heroic quests. *Broadway Danny Rose* and *The Purple Rose of Cairo,* like *Zelig* and the earlier comedies, involve inept, unselfconscious, relatively passive, incomplete, and innocent sacrificial victims as central characters, but we may also sense heroism in their pathos.

As in earlier movies, both films involve the little person in questions of authenticity and describe the frustrations involved in their predicaments—the threat to human freedom and personal integrity posed by the dehumanization of modern culture. Both films deal with lies and betrayals resulting from self-interest and/or economic pressures, which permit people to distance themselves from each other and objectify other people.

In these later films, Allen's humor also carries on a dialogue with the carnivalesque, the Rabelaisian festive comedy that served as Mikhail Bakhtin's model of subversion and revitalization in the dialogic imagination.[3] As Jack Kroll observed, even as Allen is in his "Rose Period," it is not as though he ever left his "Blue Period" and "the Chaplinesque melancholy that suffuses everything he does."[4] Allen's recent work is never the entirely negative sort of parody, with which Bakhtin contrasted his more promising carnivals of death and rebirth, but it is less festive than carnival, more aware of the limits of contemporary reality. In these films, given its bleakest interpretation, the carnival is institutionalized (a parade sponsored by businessmen) or it is dormant—the modernist machinery sits in warehouses or off-season on silent lots. Finally, perhaps as Umberto Eco observes, "Humor does not pretend, like carnival, to lead us beyond our own limits. . . . On the contrary, it warns us about the impossibility of global liberation. . . . It makes us feel the uneasiness of living under a law—any law."[5] Bakhtin's view of the carnivalesque applies to Allen's work, but with conditions. These films include the concept of the carnivalesque within a larger dialogue that also questions it.

From a less optimistic perspective than Bakhtin took in his view of the carnivalesque, Allen's films continue to question utopian possibilities even as they represent them, and mock their own moral lessons even as they espouse them. In these more recent films, Allen encourages a more intense empathy between the spectator and his innocent central character while he intensifies his use of defamiliarizing and anti-illusionistic techniques; thus, the films play on contemporary tensions—between defensive distance and human connection, between determinism and freedom, both within the narrative and outside it. As a further consequence of such intensification, both films involve larger metaphysical questions about the possibilities for knowing anything with certainty. As Robert Alter states it, "art is obviously questionable because it is understood to be ultimately arbitrary, while nature is still more problematic because it is so entrammeled with art, so universally mediated by art, shaped by art's peculiar habits of vision, that it becomes difficult to know what if anything, nature in and of itself may be."[6]

BROADWAY DANNY ROSE

In the tradition of the ancient stories retold at a rabbi's table or a tall tale told around an American cracker barrel in the nineteenth century, *Broadway Danny Rose* has an obvious narrative frame. Danny Rose's legendary adventures are reconstructed by a group of borscht-circuit comedians around a table at the Carnegie Delicatessen on New York's Seventh Avenue. The frame is a device that establishes the credibility of the story (the comedians are real-life figures who would be likely to have inside knowledge about someone in their business) but also undermines the reliability of the tale because it is told by people who deal in fictions and jokes. Moreover, the comedians' opening conversation alludes to changing audience reactions—to jokes that work in one situational context but not in another. This is another of Allen's allusions to his critics and his audiences, but it also suggests that the selective perceptions of both the spectator and the teller are implicated in coloring reality so that truth and fiction in Danny Rose's story are subject to multiple, complex perspectives. Since the tellers are real-life comedians who come out of the same background as Woody Allen (who also plays Danny Rose), the film world and the realistic frame merge with life outside the film. As if to emphasize the polysemantic nature of the frame, Allen's producer and manager, Jack Rollins, known in the industry for his personal management and concern for clients (some of whom left him when they became successful), is one of the group, and Danny Rose's story becomes a remembrance of the personal management Allen has himself enjoyed outside the film.[7]

The camera's movement and point of view in the introductory sequence also suggest a dialogic pattern. The long take and the third-person, objective camera perspective make the film appear to be realistic, as a variety of customers and waiters at the Carnegie pass randomly between the camera and its eventual goal, the comedians' table, and on into the space beyond the frame. Yet, that very realistic technique creates a disruption between beholder and his or her objective, and the camera also self-consciously passes through the plate glass window of the restaurant, denying physical limitations and alerting us to the film's apparatus. Similarly, the black-and-white photography self-consciously recalls an older film style, while giving the il-

lusion of a harsh urban reality to both the comedians' frame and
to Danny's story.

The Danny Rose story is structured as a tall tale, a little man's
story in a big man's narrative form. The inversions, dispropor-
tions, and self-conscious devices suggested by the frame and
tall-tale elements multiply as the film proceeds, notably in Allen's allusions to a film of the fifties, *Meet Danny Wilson*,[8] and
most especially to Francis Coppola's blockbuster, *The Godfather.*
Broadway Danny Rose is a little man's comical legend about love
that dares to carry on a dialogue with Coppola's grand life-
denying myth.

Comedian Sandy Baron's "Danny Rose story" describes Danny's relationship with Lou Canova (Nick Apollo Forte), an over-
the-hill Italian nightclub singer. Unsuccessful as a borscht-belt
comedian himself, Danny has turned to small-time theatrical
management, at which he barely ekes out an existence, for his
clients are mostly losers like himself. When the nostalgia craze
hits, Lou Canova becomes more popular and Danny tries to get
Lou a big break—he convinces Milton Berle to catch Lou at the
Waldorf and to consider him for the Berle TV show and a spot
at Caesar's Palace. Danny reluctantly agrees to shepherd Lou's
mistress, Tina (Mia Farrow), to the show so that Lou's third wife
won't discover his womanizing. When Danny arrives at Tina's
apartment, however, he finds her angry with Lou for flirting
with still another woman. Tina rushes from her house, consults
a fortune-teller, on whose advice she continually depends, and
goes to a large garden party given by gangster friends and
relatives.

Tina's boyfriend before Lou Canova was Johnny Rispoli, one
son in a Mafia-type family, headed not by the traditional Godfather, but by a powerful Godmother. When Danny follows Tina
to the garden party, he is mistaken for Tina's new lover, because
his name is Danny Rose and Lou has been sending Tina a white
rose each day. When her son tries to commit suicide because of
unrequited love, Mrs. Rispoli seeks revenge and a contract is set
on "Danny White Roses."

The gangsters finally catch up with Tina and Danny, but Danny tells them that a stuttering ventriloquist named Barney Dunn, not he, sent Tina the roses, and the two manage to escape and make it to the Waldorf. Lou is a success, and then he leaves Danny for another manager at Tina's encouragement. Eventually, Tina develops a conscience and on Thanksgiving Day she tries to apologize to Danny. Although he initially rejects her, he finally runs after her, finds her in front of the Carnegie Deli, and they walk off the screen together, while the comedians make their final comments about the tale over the credits.

Danny Rose's world of tough blondes, loud polyester shirts, show biz, and gangsters is a vulgar, glitzy New York of the late 1950s and early 1960s;[9] but while it is based on history, everything in it is also part of a Runyonesque exaggeration, a modern folktale. Danny's clients are carnival figures, so sadly, grotesquely real they seem unreal. They include a blind xylophone player, a one-legged tap dancer, a man with a trained penguin that performs dressed as a rabbi and a bird that pecks out "September Song" on the piano, a balloon-folding act, a cheerful woman who plays tunes on the rims of water glasses, and Canova, an overweight singer with a big ego, a temperament, a drinking problem, and two ex-wives.

The crime family's garden party resembles the wedding scene in Coppola's film. This resemblance, as well as the presence of twins and a whole array of stereotyped, cartoon figures at the festivities, heightens our sense of the carnivalesque and the confusion of reflection and realism. Several of the characters at the party conspicuously wear lots of necklaces. While the jewelry overkill helps to establish the kitschy milieu in which the film is set, the various necklaces also serve as all too obvious labels that both bespeak a meaningful truth and expose the characters as allegorical props. Danny wears the Hebrew chai, which signifies "life"; literally, it is a form of the verb to be, meaning "I am," and identifying Danny with the life force. On the other hand, Rocco, Tina's gangster uncle, whose business is cement, wears a miniature gold horse's head around his neck, reminding us of Vito Corleone's dangerous offers that couldn't be refused. If Danny is associated with life, the gangsters are associated with violence and death. Similarly, as Tina breaks up with Johnny Rispoli, she fills her glass with ice from a bucket with a horse's head on the lid. Shortly before Danny betrays Barney Dunn, Barney also appears in a tie covered with horses' heads, which mark him for the gangster's retribution. These allusions to Coppola's film are small inside jokes, but they also refer to the larger dialogues between love and death that have always been central to Allen's films.

In part, Coppola's *The Godfather* is about the distance between personal and business morality. The film is filled with schizophrenic Clemenzas, warm family men who remember to retrieve from cars, where their victims lie struggling in death throes, the cannoli their wives ordered that morning. As Tessio, about to be killed for betraying Michael, says, "Tell Mike I always liked him. It was just business." Not unlike the Corleones in Coppola's film, Rocco and his friends tell Danny they are morally outraged at dirty comedy despite their own unwholesome criminal activities, and the Rispolis' family loyalty, happy garden parties, and romantic poetry does not keep them from planning revenge kidnappings and assassinations.

Recapitulating and inverting *The Godfather*'s themes in a comic-serious context, Danny, in *Broadway Danny Rose*, devotes himself personally to all his business clients. He props his losers up with platitudes, at once corny self-parodies and serious advice. He tells them they should always think about the "3 Ss": "Star, Smile, Strong." Danny devotes himself especially to Lou. He offers to forgo commissions so Lou can make alimony payments; he agrees to pick up Tina to ensure Lou's success at the Waldorf because he is a friend. Unlike the Godfather, Danny Rose cannot keep the personal out of his business life any more than Eudora Fletcher could treat her patient impersonally in *Zelig*. As Danny puts it, "I'm in personal management—the key word is personal—so I gotta get involved."

Coppola's *Godfather* is a contemporary ironic myth of betrayals, deceptions, and revenge. In Coppola's film, none but the weakest among the criminals ever shows guilt. Similarly, despite Danny's devotion, those clients who achieve success leave him. "They don't feel guilt or anything," Danny says. "I find them, I discover them, I breathe life into them, and they split."

As Danny explains it, "It's important to feel guilt, otherwise you're capable of terrible things." In Allen's film world, however, no one is completely ethical, not even the little man. Danny participates in deceiving Lou's wife and he betrays Barney Dunn. While Danny is capable of betrayal, he also feels guilty enough to go to see Barney after the Rispolis have beaten him up; he offers to pay Barney's hospital bills, but he does not tell Barney why he is being so generous.

Danny's ethical weaknesses, however, are small compared to Lou and Tina's betrayals. Both have a history of deceptions. Lou betrays three wives and even Tina before he betrays Danny. Tina betrays Johnny with Lou and finally betrays Danny by suggesting that Lou seek another manager and by setting up the meeting that leads Lou to Sid Bachrach, Danny's replacement. When Danny asks her to intervene on his behalf, she remains silent. Allen emphasizes Tina and Lou's careless emotional dishonesty, their lack of guilt, in another referential moment. While she and Lou are playing miniature golf, Tina suggests to Lou that he see the new agent Bachrach, and the camera lingers on the golf ball and the hole in a sleazy echo of Jordan Baker's dishonesty during the golf tournament in *The Great Gatsby*.

If Danny wears a chai and Rocco wears a horse's head, Tina wears a necklace with her own name proclaimed on it, suggesting her self-centered view of life, and a philosophy that she makes explicit to Danny in another too obviously serious discussion. Talking about why Danny is a loser and why clients leave him, she says, "Guilt? What the hell is that?" Later she adds, "[Life's] over quick so have a good time. If you see what you want, go for it, and don't pay attention to anybody else." "This is a philosophy of life?" Danny retorts. "This sounds like the screenplay for *Murder Incorporated*. . . . It's important to have some laughs," he says. "But you got to suffer a little, too, because otherwise you miss the whole point of life." Such philosophizing, is difficult to take seriously, however, from a character who seems to have stepped out of one of the dime-a-dozen Picasso Don Quixote prints or cheap clown pictures that are part of Allen's mis-en-scène.

Despite Danny's sacrifices for Lou, Lou acts out Tina's philosophy. He takes her suggestion and leaves Danny for Bachrach—just after Danny has risked his life for Lou and just after Berle has assured Danny that Lou will get his big break. Tina and Lou's betrayal leaves Danny confused and embittered, martyred to his own integrity and empathy.

The Godfather ends in the ultimate deception in that film: Michael's lie to Kay about the revenge assassination of his own brother-in-law. Danny Rose's tale is one of reconciliation and forgiveness, which, if we take it seriously, is all the more emphatic because of the sleazy milieu in which the forgiveness occurs. Allen prepares for his final scenes well, however, pushing legend into fairy tale. While Tina and Danny are escaping from the Rispoli brothers, they run through a warehouse containing huge floats and over-sized balloons for Macy's Thanksgiving Day parade. The giant comic-book images filled with helium contribute to the carnivalesque, surrealistic quality of the film, and the release of the gas from a bullet-punctured tank turns murdering crooks and victims alike into cartoon characters with funny voices, even while we are to believe that the bullets are real. As in earlier scenes where a supermanlike character (who is making a commercial) helps Tina and Danny escape their pursuers after their dreamlike race through high weeds, this scene provides a defamiliarizing disruption and a confusion of fairy tale and reality. An ominous shootout suddenly becomes a farce, and again we wonder what we should take seriously.

It is on Thanksgiving Day after Tina has married and then left Lou and is growing tired of Lou's replacement that we find her watching the annual Macy's parade in New York. Riding prominently on a float is Milton Berle, dressed in one of his famous drag outfits, portraying a comic Cinderella, and accompanied by a child-prince. Next to Coppola's dark image of Michael becoming Godfather at the end of Coppola's film, Allen appears to offer up a comic muse, half-cartoon, half real-life, a male-female figure who unites opposites. We may perceive Berle as bringing grace to the conclusion of a campy modern fairy tale, perhaps a sign of hope, but done up, carnival style, in trashy organza, sequins, and shoulder-length wig. Berle is an anti-Corleone and anti-Rispoli Cinderella created by a "good" godmother; a signal of affirmation representing an optimistic perspective as he presides over the Macy's parade on a day of thanksgiving; but like other comic mythical images combining art and life in the film, he finally evokes a continuing dialogue; he is at once a reliable indication of grace and a skeptical parody of himself.

Despite the festive atmosphere, however, Tina is not able to participate in the carnival. For some time she has been moody and uncomfortable for reasons she cannot at first understand. Just after huge balloons of Woody Woodpecker and Underdog pass by in the parade, however, Tina remembers Danny. She returns to her fortune-teller—a stock fairy tale figure—but culled in this case from the neorealistic, socially conscious film *The Bicycle Thief*. Finding that the fortune-teller is not there to give her advice, however, she is forced to make a choice on her own. Having apparently developed a conscience and a sense of guilt for the first time and recognizing the injustice she has done Danny, she goes to Danny's apartment where he and his motley troup of losers are celebrating Thanksgiving with frozen turkey dinners.

In a series of close shots, the camera captures the sensitive interchange as Danny responds with a mixture of emotions to Tina's visit. These moments, like the film's final images and like the moments that portray Danny's pain at Lou's betrayal outside the Waldorf, appear to cut through all the sad artificiality and tawdriness of the city scenes, the huge parade cartoon balloons, the tinselly people in pants suits—to recall authentic human feeling. Yet even here, where we most believe, we are forced to take into account the skepticism that pervades the rest of the film, the self-parodying characters. The captured moments of real feeling circumscribed by caricature may become fleeting moments of belief in an era of doubt. They may either be more memorable because of the depressing context in which they appear or undercut by that very context.

While Danny initially rejects Tina as if to take his revenge, soon after, he changes his mind and in an echo of the end of *Manhattan*, he runs after her. While the moment inspires hope, the contrast between innocent Tracy and brassy Tina also suggests the compromises and the ironies of Allen's more recent films. Before the Carnegie Delicatessen, that realistic landmark where the comedians in the frame began their story, Danny catches Tina and they walk away together. The closing images in *Broadway Danny Rose* may make us feel a sense of resolution and forgiveness. We want to take seriously Danny's earlier explanation of the difference between his viewpoint and that of the Rispolis (or the Corleones). Not only is being personal important, not only are guilt and suffering necessary for feeling and empathy, but as Danny's platitudinous Uncle Sidney (God rest his soul) once told Danny, " 'Acceptance, Forgiveness, Love.' That's a philosophy of life." With the main characters of the story standing before the Carnegie and the camera establishing an extremely long perspective, it may become more difficult to see self-parody; and we may briefly believe in the survival of a true carnival spirit in this modern myth of reconciliation.

The film's last moments, however, draw a final comic contrast with *The Godfather*, affirm Danny's legendary nature, and reemphasize the tale's unreliability. At the end of Coppola's ironic film, Michael participates in the baptism of his sister's child while he uses that moment as an alibi for a blood bath that finally baptizes him as Godfather. In Coppola's film, that spiritual transfiguration underlines in horrifying images Michael's sacrifice upon the altar of family loyalty, his dedication to the ironic distance between business and personal roles, his commitment to revenge and his refusal to forgive. Danny Rose is also a sacrifice and becomes a legend in a comic Jewish, this-worldly inversion of Christian communion:[10] Danny and Tina are memorialized as a sandwich on the Carnegie Delicatessen menu. Probably, quips one of the comics, as cream cheese on a bagel with marinara sauce.

Our final impressions in *Broadway Danny Rose* are again within the frame. Once more we are among the comedians, and Danny Rose is absent. As the credits roll, the comedians' last remarks are filled with skepticism about Sandy Baron's story and with elaborations on it. For all his small corruptions, Danny

Rose appears to signify the vestiges of our own virtue, innocence, and humanity; his story is part of a film that contains a
simple, but meaningful lesson for our times. But Danny's tale is
mediated by interlocutors and by a visual style that mocks it,
that confuses reality and fiction, that draws us into an empathetic relationship and then questions our gullibility. Danny
may be a surviving life-affirming remnant of human kindness in
a decadent world, or like Leonard Zelig, just a legend—the
memory of an image that can no longer be part of our reality
except as fiction. His tale describes the limitations of our world
as well as the limits and possibilities of contemporary, self-conscious storytelling and myth making. *Broadway Danny Rose*,
like *The Purple Rose of Cairo*, explores our hopes and reservations regarding dreams of desire in sophisticated postmodern
times. Allen's carnivalesque film also questions its own carnival.

THE PURPLE ROSE OF CAIRO

In *The Purple Rose of Cairo*, Allen returns to the pattern of *Play
It Again, Sam*, where Humphrey Bogart came off the screen to
influence a little man's life, and where the central character is
torn between the realism of his illusions and narrative episodes
of reality. Although *The Purple Rose of Cairo* is built on the dialogic perspective of Allen's early comedy, the oppositions have
become more complex and the conclusion is more obviously
problematic. In Allen's *Purple Rose*, the smallest details of plot,
mise-en-scène, verbal interchange, lighting, and camera work
are more carefully integrated to foreground its contradictions
and inconclusiveness—the "pervasive insecurity about the relationship of fiction to reality."[11] The film nods to a series of contemporary philosophical and linguistic issues directly within
the narrative: it includes allusions to carnival in the surface
structure of images; it presents a great number of disruptions
between discourse and spectator; it includes characters as well
as actors, audience, and filmmaker as part of the problem; it has
tragic overtones and an elegiac quality, which only hovered

After an actor steps off the screen and joins the "real" world, spectators flock to see "The Purple Rose of Cairo," a film within Woody Allen's film *The Purple Rose of Cairo. Courtesy of Woody Allen and Orion Pictures.*

about the margins of the early comedies; and it features a woman in Allen's familiar little-man role. The result is, as Jack Kroll saw it, "a gem, one of the shrewdest, funniest, most plaintive explorations of movies as dream machine and escape mechanism."[12]

Allen's decision to remain behind the camera and give the central little-man role to Mia Farrow may indicate his growing sensitivity to female sensibility and perspectives. Although he could be accused of reinforcing female stereotypes because the woman is a small, wispy, sacrificial victim, he also portrays her victimization in the face of ruthless economics and alienation that are predominantly represented by males in the film. In any case, Allen makes good use of Mia Farrow's delicate beauty and vulnerability to evoke pathos and to create an empathy between spectator and little-person figure typical of his other films in this period.

The Purple Rose of Cairo is the tale of Cecilia (Mia Farrow), a poor inept waitress during the Great Depression, who lives in a dingy apartment with her domineering husband, Monk (Danny Aiello), who is out of a job. Her only escape is the Jewel, a local movie house that shows romantic 1930s comedies such as "The Purple Rose of Cairo" (quotation marks will be used throughout to distinguish the title of the film-within-a-film from the title of Allen's film, which is italicized). When she is fired for daydreaming about movies, Cecilia seeks refuge in the theater. As she is watching "The Purple Rose of Cairo" for the fifth time, Tom Baxter (Jeff Daniels), the movie's handsome explorer, suddenly steps off the Jewel's screen and enters Cecilia's world, leaving his fellow characters confused and bringing the plot of the film-within-in-the-film to a halt. Tom says that he deserted his movie because he desired freedom and wanted to talk to Cecilia. Shortly thereafter he falls in love with her.

Further complications arise when Raoul Hirsch, the film's director, and other executives get word of Tom's defection and fear for their investments. They threaten to ruin Gil Sheperd, the actor who played Baxter, if he doesn't persuade Tom, his character, to return to the screen. Afraid for his career, Sheperd travels to Cecilia's New Jersey town to make Baxter get back into the movie. Sheperd meets Cecilia and competes with Tom for her love. Finally Sheperd promises to take her to Hollywood and makes her choose between him and the character he played. Cecilia chooses reality and Tom reluctantly returns to his film. But then Sheperd betrays Cecilia and flies back to Hollywood without her. In *The Purple Rose of Cairo*'s final scene, a teary-eyed Cecilia is seeing another movie at the Jewel. As in *Manhattan*, the concluding close shot in this film is a memorable visual synecdoche that underlines the film's dialogic and inconclusive design.

All of Allen's work has to some extent dealt with a dialogue between the longing for freedom and fulfillment of desire, and the pressures that frustrate the realization of such possibilities.

In *The Purple Rose of Cairo*, Allen highlights the philosophical concern with language as a "prisonhouse" that promises fulfillment but must continually frustrate it. Allen devises dialogues around a number of related questions: What are the possibilities for escape from determinate circumstances such as those described by Wittgenstein, where the limits of one's language are the limits of one's world?[13] Can either film or reality be satisfying and authentic when each is so intertextual, when each is mediated by so many "others"—by interlocutors, perspectives, or pressures—by actors, plot, audience, producers, the ideology of a competitive society, individual self-interest, time, and history? Is meaning possible in the face of an overdetermination of meanings? Does knowledge or an understanding of the "rules of the game" make a difference? Is there such a thing as making a liberating decision when the limitations of language and experience may dominate the terms of the choice? Can art offer sustenance and the hope that may lead to risk taking and freedom, or does it merely exacerbate the problem by encouraging false illusions? Are dreams of desire by definition impossible dreams? The film both challenges or critiques its own dialogic patterns, yet remains within them.

Like so many of his films, Allen's *The Purple Rose of Cairo* exploits and deconstructs a binary pattern of oppositions, but the alternative worlds intersect in a more perplexing way than did the two mutually contradictory situations in films like *Take the Money and Run*, *Bananas*, and *Sleeper*. Both the world of the film-within-the-film Cecilia sees and Cecilia's world outside the film are represented as worlds of possibility and of restriction, and *The Purple Rose of Cairo* probes the limits of these frames. In the process, it raises questions regarding yet another frame involving Allen and the spectator of his entire metafictional presentation.

Cecilia lives an apparently hopeless life. Her territory is restricted to a small apartment, a restaurant, and a movie house. Cecilia's boss tells her to "shape up" or lose her job; her drunken husband warns her to "shape up" and beats her when she doesn't. Rather than going to movies, Monk escapes *his* powerlessness by gambling, drinking, and cheating with other women. He demonstrates his only power—over Cecilia's physical presence—even while he lives off her small earnings. On several occasions she tries to escape from Monk, "who never used to be this way," but given her timid nature and her innocence, her fear of being alone, she cannot find a viable exit. The only eligible men she meets are mousy exterminators, and she is frightened by her prospects when she observes the prostitute Emma trying "to make a buck." Cecilia's life is a closed circle, and she always returns to Monk and to their small drab apartment. Cecilia describes the real world to Tom as a difficult place where jobs are hard to find, where there are wars, where people get old and sick and never find true love, where people are not consistent or reliable.

"The Purple Rose of Cairo" appears to be a dramatic contrast to Cecilia's drab reality. The film-within-a-film is a gentle parodic pastiche of 1930s society comedies like Fred Astaire's *Flying Down to Rio* (1933), *The Gay Divorcée* (1934), and *Swing Time* (1936). It even refers to Mae West pictures. "The Purple Rose of Cairo" adheres to the codes of those thirties films—titles that look like engraved invitations to a high-society function, mandatory white telephone, white art-deco penthouse, studio sets for exotic places, New York nightlife; it showcases lively conversation, beautiful, expensive clothes, rich heiresses, elegant countesses, charming boyish explorers, suave playboys, clever playwrights, and smart-alecky servants. Initially, "The Purple Rose of Cairo" appears to represent escape from reality's limits.

But as Stephen Schiff suggests, "Mia Farrow isn't the only one playing Woody Allen in this movie."[14] Tom Baxter, the rich explorer out of the Midwest—one of the Chicago Baxters—is Cecilia's innocent counterpart in "The Purple Rose of Cairo." Tom's world is more consistent and reliable, but from his perspective, life on the screen is also restricted. The events in his plot repeat themselves in the same order, showing after showing, and his character's consciousness is conditioned by the way it has been scripted. As Cecilia seeks freedom from her oppressive world by going to the Jewel, Tom seeks freedom from the determinism of the written word and projected image by entering Cecilia's world. As the theater manager states the problem, "Those who are real want to be fictional and those who are fictional want to be real." If Cecilia sees the screen world as wonderful and romantic, Tom "stands in awe of existence" and speaks of her world as "almost magical . . . as opposed to the world of celluloid and flickering shadows." Cecilia's longings as a spectator may have inspired Tom to leave the screen, but his choice opens both their lives to the unpredictable and the apparently impossible; his escape brings them love, and his risk taking may help Cecilia to take chances.

As Tom courts Cecilia, events continually and comically remind us of his scripting and draw attention to filmic apparatus. Thus, his stage money is useless in the real world, and the car he tries to drive will not start without a key. He has trouble conceiving of lovemaking without the conventional fade-out. Although Tom says he will try to be real so that he can join Cecilia's world, Gil reminds him that one can't learn to be real. Tom does not understand the meaning of God beyond the creators of his script, R. J. Sax and Irving Levine; thus, he points to his film's construction but also lays bare the way our reality is constructed. Cecilia observes that his innocence and idealism make him unfit for the harshness of the real world, but in this he also resembles her. Although he is written to believe in love and (like Cecilia) turns down the loveless sex Emma represents, that same idealism makes him protect Cecilia. When he fights with Monk, like Cecilia, he loses because he cannot fight unfairly and Monk knows only winning and losing. However, unlike Cecilia, he is not hurt, because he is fictional.

A series of other parallels demonstrates how Tom and Cecilia and their worlds interpenetrate. When Tom first comes out of his film, a woman in the Jewel's audience faints because Tom isn't real. Similarly, when Cecilia has a date on the town with Tom and accompanies him into his plot, Kitty, Tom's intended, faints because Cecilia *is* real. While her date with Tom is wonderful, Cecilia, like Tom, remains in costume and never takes off her hat. Like Tom's discoveries that the external world is different from what he thought, Cecilia's view of the perfect film-world is also qualified as she recognizes that movie champagne is only ginger ale. While Tom has his double in Gil, Cecilia has hers in a sister (Stephanie Farrow). Finally, for all their apparent innocence, both of Allen's little-person characters are edged in minor corruptions that blur their roles as outsiders to the self-interested and betraying worlds around them. Cecilia lies to Monk about her meetings with Tom and ultimately betrays Tom when she decides to go with Gil. For his part, Tom, like Gil Sheperd, egocentrically takes offense at suggestions that he is only a minor player.

Gil Sheperd s appearance further complicates the intersecting frames. Because it is never entirely clear whether Gil actually had feelings for Cecilia or whether he was just using her to influence Tom, we cannot tell whether he is real or playing a role. Although he appears sincere, he lies to Cecilia even from their first meeting. In retrospect, after we have seen Gil betray Cecilia, Gil's re-creation with Cecilia of a scene from one of his films, where he tells her that he will have to leave her behind, seems a particularly sad moment of foreshadowing and of villainous deception. Tom buys Cecilia a ukulele, tells her how much he cares for her, and kisses her—even as he confesses paradoxically that film kisses don't mean much to acting professionals.

The film involves additional dialogues that recall a variety of contemporary arguments that attempt unsuccessfully to resolve the contradictions of film and of life. Such moments further confuse the nested frames. Economics intrude into both Cecilia's world and the film-within-the-film. Cecilia's impersonal boss's main concern is his business. The moguls who control "The Purple Rose of Cairo" have no personal interest in others involved in their production; they only seek profits and buy off the "free" press to secure their objectives. Economic depression causes problems in Cecilia's life with Monk, but economic self-interest also places pressures on Gil Sheperd and is instrumental in destroying Cecilia's relationships with both Gil and Tom. The film, however, also exposes and mocks economic and political analyses and solutions as still further constructions. The stock communist character in the 1930s film-within-the-film absurdly exhorts the other fictional characters to revolt against the moguls who exploit their work, while the producers recollect the red-baiting of the 1930s as they insist (equally absurdly) that attempts by the remaining characters to leave the screen is "communist talk."

In a similar sort of dialogue, the playwright in "The Purple Rose of Cairo" appears horrified when the Jewel's manager threatens to turn off the projector, because blackness and annihilation is the equivalent to death in the real world. But when the playwright suggests that perhaps all of this confusion points out that the distinction between fiction and reality is only a semantic issue, that perhaps the fiction is real and the real is only fiction, the countess commonsensically provides the other side of the dialogue as she tells him he has been "flickering" up on the screen too long. In yet another attempt to resolve problems, Tom tells Cecilia that he's tired of trying to figure out what life means and just wants them "to live it."

The characters on the screen also interact with the spectators in the Jewel and turn the tables on the usual conventions in Allen's films where audiences and critics analyze and criticize his and others' films. Like the intellectuals in *Zelig* or the fans in *Stardust Memories*, here, not only the movie patrons, but the characters in the movie-within-the movie disagree about the meaning their film has and what consequences will follow from Tom's actions. Here the characters are freed to attack the audience with as much fervor as their audience attacks them and their film. So, too, the audience responds to Tom's surprising exit in a variety of ways. As one disconcerted fan cries, "I want what happened in the movie last week to happen this week; otherwise, what's life all about anyway?" Just as in other Allen films, but now with an additional novel twist represented by the characters' intervention, we, as spectators outside his film, are driven into active viewing. We are forced into considering the complex interrelationships involved in any attempt to escape the contradictions of subjective perception, the overdetermination of meanings, and the several levels of illusions and interpenetrating frames, in our longing to discover what is real.

Further confusions arise because Cecilia and Tom meet and

Tom spends his nights in an amusement park with a large Ferris wheel, a carousel, and a roller coaster. But the carnival in *The Purple Rose of Cairo* is closed down "for the season." The carousels and Ferris wheel are at rest, and Tom sits alone in a roller-coaster car that never moves. On the carousel is another carnival figure, a bas-relief of a clown whose expression shows him preserved as art within a liminal gap between laughter and horror, between comedy and pathos. The mise-en-scène provides a backdrop that stresses Tom and Cecilia's peculiar position outside the carnival, yet within it. They are caught momentarily, like the clown face, in a gap between dialogues that confines them in ambiguities or presents them as though in a frozen moment beyond contradictions. The rich carnivalesque and archetypal associations of the silent amusement park with its circular imagery highlight the positive equipoise of Tom and Cecilia's moments of romantic escape from their worlds, even as they remind us of the limitations of those moments, with images of a sad reality. This juxtaposition adds to the film's poignancy—its elegiac quality.

In the climactic sequences of the film, Cecilia has to choose between Tom—the world of fictional film—and Gil's reality, which will turn out to be only another fiction. Her moment of choice emphasizes the film's central concern—whether freedom and escape from determining circumstances is possible. Cecilia's choice may contain either a serious lesson about the importance of making freeing choices and taking risks in the face of difficult options or it may only be an absurd mockery of itself. From the Jewel's screen, a character reminds Cecilia that making choices is what makes her most human. And we recall that earlier Cecilia told Tom that his actions have inspired her to be brave and to escape her usual timidity by standing up to Monk. And the film also suggests that the impossible may be possible. One of the film executives says, "Just because a thing never happened before doesn't mean it can't happen for a first time." As the characters on the screen observe, "One minor character takes some action and the whole world turns upside down." We also recall, however, that in "The Purple Rose of Cairo" Tom said, "What is life without a little risk-taking?" as he made a decision to leave his Cairo tomb for "a madcap Manhattan adventure." But that decision was, after all, scripted; it was the only choice he could make. Since there have been hints that Cecilia's reality is also constructed and we have evidence of its limitations, her world may only be as determinate as Tom's. Moreover, we will finally remember that she, like Tom, is also a character—within Allen's script. The film leaves us hoping that real liberating choices are possible—and seriously doubting that possibility at the same time.

Although we may empathize with Cecilia's decision to choose Gil and reality, Tom's exit contributes to the film's elegiac mood. From our perspective at the back of the empty Jewel theater, Tom's exit resembles Leonard Zelig's last moments on screen. Tom moves into the distance. He looks back at Cecilia and the world he is leaving and then exits from his frame while the camera lingers on the empty set to heighten our sense of loss. That is the last we see of Tom, but we suspect that Raoul Hirsh has made good his threat—that the projector has been turned off and that the negatives of the film have been destroyed.

Tom's exit leaves another option for Cecilia, who rushes home, gathers her clothes into her suitcase yet another time, and says her good-byes yet again to Monk. But when she arrives at the Jewel to meet Sheperd, suitcase and pathetic little ukulele in hand, she finds that his promise of a better reality was only another fiction and that he has abandoned her. The hope that resided in the other half of the dialogue between art and life is now no more available to Cecilia than was the outside of prison—after the inside—for Virgil Starkwell, or the San Marcos jungle—after the New York jungle—for Fielding Mellish.

And yet the ending is not entirely without hope. The film's last shots find Cecilia back at the Jewel watching Fred Astaire and Ginger Rogers in *Top Hat* (1935). At first Cecilia looks at the screen through tears, but as Astaire and Rogers dance to "Cheek to Cheek" (which brings us back in a circular manner to the music that opened *The Purple Rose of Cairo*), Cecilia's expression becomes more difficult to label. She appears in the film's last moment, in a close shot, caught between the pain of her loss and the start of a smile that signals her involvement once more in the screen images that dominate her frame and ours. In the film's last moments Cecilia appears to be poised between disillusionment and regenerating hope as she once more becomes an engrossed spectator. Although the qualifications have multiplied since Allen's earliest comedies, we are still unsure whether to reject Cecilia's dreams of desire on the screen or to see them as helpmates in her attempts to survive oppressive circumstances; we are still uncertain whether those dreams inspire hope and risk taking or whether they are only further reflections of infinitely determinate fictions—limited constructed worlds.

There are further variations within the intersecting realities and fictions from which Allen's film is fashioned. If Cecilia's predicament, despite its ambiguous final image, still strikes us as rather bleak, we also recall some special moments, characteristic of all of Allen's recent films, that suggest escape and affirmation. For instance, we share with Cecilia and Gil and the owner of a music shop a brief moment of sheer entertainment, of apparent human connection, of delight as Cecilia happily strums her ukulele while Gil sings and the elderly music shop proprietor bangs out popular tunes on a piano. In a parallel sequence—Cecilia's Copacabana date with Tom inside his film— we feel her joy as she dances the night away. Arturo, the Copa's maître d', amplifies that moment of freedom when he sees that Cecilia's entrance into the script "chucks the plot"; he does what he always wanted to do—he leaves his role, cries "Hit it," and taps an exuberant dance across the floor to the music of a big band. Like other such moments often involving music and dance in Allen's earlier films, these are mottled with conditions and qualifications—they are themselves dialogic occasions. But in the weight of emphasis they are also memorable, delicious images of possibility; they appear, from one perspective, to escape the determinate medium even as they are part of it.

Escape, of course, is not defined just in terms of Cecilia's relation to the screen image. After all, we in the audience are also watching a film—one that is also entitled *The Purple Rose of Cai-*

ro. As we watch innocent Cecilia make her choices, we empathize with her, but that empathy is offset by Allen's insistence that we remain aware of ourselves as spectators, which he accomplishes by creating Cecilia's story with enough self-conscious techniques to keep us distanced from her frame.

The sections of Allen's film that portray Cecilia's reality imitate the anti–white telephone movies, the social realism films of the 1940s—but in color. The deterministic situation, the poor wife, the drinking husband, the subversion of a potential rags-to-riches Cinderella plot are not unfamiliar codes. The lighting is stylized—curiously rosy-colored in some sequences and too washed-out or dark in others to create a wholly convincing illusion of reality. Compositions frequently involve two to three shots in a stagy fashion despite the fact that the film is shot on location. Occasionally, both in Cecilia's real world and in "The Purple Rose of Cairo," characters obviously get in the way of the camera so as to deny it, but simultaneously to remind us of Allen's apparatus and a familiar quality of his style, not typical of films in the 1930s or the 1940s. Although costuming and setting appear to be realistic, some of the characters in the restaurant and the characters who wait in line to get into the theater appear overly made-up, artificial in contrast to Cecilia's more realistic make-up. As Cecilia works in the restaurant, a voice that sounds remarkably like Woody Allen's demands a hamburger from his waitress—an intrusion from the real world, our world, which is particularly ironic because of Allen's real-life personal relationship with Mia Farrow. These devices, together with the larger narrative structure (with its reflexive, continuously intersecting frames), so disorient us, that we cannot determine whether to accept Cecilia's world as reality or as yet another level of artifice.

Thus, Cecilia, like Tom, may also be a fiction remembered out of film history; and since the whole film is set in an earlier time, we experience an acute sense of loss, not only when Tom exits from the real world, but when we recognize that we are temporally and intellectually distanced from Cecilia and her innocent engagement with films, as well. Like Zelig and Danny Rose, Cecilia's little-person character evokes an elegiac mood; like Tom, she may be the image of an image that once promised innocence.

However, our roles as spectators vis-à-vis *The Purple Rose of Cairo* also parallel Cecilia's role vis-à-vis "The Purple Rose of Cairo." Cecilia's act of imagination, her identification with the narrative, may help to free the characters from the determinism of the script; the spectator's imaginative interaction expands the narrative beyond its manifest overdetermination. But, finally, Cecilia cannot escape overdetermined conditions and returns to spectation, which may begin the whole process once more. We cannot tell whether Cecilia will be able to participate in a freeing "impossibility" again and what her choice will be if that occurs. We do not know what, if anything, she has gained from her experience with Tom and Gil, whether she will ever be able to believe in the images as well as she did before. Like Cecilia, we, as spectators, are caught between illusions and realities, between empathetic participation and intellectual distance. Like Cecilia, we gain knowledge, we become more sophisticated—in our case, both within the narrative structure of images and through the filmmaker's disruptions—but the consequences of our understanding also remain ambiguous. We are permitted to accept everything in Allen's film—its dreariest or most positive predictions—or we can see it as a mockery of its own seriousness, even its own inconclusiveness. Our own consciousness prescribes our limits, and we may believe that knowledge leads to hope for escape or that our very knowledge of the paradoxical possibilities prevents us from returning to a state of innocent involvement, belief, and empathy—the fulfillment of desire that we long for, but perhaps can never hope to achieve, given the constraints of language, time, and history. In Allen's films we participate in the carnival, and we reflect on its possible demise. We learn about ourselves as we participate in the dialogues of hope and hopelessness, and we still long to escape the struggle into a sense of sureness and unity with our world that may always be possible and may always have been the impossible dream. Knowledge or understanding, the result of experience, then, both inside and outside the film, involves both gains and losses; Allen's film describes our limits and subverts all laws.

Broadway Danny Rose and *The Purple Rose of Cairo* are films about the instabilities of our world and about the way in which art as language both reflects and constructs our realities. They depend on both the creation of illusions and the deconstruction of those illusions to make all conclusions or meanings provisional, unresolved dialogues. These small, sad, and funny films of Allen's rose period blossom into a much larger experience than any first viewing can provide. The rich weave of intertextual allusions and frames; the profound social satire that goes well beyond mere self-concern; the sophisticated integration of visual style with narrative structure; the mixture of pathos and comedy; the presentation of complex issues in popular terms; and the variations upon his central little-man characters testify to how far Woody Allen has come since he made the humbler comedy *Take the Money and Run* in 1969.

NOTES AND REFERENCES

Chapter 1

1. Woody Allen, *Without Feathers* (New York: Warner Books, 1976), 9.

2. See Roberet Stam, *Reflexivity in Film and Literature from Don Quixote to Jean-Luc Godard* (Ann Arbor, Mich.: UMI Research Press, 1985), xi. "Reflexivity subverts the assumption that art can be a transparent medium of communication. . . . [Reflexive texts] interrupt the flow of narrative in order to foreground the specific means of literary and filmic production."

3. See Mikhail Bakhtin, *The Dialogic Imagination*, ed. Michael Holquist (Austin: University of Texas Press, 1981). Also see Mikhail Bakhtin, *Rabelais and His World*, trans. Helene Iswolsky (Bloomington: Indiana University Press, 1984), Katerina Clark and Michael Holquist, *Mikhail Bakhtin* (Cambridge: Harvard University Press, 1984), and Gary Saul Morson, ed., *Bakhtin: Essays and Dialogues on His Work* (Chicago: University of Chicago Press, 1986). Bakhtin regarded individual consciousness as social. Every individual utterance and thus all texts are composed of a dynamic and diverse group of social references; therefore, all utterance is to some degree open-ended and "dialogic." More specifically, the term *dialogic* here refers to Allen's texts as they are made up of unresolved dialogues, arguments, debates, and conversations often among several interrelating texts. The term is discussed more fully later in this introduction.

4. Bakhtin, *The Dialogic Imagination*, 50. Bakhtin traces the "dialogic" imagination to the prehistory of the novel and to "the earliest stages of verbal culture," to "a primordial struggle between tribes, peoples, cultures and languages." For the little man's archetypal backgrounds, see especially Edith Kern, *The Absolute Comic* (New York: Columbia University Press, 1980), 177–208.

5. Walter Blair, *Horse Sense in American Humor* (Chicago: University of Chicago Press, 1942), 283, 300.

6. Ibid., vi.

7. Hamlin Hill, "Modern American Humor, The Janus Laugh," *College English* 25 (December 1963), 171.

8. Norris Yates, *The American Humorist, Conscience of the Twentieth Century* (New York: The Citadel Press, 1965), 39–40.

9. Hill, "Modern American Humor," 171.

10. Yates, *American Humorist*, 13.

11. Sanford Pinsker, "Jumping on Hollywood's Bones, or How S. J. Perelman and Woody Allen Found It at the Movies," *Midwest Quarterly* 21, no. 3 (Spring 1980): 374.

12. Steve Seidman, *Comedian Comedy: A Tradition in Hollywood Film* (Ann Arbor, Mich.: UMI Research Press, 1981), 69.

13. Ibid., 15–27.

14. Ibid., 59–78.

15. Dave Hirshey, "Woody Rates the Comics," *Sunday News Magazine*, 20 March 1977, 20.

16. Penelope Gilliatt, "Guilty, with an Explanation," *New Yorker*, 4 February 1974, 43.

17. Thomas Schatz, *Old Hollywood/New Hollywood: Ritual, Art, and Industry* (Ann Arbor, Mich.: UMI Research Press, 1983), 169–294.

18. Roger Ebert, *A Kiss Is Still a Kiss* (New York: Andrews, McMeel & Parker, 1984), 231. Also see Eric Lax, *On Being Funny* (New York: Manor Books, 1977), 77, 117.

19. Lax, *Being Funny*, 221–22. Allen told Lax: "The more I was introduced to Perelman and Robert Benchley, I got crazy about them. I think those two are the great comedy writers." Allen found Perelman "so utterly unique and complex [that] you can't be influenced a little by him. You have to go so deeply that it shows all over the place." Also see "Woody Allen: Rabbit Running," *Time*, 3 July 1972, 60–61.

20. Bakhtin, *Dialogic Imagination*, 47 and 49.

21. Ibid., 46.

22. Ibid., 48–49.

23. Ibid., 60.

24. Bakhtin, *Rabelais and His World* 11.

25. Patricia Waugh, *Metafiction* (New York: Methuen, 1984), 23.

26. See especially Robert Eberwein, *Film and the Dreamscreen* (Princeton, N.J.: Princeton University Press, 1985), 18–42.

27. This interpretation is supported by Stam's discussions of Buster Keaton's *Sherlock Jr.* as "an allegory of spectatorship," 37–39.

28. Bakhtin, *Rabelais and His World*, 11–12.

29. Evidence for this suggestion appears in Ralph Rosenblum and Robert Karen, *When the Shooting Stops . . . the Cutting Begins* (New York: Viking Press, 1979), 245, 259, 286.

30. See Maurice Yacowar, *Loser Take All* (New York: Frederick Ungar, 1979).

31. Waugh, *Metafiction*, 6.

32. Bakhtin, *Rabelais and His World*, 12.

Chapter 2

1. Francis du Plessix Gray, "Woody Allen: America's Melancholy Funnyman," *Cosmopolitan*, September 1974, 147–48.

2. Ibid., 148.

3. Robert F. Moss, "Creators on Creating," *Saturday Review*, *November 1980, 43*.

4. Ibid., 42.

5. Ebert, *A Kiss*, 233.

6. Gilliatt, "Guilty," 44.

7. Michael Blowen, "Woody Allen, Businessman," reprinted in *Detroit Free Press*, 18 September 1983, sec. C, p. 1, from the *Boston Globe*.

8. Moss, "Creators," 40, 42, 43.

9. Ibid., 42.

10. Blowen, "Woody Allen," 1.

11. Phil Berger, "The Business of Comedy," *New York Times Magazine*, 9 June 1985, 82.

12. Moss, "Creators," 44.

13. Blowen, "Woody Allen," 1.

14. Richard J. H. Johnston, "You Name it, Woody is Doing It," *New York Times, 14 February 1969, 26*.

15. Natalie Gittelson, "The Maturing of Woody Allen," *New York Times Magazine*, 22 April 1979, 105.

16. Ken Kelley, "A Conversation with the Real Woody Allen (or someone just like him)," *Rolling Stone*, 1 July 1976, 91.

17. Gittelson, "Maturing," 105.

18. Jack Kroll, "Woody Funny, But He's Serious," *Newsweek*, 24 April 1978, 65.

19. Kelley, "A Conversation," 35.

20. Gittelson, "Maturing," 106–7.

21. Michael Walker, "The Met Grill," *Metropolitan Home* 17 (June 1985):15.

22. Johnston, "You Name It," 26.

23. Frank Rich, "Of Love, Death, Chicken Soup, and Bob Hope," *Time*, 30 April 1979, 69.

24. Kroll, "Funny," 64.

25. Gittelson, "Maturing," 104.

26. Moss, "Creators," 43.

27. Dave Hirshey, "Woody Rates the Comics," *Sunday News Magazine, 20 March 1977, 30*.

28. Philip Oakes, "The Value of Worry," *Sunday Times* (London) 25 October 1970, 30.

29. Kroll, "Funny," 66.

30. Jim Jerome, "If Life's a Joke, Then the Punchline is Woody Allen" *People*, 4 October 1976, 40.

31. Gittelson, "Maturing," 107.

32. Gray, "Melancholy Funnyman," 148.

33. Ibid., 148.

34. Ibid., 224.

35. Gittelson, "Maturing," 32.

36. Kelley, "A Conversation," 88.

37. Gray, "Melancholy Funnyman," 147.

38. Gilliatt, "Guilty," 42.

39. Moss, "Creators," 43–44.

40. Gray, "Melancholy Funnyman," 155.

41. Gene Siskel, "Woody Allen on Love, Films, and Reagan," *Chicago Tribune*, 11 June 1982, sec. 6, 5.

42. Gray, "Melancholy Funnyman," 155.

43. Kelley, "A Conversation," 38.

44. Gittelson, "Maturing," 32.

45. Ibid., 106.

46. John Dart, "Woody Allen, Theologian," *Christian Century*, 22–29 June 1977, 585.

47. Oakes, "Value of Worry," 30.

48. Ebert, *A Kiss*, 230.

49. Kroll, "Funny," 66.

50. Ebert, *A Kiss*, 227.

51. Bernard Carragher, "Woody Allen Tells: What I Laugh at and What My Parents Laugh at," *Family Circle*, August 1974, 96.

52. Ibid.

53. Lax, *Being Funny*, 31.

54. Foster Hirsch, *Love, Sex, Death, and the Meaning of Life* (New York: McGraw-Hill, 1981), 13–14.

55. Kroll, "Funny," 64.

56. Lax, *Being Funny*, 30.

57. Ibid., 29.

58. Ibid., 28.

59. Bill Adler and Jeffrey Feinman, *Woody Allen, Clown Prince of American Humor* (New York: Pinnacle, 1975) 8.

60. Lax, *Being Funny*, 185.

61. Adler and Feinman, *Clown Prince*, 13–14.

62. Johnston, "You Name It," 26.
63. Kroll, "Funny," 71.
64. Berger, "Business of Comedy," 81, 83.
65. "Woody Allen: Rabbit Running," *Time*, 3 July 1972, 59.

Chapter 3

1. See Ruth R. Wisse, *The Schlemiel as Modern Hero* (Chicago: University of Chicago Press, 1971) and Maurice Yacowar, *Loser Take All*.
2. Eric Lax, *On Being Funny*, 65.
3. Ibid., 70.
4. Ibid., 126.
5. Rosenblum and Karen, *When the Shooting Stops*, 245, 251.
6. Lee Guthrie, *Woody Allen, a Biography* (New York: Drake, 1978), 64.
7. Woody Allen, "A Look at Organized Crime," in *Getting Even* (New York: Warner, 1972), 16–20.
8. Rosenblum and Karen, *When the Shooting Stops*, 259.
9. Richard Anobile, ed., *Woody Allen's "Play It Again Sam"* (New York: Grosset & Dunlap, 1977), 7.
10. Ibid., 7.
11. Yacowar, *Loser Take all*, 52.
12. Diane Jacobs, . . . *but we need the eggs: The Magic of Woody Allen* (New York: St. Martin's Press, 1982), 46.

Chapter 4

1. Penelope Gilliatt, "Meanwhile Back at the Uterus," *New Yorker*, 19 August 1971, 58.
2. David Reuben, *Everything You Always Wanted to Know about Sex* (New York: Bantam, 1971), 8, 43.
3. Ibid., 13–14.
4. Lax, *Being Funny*, 96.
5. Ibid., 102.
6. Ibid., 112.
7. Ibid., 230–31.
8. Yacowar, *Loser Take All*, 169.

Chapter 5

1. Michiko Kakutani, "How Woody Allen's *Zelig* Was Born in Anxiety and Grew into Comedy," *New York Times*, 18 July 1983, sec. C, p. 13.

2. Yacowar, *Loser Take All*, 177 and 180.

3. Thomas Schatz, *Old Hollywood/New Hollywood*, 225.

4. Andrew Bergman, *We're in the Money* (New York: Harper Colophon, 1972), 133.

5. Stanley Cavell, *Pursuits of Happiness* (Cambridge: Harvard Univ. Press, 1981), 17.

6. See especially the visual and verbal references to theater and performance in *Adam's Rib*.

7. Cavell, *Pursuits*, 1.

8. Ibid., 60.

9. Ibid., 56.

10. Robert Alter, *After the Tradition*, (New York: Dutton, 1969), 111.

Chapter 6

1. Peter Cowie, *Ingmar Bergman* (London: Secker & Warburg, 1982), 277.

2. Ibid.

3. Paisley Livingston, *Ingmar Bergman and the Rituals of Art* (Ithica, N.Y.: Cornell University Press, 1982), 242.

4. Roger Ebert, "Interiors of Woody's Mind," sec. 3, col. 1. *Chicago Sun-Times* 10 September 1978.

5. Penelope Gilliatt, "Woody Reverberant," *New Yorker*, 7 August 1978, 77.

6. Yacowar, *Loser Take All*, 189.

7. Ira Halberstadt, "Scenes from a Mind," *Take One*, November 1978, 17.

8. Ibid.

9. Ibid.

10. Gilliatt, "Woody Reverberant," 77.

11. Jack Kroll, "The Inner Woody," *Newsweek*, 7 August 1978, 83.

12. Richard Goldstein, "Ten Minutes with Woody," *Village Voice*, 7 August 1978, 31.

13. Halberstadt, "Scenes," 16.

14. Ibid.

15. Ibid.

16. Ibid., 17.

Chapter 7

1. Gittelson, "Maturing," 106.

2. Thomas Schatz, *Hollywood Genres* (Philadelphia: Temple University Press, 1981), 198–199.

3. Janey Place, "Women in Film Noir," in E. Ann Kaplan, ed., *Women in Film Noir,* rev. ed. (London: British Film Institute, 1980), 41.

4. Richard Schickel, "Woody Allen Comes of Age," *Time,* 30 April 1979, 65.

5. Gittelson, "Maturing," 32.

6. Ibid., 102.

7. Place, "Film Noir," 50.

8. Yacowar, *Loser Take All,* 205.

9. Kaplan, introduction to *Women in Film Noir,* 14.

10. Dave Hirshey, "The Unlikely Titan," *Leisure,* 22 April 1979, 7.

Chapter 8

1. Veronica Geng, "Tsuris Memories," *Soho News,* 1 October 1980, 17.

2. Pauline Kael, "The Frog Who Turned into a Prince/The Prince Who Turned into a Frog," *New Yorker,* 27 October 1980, 184.

3. Janet Maslin, "Screen: The Acid Humor of Woody Allen's *Stardust Memories,*" *New York Times,* 26 September 1980, sec. C, p. 66.

4. Stephen Schiff, "Inferiors," *Boston Phoenix* 7 October 1980, sec. 3, p. 4.

5. Stephen Farber, "Woody Allen," *Moviegoer,* May 1985, 18.

6. Gene Siskel, "Woody," *Detroit Free Press* 7 June 1981, sec. E, p. 1, reprinted from the *Chicago Tribune.*

7. Vincent Canby, "The Humor, Hostility, and Mystery of Woody Allen," *New York Times,* 28 November 1980, sec. D, p. 33.

8. Deena Boyer, *The Two Hundred Days of 8½,* trans. Charles Ian Markman (New York: Macmillan, 1964), 130–31.

9. Ted Perry, *Filmguide to "8½"* (Bloomington: Indiana University Press, 1975), 64–66.

10. Siskel, "Woody," 1.

Chapter 9

1. See Ellen Pfeifer, "Allen's Latest: Amiable, Imitation," *Boston Herald American,* 16 July 1982, sec. B, p. 12, and Janet Maslin, "Film: A New Woody Allen," *New York Times,* 16 July 1982, sec. C, p. 4.

2. Mark Goodman, "The World According to Woody," *Family Weekly,* 11 July 1982, 7.

3. Andre Bazin, *Jean Renoir* (New York, Simon & Schuster, 1971), 298.

4. Ibid.

5. Arnold Hauser, *The Social History of Art,* (New York: Vintage, 1951), 4:169.

6. Alexander Sesonske, *Jean Renoir* (Cambridge: Harvard University Press, 1980), 382–83.

7. Ibid., 383.

8. David A. Cook, *A History of Narrative Film* (New York: Norton, 1981), 342.

9. Gavin Lambert, *"La Regle du jeu," London Film Society Notes* (11 August 1949), quoted in Raymond Durgnat, *Jean Renoir* (Berkeley: University of California Press, 1974), 197.

10. Hauser, *Social History of Art*, 167.

Chapter 10

1. Kakutani, "How Woody Allen's *Zelig* Was Born," 13.

2. The title may also have ironic overtones. One possible source for the title, which suggests this ambiguity, is Benjamin Rosenblatt's "Zelig," an obscure short story about a lonely and alienated Russian Jewish immigrant. It originally appeared in the *Bellman*, and was collected in *The Best Short Stories of 1915*, ed. Edward J. O'Brien (Boston: Small Maynard & Co., 1916), 219–25.

3. Pauline Kael, "Anybody Home?", *New Yorker*, 8 August 1983, 84–89.

4. Stam, *Reflexivity*, 254.

5. William Johnson, "Orson Welles: Of Time and Loss," *Film Quarterly* 21 (Fall 1967): 15, 19.

6. See especially Stewart Brand, Kevin Kelly, and Jay Kinney, "Digital Retouching: The End of Photography as Evidence of Anything," *Whole Earth Review*, July 1985, 42–49.

7. Bruce Kawin, "Time and Stasis in *La Jetée*," *Film Quarterly* 36, no. 1 (Fall 1982): 19.

8. Ibid., 20.

9. Stam, *Reflexivity*, 251, 253.

Chapter 11

1. See Roland Penrose, *Picasso: His Life and Work* (Berkeley: University of California Press, 1981), 107–13, and Anne Grelle, "Pablo Picasso," in *Encyclopedia of World Art*, vol. 11 (New York: McGraw-Hill, 1966), cols. 331–37.

2. For additional discussion of Fitzgerald and Allen, see Douglas Brode, *Woody Allen: His Films and Career*, (Secaucus, N.J.: Citadel Press, 1985).

3. Bakhtin traced the multiplicity of voices and the subversive quality of utterance in the dialogic novel to the spirit of the cyclic medieval folk carnival, in which people took to the streets in costume, in

which the vulgar parodied the polite and sacred to symbolically destroy all convention and restriction. Bakhtin sees the survival of carnival in the profoundly subversive and often grotesque festive comedy of Rabelais, in which the imagination grabs victory over oppression and mortality. For Bakhtin, the carnival was a drama of death and rebirth, a tapestry of voices and images that reveled in contradiction, but that suggested the triumph of a life-affirming spirit in its very form. See Bakhtin, *Rabelais and His World*.

4. Jack Kroll, "Woody's Bow to Broadway," *Newsweek*, 30 January 1984, 69.

5. Umberto Eco, "Frames of Comic Reference," in Umberto Eco, V. V. Ivanov, and Monica Rector, *Carnival!* (New York: Mouton Publishers, 1984), 8.

6. Robert Alter, *Partial Magic: The Novel as Self-conscious Genre* (Berkeley: University of California Press, 1975), 28–29.

7. See Berger, "Business of Comedy," 76.

8. *Broadway Danny Rose* may have been inspired in part by *Meet Danny Wilson*, starring Frank Sinatra (Mia Farrow's ex-husband). That film is a black-and-white film-noir musical. It focuses on Danny Wilson, a singer with a weak character, who becomes entangled with organized crime and betrays his personal manager and lifelong friend.

9. Fred Ferretti, "How Woody Allen's Old World Inspired His New Film," *New York Times* 19 February 1984, sec. H, 1, 16.

10. Also see Brode, *Allen: His Films*, 239.

11. Waugh, *Metafiction*, 2.

12. Jack Kroll, "Reel Life versus Real Life", *Newsweek*, 25 February 1985, 84.

13. Ludwig Wittgenstein, *Tractatus Logico-Philosophicus*, trans. D. F. Pears and B. F. McGinness, (London: Routledge & Kegan Paul, 1961), 115.

14. Stephen Schiff, "Woody-One-Note," *Vanity Fair* 48, no. 3 (March 1985): 101.

SELECTED BIBLIOGRAPHY

Primary Sources

1. Plays
Don't Drink the Water. New York: Random House, 1967.
The Floating Light Bulb. New York: Random House, 1982.
Play It Again, Sam. New York: Random House, 1969.

2. Screenplays
Four Films of Woody Allen. New York: Random House, 1982. Contains
    Annie Hall, Interiors, Manhattan, and *Stardust Memories.*
Woody Allen's "Play It Again, Sam." edited by Richard J. Anobile. New
    York: Grosset & Dunlap, 1972. A frame-by-frame reproduction of
    the film with a critical introduction by the editor and an interview
    with film director Herbert Ross.

3. Stories and Essays
Getting Even. New York: Random House, 1971.
Side Effects. New York: Random House, 1980.
Without Feathers. New York: Random House, 1975.

Secondary Sources

1. Books
Adler, Bill, and Feinman, Jeffrey. *Woody Allen, Clown Prince of American
    Humor.* New York: Pinnacle Books, 1975. A readable, early light-
    weight overview that covers Allen's work through *Love and Death.*
Benayoun, Robert. *The Films of Woody Allen.* New York: Harmony
    Books, 1986. The newest book on Allen, translated from the french
    version, *Au-Delá du Language.* Paris: Editions Herscher, 1985. Ben-
    ayoun emphasizes Allen's growth as a visual artist who is always
    testing the limits of his medium.
Brode, Douglas. *Woody Allen: His Films and Career.* Secaucus, New Jer-
    sey: Citadel Press, 1985. An astute popular book with many illus-
    trations that portrays Allen as a paradoxical romantic idealist and
    a pessimistic realist. The book avoids serious consideration of re-
    flexivity and intertextuality and dismisses *Interiors, Stardust Mem-
    ories,* and *A Midsummer Night's Sex Comedy* as weak films.
    Filmography, but no notes or bibliography.

Burton, Dee. *I Dream of Woody*. New York: William Morrow & Co., 1984. Eighty fans' dreams of Allen and brief interpretations of the subjects' perceptions of him.

Guthrie, Lee. *Woody Allen, a Biography*. New York: Drake Publishers, 1978. This unauthorized and untrustworthy biography was taken off the market shortly after publication when Allen sued Guthrie and Drake Publishers because Guthrie appropriated materials from Allen, from Eric Lax, and from other secondary sources without attribution.

Hample, Stuart. *Non-Being and Somethingness*. New York: Random House, 1978. Selections from the comic strip *Inside Woody Allen*. Includes introduction by R. Buckminster Fuller.

Hirsch, Foster. *Love, Sex, Death, and the Meaning of Life*. New York: McGraw-Hill, 1981. Discusses films through *Stardust Memories* and is strong on comedy backgrounds to Allen's work. Takes pride in creating a lighter reading of Allen's work than Yacowar, but dismisses several Allen films summarily. Bibliography.

Jacobs, Diane. . . . *but we need the eggs: The Magic of Woody Allen*. New York: St. Martin's Press, 1982. Sees the tension between reality and magic as the structure of Allen's work. The book covers material through *Stardust Memories*. Filmography.

Lax, Eric. *On Being Funny: Woody Allen and Comedy*. New York: Charterhouse Press, 1975. Paperback edition. Manor Books, 1977. Lax spent many months with Allen while he was making *Sleeper* and is a good source for understanding Allen's attitudes and his work during that time. Reportorial treatment allows few critical evaluations, but portrays Allen as a "survivor" and a hard-working, conscientious filmmaker.

Palmer, Myles. *Woody Allen: An Illustrated Biography*. New York: Proteus, 1980. Includes several photographs not reprinted elsewhere and a popular biographical overview.

Yacowar, Maurice. *Loser Take All*. New York: Frederick Ungar, 1979. Pioneering scholarly study of Allen's work is a penetrating, coherent account of Allen's writings and films (no biography) through *Manhattan*. Yacowar takes Allen's humor seriously; he portrays Allen's central character as the eternal outsider who nevertheless consistently wins the day. Includes a filmography, discography, and selected bibliography.

2. Parts of Books

Berger, Phil. *The Last Laugh: The World of Stand Up Comics*. New York: Wm. Morrow & Co., 1975. Interview with Jack Rollins about Allen's nightclub debut.

Byron, Stuart, and Elizabeth Weis, eds. *The National Society of Film Critics on Movie Comedy*. New York: Grossman Publishers, 1977.

Reprint. Penguin, 1977. An overview and discussions of *Bananas, Sleeper, Love and Death;* also a section on Allen vs. Mel Brooks.

Coursodon, Jean-Pierre. *American Directors,* vol. 2. New York: McGraw-Hill, 1983. Includes a short analytical discussion of Allen's films from *Take the Money and Run* to *Stardust Memories.*

Ebert, Roger. *A Kiss Is Still a Kiss: Roger Ebert at the Movies.* Kansas City and New York: Andrews, McMeel & Parker, 1984. Includes 1982 Allen interview primarily about *A Midsummer Night's Sex Comedy.*

Erens, Patricia. *The Jew in American Cinema.* Bloomington: Indiana University Press, 1984.

Friedman, Lester D. *Hollywood's Image of the Jew.* New York: Frederick Ungar, 1982. Appreciation of Allen as a Jewish humorist and creator of Jewish film characters.

Kael, Pauline. *Reeling.* Boston: Little, Brown and Co., 1976. Includes four-page review of *Sleeper.*

———. *Taking It All In.* New York: Holt Rinehart and Winston, 1982. Includes negative review of *A Midsummer Night's Sex Comedy.*

———. *When the Lights Go Down.* New York: Holt, Rinehart and Winston, 1980. Negative review of *Interiors.*

Kauffmann, Stanley. *Before My Eyes: Film Criticism and Comment.* New York: Harper & Row, 1980. Includes reviews of *Love and Death, Annie Hall, Interiors,* and *Manhattan.*

Lasch, Christopher. *The Culture of Narcissism: American Life in an Age of Diminishing Expectations.* New York: W. W. Norton, 1978. Sees Allen's work as an example of self-conscious, pseudoconfessional narcissistic style.

Leyda, Jay, ed.. *Film Makers Speak: Voices of Film Experience.* New York: Macmillan, 1977. Reprint, with update by Doug Tomlinson. New York: Da Capo Press, 1984. Just two paragraphs of quotations.

Manchel, Frank. *The Box-Office Clowns.* New York: Franklin Watts, 1979.

Mellen, Joan. *Big Bad Wolves: Masculinity in the American Film.* New York: Pantheon, 1977. "Woody Allen's comedies about the puny neurotic male in glasses attempting to be a man in a culture glorifying John Wayne and Humphrey Bogart have honest moments despite Allen's failure to transcend the values of Wayne."

Monaco, James. *American Film Now.* New York: Oxford University Press, 1979. Rev. ed. New York: Zoetrope, 1984.

Probst, Leonard. *Off Camera.* New York: Stein & Day, 1975. Includes a chapter-length interview with Allen.

Rosenblum, Ralph, and Robert Karen. *When the Shooting Stops . . . the Editing Begins.* New York: Viking Press, 1979. Firsthand insights into the relationship between Allen and his editor on *Take the Money and Run, Bananas, Sleeper, Love and Death,* and *Annie Hall.*

Schatz, Thomas. *Old Hollywood/New Hollywood: Ritual, Art, and Industry.* Ann Arbor: UMI Research Press, 1983. Includes a reading of *Annie Hall* as a modernist, reflexive film (also see *Literature/Film Quarterly* [January 1982]).

Schechner, Mark. "Woody Allen: The Failure of the Therapeutic." In *From Hester Street to Hollywood*, edited by Sarah Blacher Cohen, 231–44. Bloomington: Indiana University Press, 1983. Laments Allen's recent tendency to "smother" comedy "in the wet blankets of *significance* and "high school existentialism," thus losing touch with "the particular genius of Yiddish comedy."

Seidman, Steve. *Comedian Comedy: A Tradition in Hollywood Film.* Ann Arbor: UMI Research Press, 1981. Attempts to "establish that films with comedians can be seen as an identifiable American film genre." Places Allen within this genre and cites many examples from his films.

Simon, John. *Reverse Angle: A Decade of American Films.* New York: Clarkson N. Potter Inc./Crown Publishers, 1982. Reviews *Bananas, Play It Again, Sam, Sleeper, Love and Death, The Front, Interiors,* and *Stardust Memories.*

Smith, Dian G. *American Filmmakers Today.* Poole, England: Blandford Press, 1983. Discussions of filmmakers who exercise control over their films includes a 16 page overview of Allen's work.

Stam, Robert. *Reflexivity in Film and Literature: From Don Quixote to Jean-Luc Godard.* Ann Arbor: UMI Research Press, 1985. A lucid and incisive study of reflexivity that includes a reading of *Stardust Memories* as "self-conscious" cinema.

Wilde, Larry. *Great Comedians Talk about Comedy.* New York: Citadel Press, 1968. Interview with Allen.

3. Articles

Berger, Phil. "The Business of Comedy." *New York Times Magazine,* 9 June 1985, 55 and passim. About Allen's managers.

Bester, Alfred. "Conversation with Woody Allen." *Holiday* (May 1969): 70–71 and passim.

Blowen, Michael. "Woody Allen, Businessman." Reprinted in *Detroit Free Press,* 18 September 1983, 1, from the *Boston Globe.*

Canby, Vincent. "Woody Allen Continues to Refine His Cinematic Art." *New York Times,* 17 July 1973, 15. About *Zelig.*

———. "The Screen: Woody Allen's *Manhattan.*" *New York Times,* 25 April 1979, 17.

———. "Notes on Woody Allen and American Comedy." *New York Times,* 13 May 1979, 1.

———. "The Humor, Hostility and Mystery of Woody Allen." *New York Times,* 28 September 1980, 1. About *Stardust Memories.*

————. "Woody Allen: Risking It without Laughs." *New York Times,* 6 August 1978, 1. About *Interiors.*

Dart, John. "Woody Allen, Theologian." *Christian Century* 94 (22 June 1977): 585–90.

Davis, J. Madison. "The Literary Skills of Woody Allen." *West Virginia University Philological Papers* 29 (1983): 105–11.

Dempsey, Michael. "The Autobiography of Woody Allen." *Film Comment* 15 (May–June 1979): 9–16.

Denby, David. "Kvetches and Whispers," *New York,* 14 August 1978, 60–62. About *Interiors.*

Didion, Joan. "Review of *Annie Hall, Interiors,* and *Manhattan.*" *New York Review of Books* 16 (August 1979): 18. Sees *Manhattan, Interiors,* and *Annie Hall* as evidence that Allen's films exemplify the inauthenticity and self-absorption that he appears to criticize.

Drew, Bernard. "Woody Allen Is Feeling Better." *American Film* 2 (May 1977): 10–15. Interview.

Farber, Stephen. "Woody Allen." *Moviegoer* 4 (May 1985): 14–19. Interview on *The Purple Rose of Cairo.*

Feldstein, Richard. "The Dissolution of the Self in *Zelig*" *Literature/Film Quarterly* 13 (January 1985): 155–160. A provocative discussion of identity issues in *Zelig* with reference to Jacque Lacan's "mirror phase."

Ferretti, Fred. "How Woody Allen's Old World Inspired His New Film." *New York Times* 19 February 1985, 1 and passim. Describes New York of the 1950s and 1960s that inspired *Broadway Danny Rose.*

Gilliatt, Penelope. "Guilty, with An Explanation." *New Yorker,* 4 February 1974, 39. Interview.

————. "Meanwhile, Back at the Uterus." *The New Yorker,* 19 August 1971, 58–61. Allen's *Everything You Always Wanted to Know about Sex* and Dr. David Reuben's book.

————. "Woody Reverberant." *New Yorker,* 7 August 1978, 76–78. About *Interiors.*

Gittelson, Natalie. "The Maturing of Woody Allen." *New York Times Magazine,* 22 April 1979, 30–32 and passim. In-depth interview.

Gray, Francis du Plessix. "Woody Allen: America's Melancholy Funnyman." *Cosmopolitan* 177 (September 1974): 146 and passim. Interview.

Grenier, Richard. "Woody Allen on the American Character." *Commentary* 76 (November 1983): 61–65. Claims *Zelig* was "lifted from *Reds*" and alludes to Stephen Jacob Weinberg, a great imposter of the 1920s.

Halberstadt, Ira. "Scenes from a Mind." *Take One,* November 1978, 16–20. Interview on *Interiors.*

Hirshey, Dave. "Woody Rates the Comics." *Sunday News Magazine,* 20 March 1977, 20 and passim.

Jacobs, Diane. "Ineffable Dreams." *Horizon* 23 (December 1980): 70–72. *Stardust Memories* and the American dream.

James, Caryn. "Auteur! Auteur!" *New York Times Magazine,* 10 January 1986, 18–30.

Johnston, Richard J. H.. "You Name It, Woody Is Doing It." *New York Times Magazine,* 22 April 1979, 6 and passim.

Kael, Pauline. "Anybody Home?" *New Yorker,* 8 August 1983, 84–88. Review of *Zelig.*

———. "The Frog Who Turned into a Prince/The Prince Who Turned into a Frog." *New Yorker,* 27 October 1980, 183–90. Review of *Stardust Memories.*

Kakutani, Michiko. "How Woody Allen's *Zelig* Was Born in Anxiety and Grew into Comedy." *New York Times, 18 July 1983, 13.* Includes interview.

Kelley, Ken. "A Conversation with the Real Woody Allen or Someone Just Like Him. *Rolling Stone,* 1 July 1976, 34 and passim. Interview.

Kroll, Jack. "Woody Funny, But He's Serious." *Newsweek,* 24 April 1978, 62–66 and passim.

Liebman, Robert L. "Rabbis or Rakes, Schlemiels or Supermen? Jewish Identity in Charles Chaplin, Jerry Lewis, and Woody Allen." *Literature/Film Quarterly* 12 (January 1984): 195–201. Jewish identity and the relationship between schlemiel characters and superheroes.

Lerman, Leo. "Woody the Great: The Funniest Man of the Year." *Vogue* 160 (December 1972): 144–51. Exceptional photos of Allen mimicking Chaplin, Keaton, Groucho, and Harpo, and a short interview with Allen about these comics.

Londre, Felicia Hardison. "Using Comic Devices to Answer the Ultimate Questions: Tom Stoppard's *Jumpers* and Woody Allen's *God,*" *Comparative Drama* 14 (1980–81): 346-54. Both playwrights use comic devices not to provide answers to the question about the nature of God, but "to wonder at its continuing importance in the mind of modern man."

Moss, Robert F. "Creators on Creating: Woody Allen." *Saturday Review* 7 (November 1980): 40–44. Interview.

Mundy, Robert. "Woody Allen." *Cinema* (Los Angeles) 7 (Winter 1972–73): 6–8.

———, and Mamber, Stephen. "Woody Allen: An Interview." *Cinema* (Los Angeles) 7 (Winter 1972–73): 14–21.

Pinsker, Sanford. "Jumping on Hollywood's Bones, or How S. J. Perelman and Woody Allen Found It at the Movies." *Midwest Quarterly* 21 (Spring 1980): 371–83. Allen recognizes "movies' artificiality on one hand and the continuing power of their artifice on the other."

Rich, Frank. "An Interview with Woody." *Time,* 30 April 1979, 68–69. Especially about *Manhattan.*

———. "Woody Allen Wipes the Smile off His Face." *Esquire* 87 (May 1977): 72 and passim. Interview.

Roth, Evelyn. "Photo Fictions: Brilliantly Faked Pictures of Woody Allen's *Zelig* Invent a Non-existent Past." *American Photographer* 12 (May 1984): 68–73.

Sarris, Andrew. " 'S Wonderful." *The Village Voice*, 30 April 1979, 51 and passim. Review of *Manhattan*.

———. "Woody Allen's Funny Valentine." *The Village Voice*, 25 April 1977, 45. Review of *Annie Hall*.

Schatz, Thomas. "Annie Hall and the Issue of Modernism." *Literature/Film Quarterly* 10 (January 1982): 180–87. Discusses the film's reflexivity.

Schickel, Richard. "The Basic Woody Allen Joke: 'Not Only is God Dead but Try Getting a Plumber on Weekends.' " *New York Times Magazine*, 7 January 1973, 10 and passim. A penetrating discussion of Allen's appeal in our time.

———. "Woody Allen Comes of Age." *Time*, 30 April 1979, 62–65. Review of *Manhattan* includes interview with Marshall Brickman.

Schwartz, Tony. "The Conflicting Life and Art of Woody Allen." *New York Times*, 19 October 1980, 28.

Shapiro, Barbara, "Woody Allen's Search for Self." *Journal of Popular Culture* 19 (Spring 1986): 47–62.

Siskel, Gene. "Woody Allen on Love, Life, and Ronald Reagan." *Chicago Tribune*, 11 June 1982, 5.

Spiegel, Alan. "American Flim-Flam." *Salamagundi* 41 (Spring 1978): 153–69. *Annie Hall* exemplifies the fact that "movies have arrived at a stymied point in their development . . . where paradoxically the old formulas can neither be viably used nor fully relinquished."

Trotsky, Judith. "The Art of Comedy: Woody Allen and *Sleeper*." *Film-makers Newsletter*, Summer 1974, 20–24.

Turan, Kenneth. "The Comic Genius of Woody Allen." *Progressive*, 37 (March 1973): 44–46.

Wasserman, Harry. "Woody Allen: Stumbling through the Looking Glass." *The Velvet Light Trap Review of Cinema* 7 (Winter 1972–73): 37–40.

Young, Vernon. "Interiors." *Commentary* 67 (January 1979): 60–64.

Zoglin, Richard. "Manhattan's Methusalah." *Film Comment* 22 (May–June 1986): 16–20.

FILMOGRAPHY

What's New, Pussycat? (Famous Artists, 1965)
Producer: Charles K. Feldman
Director: Clive Donner
Assistant Director: Enrico Isacco
Screenplay: Woody Allen
Photography: Jean Badal (Technicolor, Scope)
Art Direction: Jacques Saulnier
Special Effects: Bob MacDonald
Music: Burt Bacharach
Editor: Fergus McDonnell
Sound: William-Robert Sivel
Cast: Peter Sellers (Fritz Fassbender), Peter O'Toole (Michael James), Romy Schneider (Carol Werner), Capucine (Renée Lefedvre), Paula Prentiss (Liz Bien), Woody Allen (Victor Shakapopolis), Ursula Andress (Rita), Edra Gale (Anna Fassbender)
Running time: 108 minutes
16 mm. rental: MGM/United Artists

What's Up, Tiger Lily? (American International Pictures, 1966)
English adaptation of *Kagi No Kagi* ((Key of Keys [Japan, 1964])
Producer: Tomoyuki Tanaka
Director: Senkichi Taniguchi
Screenplay: Hideo Ando
Photography: Kazuo Yamado (Eastmancolor, Scope)
Running Time: 94 minutes
Re-release Director: Woody Allen
Production Conception: Ben Shapiro
Executive Producer: Henry G. Saperstein
Screenplay and Dubbing: Woody Allen, Frank Buxton, Len Maxwell, Louise Lasser, Mickey Rose, Julie Bennett, Bryna Wilson
Music: The Lovin' Spoonful
Cast: Tatsuya Mihasha (Phil Moskowitz), Mie Hana (Terry Yaki), Akiko Wakayabayashi (Suki Yaki), Tadao Nakamura (Shepherd Wong), Susumu Kurobe (Wing Fat)
Running Time: 79 minutes
16 mm. rental: Twyman

Casino Royale (A Famous Artists Production, released by Columbia Pictures, 1967)

Producers: Charles K. Feldman, Jerry Bresler

Directors: John Huston, Kenneth Hughes, Val Guest, Robert Parrish, Joseph McGrath

Screenplay: Wolf Mankowitz, John Law, Michael Bayers, from an Ian Fleming novel

Photography: Jack Hildyard (Panavision, Technicolor)

Special Effects: Cliff Richardson, Roy Whybrow

Production Design: Michael Ayringer

Music: Burt Bacharach

Editor: Bill Lenny

Cast: Peter Sellers (Evelyn Tremble), Ursula Andress (Vesper Lynd), David Niven (Sir James Bond), Orson Welles (Le Chiffre), Joanna Pettet (Mata Bond), Deborah Kerr (Widow McTarry), Daliah Lavi (Detainer), Woody Allen (Jimmy Bond), William Holden (Ransome), Charles Boyer (LeGrand), John Huston (M), Kurt Kaznar (Smernov), George Raft (himself), Jean Paul Belmondo (French Legionnaire), Terrence Cooper (Cooper), Barbara Bouchet (Moneypenny)

Running Time: 130 minutes

16 mm. rental: Films Inc., Twyman, Clem Williams

Don't Drink the Water (Avco Embassy, 1969)

Producer: Charles Joffe

Director: Howard Morris

Screenplay: R. S. Allen and Harvey Bullock, based on stageplay by Woody Allen

Photography: Harvey Genkins

Art Director: Robert Gundlach

Music: Pat Williams

Editor: Ralph Rosenblum

Assistant Director: Louis Stroller

Cast: Jackie Gleason (Walter Hollander), Estelle Parsons (Marion Hollander), Ted Bessell (Axel Magee), Joan Delaney (Susan Hollander), Richard Libertini (Drobney), Michael Constantine (Krojack), Avery Schreiber (Sultan)

Running time: 98 minutes

16 mm. rental: Films, Inc.

Take the Money and Run (Palomar Pictures, 1969)

Producer: Charles H. Joffe

Director: Woody Allen

Assistant Directors: Louis Stroller, Walter Hill
Screenplay: Woody Allen, Mickey Rose
Photography: Lester Shorr (Technicolor)
Art Direction: Fred Harpman
Special Effects: A. D. Flowers
Music: Marvin Hamlisch
Editors: Paul Jordan, Ron Kalish
Cast: Woody Allen (Virgil Starkwell), Janet Margolin (Louise), Marcel
     Hillaire (Fritz), Jacqueline Hyde (Miss Blair), Lonnie Chapman
     (Jake), Jan Merlin (Al), James Anderson (Chain Gang Warden),
     Howard Storm (Red), Mark Gordon (Vince), Micil Murphy (Frank),
     Minnow Moskowitz (Joe Agneta), Nate Jacobson (Judge), Grace
     Bauer (Farm-House lady), Ethel Sokolow (Mother Starkwell), Hen-
     ry Leff (Father Starkwell), Don Frazier (Psychiatrist), Mike O'Dowd
     (Michael Sullivan), Jackson Beck (Narrator), Louise Lasser (Kay
     Lewis)
Running time: 85 minutes
16 mm. rental: Films, Inc.

Bananas (United Artists, 1971)

Producer: Jack Grossberg
Director: Woody Allen
Assistant Director: Fred T. Gallo
Associate Producer: Ralph Rosenblum
Screenplay: Woody Allen, Mickey Rose
Photography: Andrew M. Costikyan (Deluxe Color)
Production Design: Ed Wittstein
Special Effects: Don B. Courtney
Music: Marvin Hamlisch
Editor: Ron Kalish
Cast: Woody Allen (Fielding Mellish), Louise Lasser (Nancy), Carlos
     Montalban (General Vargas), Natividad Abascal (Yolanda), Jacobo
     Morales (Esposito), Miguel Suarez (Luis), David Ortiz (Sanchez),
     Rene Enriquez (Diaz), Jack Axelrod (Arroyo), Howard Cosell (Him-
     self), Roger Grimsby (Himself), Don Dunphy (Himself), Charlotte
     Rae (Mrs. Mellish), Stanley Ackerman (Dr. Mellish)
Running Time: 81 minutes
16 mm. rental: MGM/United Artists

Play It Again, Sam (Paramount Pictures, 1972)

Producer: Arthur P. Jacobs
Production Supervisor: Roger M. Rothstein
Director: Herbert Ross

Assistant Director: William Gerrity
Screenplay: Woody Allen, based on his stageplay
Photography: Owen Roizman
Music: Billy Goldenberg
Editor: Marion Rothman
Cast: Woody Allen (Allan Felix), Diane Keaton (Linda), Tony Roberts
    (Dick), Jerry Lacy (Bogart), Susan Anspach (Nancy), Jennifer Salt
    (Sharon), Joy Bang (Julie), Viva (Jennifer)
Running Time: 86 minutes
16 mm. rental: Films, Inc.

Everything You Always Wanted to Know about Sex (*but were
afraid to ask)* (United Artists, 1972)
Producer: Charles H. Joffe
Director: Woody Allen
Assistant Directors: Fred T. Gallo, Terry M. Carr
Screenplay: Woody Allen, from the book by David Reuben
Photography: David M. Walsh
Production Design: Dale Hennesy
Music: Mundell Lowe
Editor: Eric Albertson
Cast: Woody Allen (Fool, Fabrizio, Victor, Sperm), John Carradine (Dr.
    Bernardo), Lou Jacobi (Sam), Louise Lasser (Gina), Anthony
    Quayle (King), Tony Randall (Operator), Lynn Redgrave (Queen),
    Burt Reynolds (Switchboard), Gene Wilder (Dr. Ross), Jack Barry
    (Himself), Toni Holt (Herself), Robert Q. Lewis (Himself), Heather
    Macrae (Helen), Pamela Mason (Herself), Regis Philbin (Himself),
    Titos Vandis (Milos), Geoffrey Holder (Sorcerer), Baruch Lumet
    (Rabbi Baumel), Robert Walden (Sperm), H. E. West (Bernard
    Jaffe)
Running Time: 87 minutes
16 mm. rental: MGM/United Artists

Sleeper (United Artists, 1973)
Producer: Jack Grossberg
Director: Woody Allen
Assistant Directors: Fred T. Gallo, Henry J. Lange, Jr.
Screenplay: Woody Allen, Marshall Brickman
Editor: Ralph Rosenblum
Photography: David M. Walsh
Production Design: Dale Hennesy
Special Effects: A. D. Flowers
Music: Woody Allen, with the Preservation Hall Jazz Band and the New
    Orleans Funeral Ragtime Orchestra

Cast: Woody Allen (Miles Monroe), Diane Keaton (Luna Schlosser), John Back (Erno Windt), Mary Gregory (Dr. Melik), Don Keefer (Dr. Tyron), John McLiam (Dr. Agon), Bartlett Robinson (Dr. Orva), Marya Small (Dr. Nero), Chris Forbes (Rainer Krebs)

Running Time: 88 minutes

16 mm. rental: MGM/United Artists

Love and Death (United Artists, 1975)

Producer: Charles H. Joffe

Director: Woody Allen

Assistant Directors: Paul Feyder, Bernard Cohn

Screenplay: Woody Allen

Photography: Ghislain Cloquet

Art Direction: Willy Holt

Special Effects: Kit West

Music: S. Prokofiev

Editor: Ralph Rosenblum

Costume Design: Gladys De Segonzac

Cast: Woody Allen (Boris), Diane Keaton (Sonia), Georges Adet (Old Nehamken), Frank Adu (Drill Sergeant), Edmond Ardisson (Priest), Feodor Atkine (Mikhail), Lloyd Battista (Don Francisco), Jack Berard (General Lecoq), Yves Brainville (Andre), Brian Coburn (Dmitri), Henri Coutet (Minskov), Henry Czarniak (Ivan), Despo Diamantidou (Mother), Florian (Uncle Nickolai), Olga Georges-Picot (Countess Alexandrovna), Harold Gould (Count Anton), Harry Hankin (Uncle Sasha), Jessica Harper (Natasha), Tony Jan (Vladimir Maximovitch), Tutte Lemkow (Pierre), Jack Lenoir (Krapotkin), Leib Lensky (Father Andre), Alfred Lutter (Young Boris), Ed Marcus (Raskov), Howard Vernon (General Leveque), James Tolkan (Napoleon), Jacob Witkin (Sushkin)

Running Time: 85 minutes

16 mm. rental: MGM/United Artists

The Front (Columbia Pictures, 1976)

Producer: Martin Ritt

Director: Martin Ritt

Assistant Directors: Peter Scoppa, Ralph Singleton

Screenplay: Walter Bernstein

Photography: Michael Chapman

Art Direction: Charles Bailey

Music: Dave Grusin

Editor: Sidney Levin

Cast: Woody Allen (Howard Prince), Zero Mostel (Hecky Brown), Herschel Bernardi (Phil Sussman), Michael Murphy (Alfred Miller),

Andrea Marcovicci (Florence Barrett), Remak Ramsay (Hennessey), Marvin Lichterman (Myer Prince), Lloyd Gough (Delaney), David Marguiles (Phelps), Joshua Shelley (Sam), Normal Rose (Howard's attorney)
Running Time: 94 minutes
16 mm. rental: Films, Inc., Clem Williams

Woody Allen: An American Comedy (Films for the Humanities, Inc., 1977) (Documentary)
Producer: Harold Mantell
Director: Harold Mantell
Narrator: Woody Allen
Running Time: 30 minutes
16 mm. rental: Films for the Humanities, Inc., P.O. Box 2053, Princeton, New Jersey 08540

Annie Hall (United Artists, 1977)
Producer: Charles H. Joffe
Director: Woody Allen
Assitant Directors: Fred T. Gallo, Fred Blankfein
Screenplay: Woody Allen, Marshall Brickman
Photography: Gordon Willis
Art Direction: Mel Bourne
Animated Sequences: Chris Ishii
Editor: Ralph Rosenblum
Costume Design: Ruth Morley
Cast: Woody Allen (Alvy Singer), Diane Keaton (Annie Hall), Tony Roberts (Rob), Carol Kane (Allison), Paul Simon (Tony Lacy), Shelley Duvall (Pam), Janet Margolin (Robin), Colleen Dewhurst (Mom Hall), Christopher Walken (Duane), Donald Symington (Dad Hall), Helen Ludlam (Grammy Hall), Mordecai Lawner (Alvy's Father), Joan Newman (Alvy's Mother), Jonathan Munk (Alvy, aged 9), Russell Horton (Man in theater line), Marshall McLuhan (Himself)
Running Time: 93 minutes
16 mm. rental: MGM/United Artists

Interiors (United Artists, 1978)
Producer: Charles H. Joffe
Director: Woody Allen
Assistant Director: Martin Berman
Screenplay: Woody Allen
Photography: Gordon Willis
Production Design: Mel Bourne

Editor: Ralph Rosenblum
Costume Design: Joel Schumacher
Cast: Kristin Griffith (Flyn), Marybeth Hurt (Joey), Richard Jordan
    (Frederick), Diane Keaton (Renata), E. G. Marshall (Arthur), Ger-
    aldine Page (Eve), Maureen Stapleton (Pearl), Sam Waterston
    (Mike)
Running Time: 93 minutes
16 mm. rental: MGM/United Artists

Manhattan (United Artists, 1979)

Executive Producer: Robert Greenhut
Producer: Charles H. Joffe
Director: Woody Allen
Assistant Directors: Frederic B. Blankfein, Joan Spiegel Feinstein
Screenplay: Woody Allen, Marshall Brickman
Photography: Gordon Willis
Production Design: Mel Bourne
Music: George Gershwin, adapted and arranged by Tom Pierson,
    performed by the New York Philharmonic, conducted by Zubin
    Mehta, and the Buffalo Philharmonic, conducted by Michael Tilson
    Thomas
Editor: Susan E. Morse
Costume Design: Albert Wolsky
Cast: Woody Allen (Isaac Davis), Diane Keaton (Mary Wilke), Michael
    Murphy (Yale), Mariel Hemingway (Tracy), Meryl Streep (Jill),
    Anne Byrne (Emily), Karen Ludwig (Connie), Michael O'Donoghue
    (Dennis), Bella Abzug (Guest of honor)
Running Time: 96 minutes
16 mm. rental: MGM/United Artists

Stardust Memories (United Artists, 1980)

Executive Producers: Jack Rollins, Charles H. Joffe
Producer: Robert Greenhut
Director: Woody Allen
Assistant Director: Frederic B. Blankfein
Screenplay: Woody Allen
Photography: Gordon Willis
Production Design: Mel Bourne
Music: Dick Hyman
Editor: Susan E. Morse
Costume Design: Santo Loquasto
Cast: Woody Allen (Sandy Bates), Charlotte Rampling (Dorrie), Jessica
    Harper (Daisy), Marie-Christine Barrault (Isobel), Tony Roberts

(Tony), Daniel Stern (Actor), Amy Wright (Shelley), Helen Hanft (Vivian Orkin), John Rothman (Jack Abel), Anne De Salvo (Sandy's sister), Bob Maroff (Jerry Abraham), Gabrielle Strasun (Charlotte Ames), Robert Munk (Boy Sandy)
Running Time: 89 minutes
16 mm. rental: MGM/United Artists

A Midsummer Night's Sex Comedy (Orion Pictures, 1982)
Executive Producer: Charles H. Joffe
Producer: Robert Greenhut
Associate Producer: Michael Peyser
Director: Woody Allen
Assistant Director: Frederic B. Blankfein
Screenplay: Woody Allen
Photography: Gordon Willis
Production Design: Mel Bourne
Casting: Juliet Taylor
Music: Felix Mendelssohn
Editor: Susan E. Morse
Costume Design: Santo Loquasto
Cast: Woody Allen (Andrew Hobbes), Mary Steenburgen (Adrian Hobbes), Jose Ferrer (Leopold), Mia Farrow (Ariel Weymouth), Tony Roberts (Dr. Jordan Maxwell), Julie Hagerty (Dulcy Ford)
Running Time: 88 minutes
16 mm. rental: Films Inc.

Zelig (Orion Pictures, 1983)
Executive Producers: Charles H. Joffe and Jack Rollins
Producer: Robert Greenhut
Associate Producer: Michael Peyser
Director: Woody Allen
Photography: Gordon Willis
Screenplay: Woody Allen
Production Design: Mel Bourne
Music: Dick Hyman
Editor: Susan E. Morse
Costume Design: Santo Loquasto
Casting: Juliet Taylor
Optical Effects: Joel Hyneck and Stuart Robertson
Stills Animation: Steven Plastrik and Computer Opticals, Inc.
Cast: Woody Allen (Leonard Zelig), Mia Farrow (Eudora Fletcher), Mary Louise Wilson (Sister Ruth), Stephanie Farrow (Young Sister Meryl), Ellen Garrison (Older Dr. Fletcher), Jean Trowbridge (Eu-

dora's mother), Deborah Rush (Lita Fox), Susan Sontag, Irving Howe, Saul Bellow, Bricktop, Dr. Bruno Bettelheim, John Morton Blum (Themselves).
Running Time 79 minutes
16 mm. rental: Films Inc., Swank

Broadway Danny Rose (Orion Pictures, 1984)
Producer: Robert Greenhut
Associate Producer: Michael Peyser
Director: Woody Allen
Screenplay: Woody Allen
Photography: Gordon Willis
Production Design: Mel Bourne
Editor: Susan E. Morse
Costume Design: Jeffrey Kurland
Music: Dick Hyman
Casting: Juliet Taylor
Cast: Woody Allen (Danny Rose), Mia Farrow (Tina Vitale), Nick Apollo Forte (Lou Canova), Corbett Monica, Howard Storm, Morty Gunty, Sandy Baron, Will Jordan, Jackie Gayle, Jack Rollins (Themselves—comics in the Carnegie Deli frame), Milton Berle (Himself), Joe Franklin (Himself), Hugh Reynolds (Barney Dunn), Craig Vanderburgh (Ray Webb), Paul Greco (Vito Rispoli), Frank Renzulli (Joe Rispoli), Edwin Bordo (Johnny Rispoli), Gina De Angelis (Johnny's mother), Gloria Parker (Water glass musician), Bob and Etta Rollins (Balloon act)
Running Time: 85 minutes
16 mm. rental: Films, Inc.

The Purple Rose of Cairo (Orion Pictures/Jack Rollins and Charles H. Joffe Production, 1985)
Executive Producer: Charles H. Joffe
Producer: Robert Greenhut
Associate Producers: Michael Peyser, Gayle Sicilia
Director: Woody Allen
Screenplay: Woody Allen
Photography: Gordon Willis
Production Designer: Stuart Wurtzel
Costume Designer: Jeffrey Kurland
Editor: Susan E. Morse
Original Music: Dick Hyman
Casting: Juliet Taylor
Cast: Mia Farrow (Cecilia), Jeff Daniels (Tom Baxter, Gil Sheperd),

Danny Aiello (Monk), Irving Metzman (Theatre Manager), Stephanie Farrow (Cecilia's Sister), David Kieserman (Diner Boss), Ed Herrmann (Henry), John Wood (Jason), Deborah Rush (Rita), Van Johnson (Larry Wilde), Zoe Caldwell (Countess), Eugene Anthony (Arturo), Karen Akers (Kitty Haynes), Dianne Wiest (Emma), Alexander H. Cohen (Raoul Hirsh), Loretta Tupper (Music store owner), Helen Hanft (Movie viewer)

Running Time: 81 minutes
16 mm. rental: Films, Inc.

Hannah and Her Sisters (Orion Pictures, 1986)

Executive Producer: Jack Rollins and Charles H. Joffe
Producer: Robert Greenhut
Associate Producer: Gail Sicilia
Director: Woody Allen
Screenplay: Woody Allen
Photography: Carlo DiPalma
Production Designer: Stuart Wurtzel
Costume Designer: Jeffrey Kurland
Editor: Susan E. Morse
Casting: Juliet Taylor
Cast: Woody Allen (Mickey), Michael Caine (Elliot), Mia Farrow (Hannah), Carrie Fisher (April), Barbara Hershey (Lee), Lloyd Nolan (Hannah's father), Maureen O'Sullivan (Hannah's mother), Daniel Stern (Dusty), Max Von Sydow (Frederick), Dianne Wiest (Holly), Tony Roberts and Sam Waterston (cameos)
Running Time: 106 minutes

INDEX

Abzug, Bella, 125
Adam's Rib, 84, 87, 96
Adu, Frank, 73
Agnew, Spiro, 41
Aiello, Danny, 202
Aimee, Anouk, 141
Albeck, Andy, 137
Alber, David O., 28
Alexander Nevsky, 72
Alger, Horatio, 36
Allen, Woody, and American humor traditions, 1–7; and dialogues, intertextuality, reflexivity, 8–9, 12–14; and little men figures, 10–12, 17–26; as businessman, 19–20; attitudes about art, 9, 101, 108; about mixing comedy and drama, 21–22; about politics, 24; about problems in modern culture, 23, 118; about reading, 29; about personal and artistic integrity, 20–22, 24; about religion, 25; about visual quality of his films, 21; about women, 25, 201; and managers, 29–30; as comedy writer, 28–29; early interest in magic, 28; early interest in radio comedy, 27; early interest in films, 27; early years, 26–28; fear of death, 23, 109; in psychotherapy, 22; lack of narcissism, 9; work habits, 18–19; New York vs Hollywood, 26; music, 28; nightclub years, 30; realism and illusionism in his films, 13–14; time and self-consciousness in his films, 14–15. *See also* discussions of individual works

WORKS:
ESSAYS AND WRITINGS
Getting Even, 31, 35, 43
"Selections from the Allen Notebooks," 1
Side Effects, 31, 145
"Viva Vargas," 43
Without Feathers, 31

FILM WORK
Annie Hall, 18, 19, 20, 21, 22, 35, 42, 47, 72, 73, 81–97, 105, 108, 119, 122, 123, 129, 135, 140, 142, 146, 147, 164, 169, 171, 185
Bananas, 19, 33–34, 35, 39–47, 48, 51, 68, 69, 93, 203
Broadway Danny Rose, 29, 169, 172, 189–200, 211, 213
Casino Royale, 31
Don't Drink the Water, 30
Everything You Always Wanted to Know About Sex*, 20, 57–65
Front, The, 81–82
Kagi No Kagi. See What's Up Tiger Lily?
Interiors, 19, 20, 21, 35, 93, 99–115, 119, 120, 123, 124, 129, 142, 146, 163, 190
Love and Death, 57–58, 70–78, 82, 147
Manhattan, 19, 20, 21, 22, 117–31, 133, 139, 142, 164, 165, 167, 168, 169, 173, 198, 202
Midsummer Night's Sex Comedy, A, 19, 153–69, 175
Play It Again, Sam, 31, 39, 47–54, 82, 89, 119, 122, 200
Purple Rose of Cairo, The, 39, 169, 172, 189–91, 200–13

Sleeper, 21, 35, 57–58, 65–70, 90, 108, 174, 203
Stardust Memories, 73, 84, 133–150, 164, 165, 168, 173, 174, 179, 207
Take the Money and Run, 31, 33–39, 40, 43, 47, 48, 147, 178, 203, 213
What's New Pussycat?, 31, 34
What's Up Tiger Lily, 31
Zelig, 19, 73, 167, 169, 171–86, 190, 195, 200, 207, 209, 211

PLAYS
Don't Drink the Water, 30
Play It Again, Sam, 31, 47

RECORDINGS
"Woody Allen: The Nightclub Years," 30

Alter, Robert, 96, 191
American humor, filmic tradition, 4–8, 37–38; oral/literary tradition, 2–4, 6, 37–38, 48, 191; *See* Comedian comedy
Anderson, Michael, *1984*, 67
Annie, 153
Anti-semitism, 90, 175
Anna Karenina (Tolstoy), 71, 75
Antonioni, Michelangelo, 63
Arendt, Hannah, 24
Armstrong, Louis, 146
Asphalt Jungle, The, 37
Astaire, Fred, 204, 209

Bakhtin, Mikhail, 8, 9, 190–91, 215n3, 216n20–24, 217n32, 222–23n3
Baron, Sandy, 193, 199
Barrault, Marie-Christine, 135
Battleship Potemkin, The, 40, 74
Bazin, Andre, 160
Beck, Jackson, 36
Beckett, Samuel, 29
Bellow, Saul, 96, 177, 179, 185
Benchley, Robert, 3, 6, 7, 8, 29
Benny, Jack, 7
Berdyayev, Nikolai Aleksandrovich, 29, 71

Bergman, Ingrid, 50
Bergman, Ingmar, 25, 153; *Cries and Whispers*, 99–101, 103, 109, 111, 114; *Face to Face*, 88–89; *Seventh Seal, The*, 72, 76, 77; *Smiles of a Summer Night*, 156, 157–59
Berle, Milton, 192, 197–98
Bertolucci, Bernardo, 63
Best Short Stories of 1915, The (O'Brien), 222
Bettelheim, Bruno, 179
Bicycle Thief, The, 198
Big House, The, 37
Blair, Walter, 2
Blob, The, 67
Bloom, John Morton, 179
Bogart, Humphrey, 48–50, 52–54, 200
Bondarchuk, Sergei, 73
Boone, Pat, 29
Bond, James, 31
Bonnie and Clyde, 35, 40
Bourne, Mel, 21
Borges, George Luis, 29
Bow, Clara, 180
Brice, Fanny, 180
Brickman, Marshall, 67
Bricktop, 178
Bringing Up Baby, 84, 90, 96
Brooks, Mel, 29
Brothers Karamazov, The (Dostoevsky), 71, 73, 76
Byrne, Anne, 118

Caesar, Sid, 29
Cagney, James, 36
Camus, Albert, 25, 29, 71
Canby, Vincent, 133
Capra, Frank, 87, 90
Carney, Art, 29
Carnival, 189, 191, 194, 197–200, 208, 212
Carradine, John, 64
Carrie, 60
Casablanca, 48–50, 53–54
Castro, Fidel, 39, 70
Cavell, Stanley, 89, 92

Cavett, Dick, 88
Cezanne, Paul, 129, 154
Chaplin, Charlie, 5–7, 20, 22, 66, 74, 173, 180, 186, 190; and McCarthyism, 90; *Gold Rush, The*, 6; *Modern Times*, 6, 42, 66
Childhood, Boyhood, Youth (Tolstoy), 72
Chekhov, Anton, 29
Christianity, 102–3, 140, 190, 199
Chushuingura, 125
Cinema-verite, 36, 178
Clayton, Jack, 190
Clockwork Orange, A, 58, 67–70, 174
Citizen Kane, 174–81
Cloquet, Ghislain, 73
Cool Hand Luke, 37
Comedian comedy, 4–8
Commentary, 42, 44
"Country Excursion, A," (de Maupassant), 160
Cook, David A., 163
Coppola, Francis, 87, 193–99
Cosell, Howard, 40, 46
Court Jester, A, 62
Cries and Whispers, 99–101, 103, 109, 111, 114
Crime and Punishment (Tolstoy), 71, 76
Crist, Judith, 135–36, 137
Crosby, Bing, 27
Cugar, Xavier, 68
Cukor, George, 87, 90

Daniels, Jeff, 202
Davies, Marion, 174, 180
Day in the Country, A, 156, 159–60
De Sica, Vittorio, 52
Defiant Ones, The, 37
Dewey, John, 29, 71
Dickinson, Emily, 1
Dillinger, 37
Dillinger, John, 35, 38, 70
Dirty Dozen, The, 73
Dr. Zhivago, 74
Documentary style, 35–36, 172
Don Quixote (Cervantes), 38, 196
Dostoevsky, Feodor, 29, 58, 71–73, 76–77

Dovzhenko, Alexander, 125
Dressler, Marie, 5
Duck Soup, 45, 74
Dunphy, Don, 40

E.T., 153
Earth, 125
Ebert, Roger, 25, 100
Eco, Umberto, 191
8 1/2, 9, 133–49, 174
Einstein, Albert, 154
Eisenstein, Sergei, 74
Eliot, T. S., 107
Evergreen Review, The, 43
*Everything You Always Wanted to Know about Sex** (Reuben), 59–60, 64
Existentialism, 8, 9, 25, 29, 70, 72

Face to Face, 88
Fascism, 24, 39, 68, 184–85, 186
Fahrenheit 451, 67
Fantastic Voyage, 64
Farrow, Mia, 17, 153, 166, 172, 193, 201, 202, 204, 211, 223n8
Farrow, Stephanie, 206
"Father Knows Best," 61
Feldman, Charles, 31
Fellini, Federico, 89; *8 1/2*, 9, 133–49
Ferrer, Jose, 153
Fields, W. C., 22, 124, 125
Film Noir, 118, 122, 123, 127, 128
Fitzgerald, F. Scott, 180; *Great Gatsby, The*, 39, 127, 143, 173, 180, 190, 196
Fitzgerald, Zelda, 127
Flaubert, Gustave, 29; *Sentimental Education*, 129
Flying Down to Rio, 204
Forte, Nick Apollo, 193
Freud, Sigmund, 28, 29
Frozen Dead, The, 66

Gallo, Fred, 35
Gay Divorcee, The, 204
Gelbert, Larry, 29
Genet, Jean, 29

Genre films; detective, 177, gangster, 34–39; gothic, 64, 177; film noir, 117, 119, 122–23, 127, 128; musicals, 117, 123, 130; romances, 44; science fiction, 64, 65–70, 144–45; war, 64; *See* Comedian comedy. *See also* Screwball comedy

Georgy Girl, 144

Gershwin, George, 117, 129, 130

Gilliatt, Penelope, 18, 59, 100, 105

Gittelson, Natalie, 25, 119–20, 122

Gleason, Jackie, 30

Godard, Jean-Luc, 138

Godfather, The, 88, 193–99

Gold Rush, The, 6

Goldberg, Rube, 165

Graduate, The, 130

Graham, Billy, 25

Grant, Cary, 90

Great Gatsby, The (Fitzgerald), 39, 127, 143, 173, 180, 196

Great Gatsby, The (Clayton film), 190

Griffith, Kristin, 101

Grossberg, Jack, 35

Hagerty, Julie, 154

Halberstadt, Ira, 105

Hamlet (Shakespeare), 62, 128

Harlow, Jean, 180

Harper, Jessica, 135

Hasidism, 37, 77–78, 91; *See* Jewishness

Hauser, Arnold, 162, 169

Hawkes, Howard, 87

Hawthorne, Nathaniel, 103

Hayworth, Rita, 123

Hearst, William Randolph, 174

Hegel, Georg, 29, 71

Heidegger, Martin, 29

Hirsch, Foster, 27

Heisenbergian uncertainty principle, 168

Hemingway, John, 180

Hemingway, Mariel, 118, 123, 124

Hennessey, Dale, 65

Henreid, Paul, 53

Hepburn, Katharine, 90–91

Hill, Hamlin, 2

His Girl Friday, 84, 96

Hitler, Adolf, 90, 163, 167, 184

Hobbes, Thomas, 165

Holocaust, 25, 88

Holt, Toni, 61

Hope, Bob, 7, 27, 74

House Un-American Activities Committee, The, 81

Howe, Irving, 179

Hurt, Marybeth, 101

Hustler, The, 36

I Was a Fugitive from a Chain Gang, 37

Impressionist painting, 161–62

Inherit the Wind, 45

Jazz Age, The, 172

Jessel, George, 27

Jewishness, 87, 91, 121, 140, 175, 176, 191, 194, 199; *See* Hasidism. *See also* Antisemitism. *See also* Holocaust

Joffe, Charles, 29, 30, 34

Johnson, William, 177

Johnston, Richard J. H., 20

Joan of Arc (Twain), 122

Jones, Jennifer, 60

Jordan, Richard, 101

Joyce, James, 29

Jung, Carl, 29

Kael, Pauline, 133, 173

Kafka, Franz, 29

Kaye, Danny, 62

Kawin, Bruce, 182–83

Kaye, Sammy, 28

Kazan, Elia, 21

Kean, Walter, 68

Keaton, Buster, 5, 66, 216

Keaton, Diane, 31, 51, 67, 71, 83, 84, 100, 118

Kierkegaard, Søren, 29, 71

Kinsey, Alfred, 59

Kroll, Jack, 21, 25, 27, 29, 105, 190, 201

Konigsberg, Allen Stewart. *See* Allen, Woody

Konigsberg, Martin and Nettie, 26

Ku Klux Klan, 176
Kubrick, Stanley, *Clockwork Orange, A*, 58, 67–70, 174; *2001*, 66

La Jetee, 174, 181–86
La notte, 63
La regle du jeu. See Rules of the Game, The
Lake, Veronica, 123
Lambert, Gavin, 168
Langdon, Harry, 5
Lasser, Louise, 30, 43, 62
Laurel and Hardy, 5
Lax, Eric, 27, 34, 65–66, 71, 216n19
Le Dejeuner sur l'herbe. See Picnic on the Grass
"Leave It to Beaver," 61
Lewis, Jerry, 7
Lewis, Robert Q., 61
Lindbergh, Charles, 180
Lindsay, John, 24
Little Caesar, 35
Lloyd, Harold, 5, 66
Lolita (Nabakov), 122
Lombardo, Guy, 28
Long Day's Journey into Night, 35
"Love Song of J. Alfred Prufrock, The," (Eliot), 107
Lucas, George, 144

Macbeth (Shakespeare), 62
McCarthyism, 81, 90
McCarthy, Eugene, 24
McGovern, George, 24
McKuen, Rod, 68
McLuhan, Marshall, 89
Maltese Falcon, The, 119
Man for All Seasons, A, 62
Mao Tse-Tung, 107, 110, 115
Marker, Chris, 174, 181–86
Marshall, E. G., 100
Marvin, Lee, 73
Marx Brothers, The, 7, 27, 44, 74, 137
Marx, Groucho, 129, 137
Marx, Harpo, 74
Maslin, Janet, 133
Mason, Pamela, 61
Mastroianni, Marcello, 63

Maupassant, Guy de, 160
Mays, Willie, 129
Meet Danny Wilson, 193, 223
Meltzer, Harvey, 29
Mendelssohn, Felix, 154
Midsummer Night's Dream, A (Reinhardt film), 156–57, 167
Midsummer Night's Dream, A (Shakespeare), 156, 175
Milo, Sandra, 141
Minnelli, Liza, 35
Mishima, Yukio, 29
Modern Times, 6, 43, 66
Moss, Robert F., 18
Murder Incorporated, 196
Murphy, Michael, 118
Murray, Arthur, 28

Nazis, 88–89, 120, 179, 184
Neorealism, 52
Newsreels, 36, 179
Nichols, Mike, 130
Night and Fog, 178
Never Say Die, 74
New Yorker, 3, 31, 144
Newman, Paul, 36
1984 (Orwell), 67
Normand, Mabel, 5

On Revolution (Arendt), 24
Ophüls, Marcel, 88–89
Orion Pictures, 30

Page, Geraldine, 100
Palomar Pictures, 34
Pawnbroker, The, 35
Perelman, S. J., 3, 4, 6, 8, 23, 29
Perry, Ted, 145
Philbin, Regis, 61
Photography, 92–93, 123, 142, 162, 180–85
Picasso, Pablo, 189, 196
Picnic on the Grass, 156, 159–60
Pinsker, Sanford, 4
Place in the Sun, A, 60
Plath, Sylvia, 29
Prokofiev, S., 70
Public Enemy, 36
Pursuits of Happiness (Cavell), 89

Rabelaisian comedy, 190
Rampling, Charlotte, 135, 144
Randall, Tony, 64
Reagan, Ronald, 24
Reinhardt, Max, 156–57, 167
Renoir, Jean, 161, *Day in the Country, A*, 156, 159–60; *Picnic on the Grass*, 156, 159–60; *Rules of the Game, The*, 156, 159, 163–65, 167–68
Renoir, Pierre-Auguste, 161
Resnais, Alain, 178
Reuben, David, 59–60, 64
Reynolds, Burt, 64
Rich, Frank, 21
Ritt, Martin, 81
Roberts, Tony, 31, 90, 154
Rogers, Ginger, 209
Rollins, Jack, 29, 30, 34, 137, 192
Rose, Mickey, 35
Rosen, Harlene, 29
Rosenblatt, Benjamin, 222n2
Rosenblum, Ralph, 19, 35, 46, 216n29
Roses, 189–90
Ross, Herbert, 48, 50, 53
Rules of the Game, The, 156, 163–65, 167–68
Runyon, Damon, 194
Russell, Bertrand, 29, 71

San Francisco, 50
Sartre, Jean Paul, 25, 29
Scarlet Letter, The (Hawthorne), 103
Schatz, Thomas, 83–84
Schiff, Stephen, 133, 204
Schorr, Lester, 35
Screwball comedy, 84–97
Seidman, Steve, 4
Sentimental Education (Flaubert), 129
Separate Tables, 52
Seventh Seal, The, 72, 76
Shakespeare, William, 89, 90; *Hamlet*, 62, 128; *Macbeth*, 62; *Midsummer Night's Dream, A*, 156
Shawn, Wallace, 121

Sherlock Jr., 5, 216n27
Shriner, Herb, 29
Siskel, Gene, 148
Shulman, Max, 29
Simon, Danny, 29
Simon, Paul, 18, 94
Sinatra, Frank, 223n8
Smiles of a Summer Night, 156, 157–59
Sontag, Susan, 179
Sorrow and the Pity, The, 88
Spielberg, Steven, 144, 153
Spock, Benjamin, 24
Stam, Robert, 186, 215n2, 216n27
Stapleton, Maureen, 100
Starkweather, Charles, 35
Steenburgen, Mary, 153
Streep, Meryl, 121
Streetcar Named Desire, A (Williams), 69
Sullivan, Ed, 28
Sun Also Rises, The (Hemingway), 180
Surrealism, 27, 197
Swing Time, 204

Take One, 102
Taylor, Elizabeth, 60
Television, 23, 40, 57, 59, 60–61, 88, 89, 101, 103, 108
Things to Come, 66
Thurber, James, 3
Tolstoy, Leo, 58, 71–77
Tom Jones, 45
Top Hat, 209
Truffaut, Francois, 67
Twain, Mark, 122
20,000 Years in Sing-Sing, 37
2001, 66

Une partie de campagne. See Day in the Country, A
"Unicorn in the Garden, The," (Thurber), 3
United Artists, 19, 30, 137

Vidor, King, 73
Viet Nam, 39

Viva Zapata!, 43
Vitti, Monica, 63

Walk East on Beacon, 36
Walsh, David, 65
War and Peace (Tolstoy), 71, 73–76
War and Peace (films), 73
Waterston, Sam, 101
Welles, Orson, 174–80
West, Mae, 7, 204
West Side Story, 36
"What's My Line," 60–61
Wilder, Gene, 60, 61
William Morris Agency, 28, 29

Williams, Tennessee, 69
Willis, Gordon, 18, 161
Wilson, Earl, 28
Winchell, Walter, 28
Witness for the Prosecution, 45
Wittgenstein, Ludwig, 29, 203
Woman of the Year, 84
Woolf, Virginia, 29

Yacowar, Maurice, 49, 77, 82, 83, 84, 101
Yates, Norris, 3, 4

"Zelig," (Rosenblatt), 222n2